THE EDUCATION OF EROS

"Dennis L. Carlson's latest book is nothing less than magisterial. Working across a broad swath of historical and theoretical material, he illuminates a century of discussions around sex and sexuality education in fresh and exciting ways. This book is absolutely essential for anyone attempting to understand and intervene in these important debates. This book is 'ground zero' for all future discussions around the cultural politics of sex and sexuality education."

Greg Dimitriadis, University at Buffalo/The State University of New York

The Education of Eros is the first and only comprehensive history of sexuality education and the "problem" of adolescent sexuality from the mid-20th century through the first decade of the 21st. It explores how professional health educators, policy makers, and social and religious conservatives framed the problem and articulated educational responses. Although they differed in their approaches, and battled over what got taught about sexuality in schools, these groups all shared a common understanding of the adolescent body and adolescent desire as a problem that required a regulatory and disciplinary education. The latter half of the 20th century also witnessed the rise of new social movements in civil society and the academy that began to reframe the "problem" of adolescent sexuality in a language of rights, equity, and social justice. The century ended with sexuality education in a moribund state in public schools, but with new discourses emerging that pointed toward a democratic reconceptualization of education and the problem of adolescent sexuality.

Situated within critical social theories of sexuality, this book offers a tool for reframing the conversation about adolescent sexuality and reconstructing the meaning of sexuality education in a democratic society. It speaks to a wide audience, including university faculty and graduate students in curriculum studies, sociocultural foundations of education, cultural studies of education, and health education. It is written to be broadly accessible and useful to education faculty, students, teachers, community activists, and all those interested in adolescent education and sexuality education.

Dennis L. Carlson is Professor of Curriculum, Cultural Studies of Education, and the Social Foundations of Education, Miami University.

STUDIES IN CURRICULUM THEORY
William F. Pinar, Series Editor

For additional information on titles in the Studies in Curriculum Theory series visit **www.routledge.com/education**

THE EDUCATION OF EROS

A History of Education and the Problem of Adolescent Sexuality

Dennis L. Carlson

MIAMI UNIVERSITY

Routledge
Taylor & Francis Group

NEW YORK AND LONDON

First published 2012
by Routledge
711 Third Avenue, New York, NY 10017

Simultaneously published in the UK
by Routledge
2 Park Square, Milton Park, Abingdon, Oxon OX14 4RN

Routledge is an imprint of the Taylor & Francis Group, an informa business

Library of Congress Cataloging in Publication Data
Carlson, Dennis.
The education of eros : a history of education and the problem of
adolescent sexuality / Dennis L. Carlson.
p. cm. -- (Studies in curriculum theory series)
Includes bibliographical references and index.
1. Youth--Sexual behavior--United States. 2. Youth--United
States--Attitudes. 3. Adolescent psychology. I. Title.
HQ27.C362 2012
306.70835'0973--dc23
2011035478

ISBN13: 978-0-415-80851-4 (hbk)
ISBN13: 978-0-203-14017-8 (ebk)

Typeset in Bembo
by Taylor & Francis Books

Printed and bound in the United States of America by Publishers Graphics,
LLC on sustainably sourced paper.

CONTENTS

ACKNOWLEDGEMENTS

This book would have never been possible without the support of a grant from the Ford Foundation. In particular, I would like to thank Dorinda Welle, the program officer at Ford, who encouraged me in pursuing this historical study. It was she who invited me to participate in a convention on sexuality education held at the Ford Foundation in mid-town Manhattan in 2007 to discuss my previous work on the history of sexuality education with a group of grantees who were actively involved in forging a sexuality curriculum that addressed issues of equity, rights, social justice, and community engagement. I learned much at that convening, and in follow-up conversations with Dorinda this cultural studies history project began to take shape. Aside from providing me with course release time over two years to conduct research, the Ford Foundation also supported two national "summits" on cultural studies, sexuality education, and the "problem" of adolescent sexuality with scholars from around the U.S. and Canada in attendance. The first of these "summits" was held at Miami University, Oxford, Ohio, in late May 2009; and that gathering would demonstrate to all of us involved, if we needed a demonstration, that any discussion of sexuality education is bound to generate interest and concern, including interest by the local news media and by some Christian conservative groups (such as Citizens for Community Values). The university even received threats from some alumni to suspend their financial contributions. If this was a lesson in the politics of sexuality education, it also reminded us of the importance of this work, and the importance of bringing together scholars and practitioners in an environment in which they could talk openly and share ideas. Consequently, the second national summit, in February 2010, was held near Wilmington, North Carolina, as a closed event. I would like to thank all those who participated in those "summits" for providing the kind of input and feedback needed to bring this book to press. I would also like to thank the Ford Foundation for giving me the opportunity to present initial findings from this study at several other conventions on sexuality education held in New York City over the past two years, and for supporting my travel to several conferences. Finally, I would like to thank the three doctoral students who served as graduate assistants for this book project, and who assumed much of the responsibility for collecting and assessing the books and journal articles that have been written on adolescent sexuality education since 1950. They are Jamal Abu-Attiyeh, Jennifer Bondy, and Adisa Price.

INTRODUCTION

The modern era was governed by a great binary that set reason off against desire and the mind off against the body. Education was conceived as a project of making desire submit to reason, the body submit to the mind. It was thus never a question of educating the mind and forgetting the body, but always a question of a dual education: the education of reason, and the education of *eros*. In the language of Freud, education was to teach the young "the reality principle" and teach them to sublimate, repress, and gain mastery over the "pleasure principle." Civilization itself seemed to rest on the success of this project. But the pleasure principle was not, Freud believed, to be overly-repressed or completely blocked, for it represented the great Other within the modernist project, an Other that technical-rational, bureaucratic, capitalist society needed for its creativity, its life force, its will to power. In fact, overrepression, he argued, was the cause of more personal and social maladjustments and neuroses than was underrepression. The modernist trick was to "sublimate" desire, particularly sexual desire, into "healthy" channels and guide it in the direction of marriage, "normal" family life, and "healthy living." From the start, sexuality education would be defined as a health concern, and one that attached itself to the adolescent body in particular, as a problem body. "Adolescence" was a psychological developmental name for a period in upbringing when the modernist project was most at risk, for it was the age of *eros*: of awakened sexual drives, passions, and romantic obsessions that, if left unmanaged, were not only dangerous, but threatened the foundations of authority and discipline in society. The fear was always there, in the back of the modernist mind, that outside such careful management and guidance by highly trained professionals, adolescent sexuality was a "problem," both personal and societal. But brought under the control of a regulatory, professional discourse, adolescent sexuality could finally make the promise of educating the "whole person" complete, to think of educating young people's bodies and their minds, their desires, and their reason as part of a common project of constructing the "normal" citizen, worker, and family member.

This is a history of the emergence and growth, and also gradual decline, of sexuality education as a movement in the U.S. since the mid-20th century, and thus it is also the history of a socially constructed "problem," that of adolescent sexuality. The modernist project of sexuality education can be traced back to the early 20th century progressive era in the U.S., but it was not until the mid-20th century that sexuality education became a broad movement in American education and society.[1] It arrived on the scene as the fulfillment of the promise of progressive education, to take on the challenge of educating young people about their own sexuality and to lead them in the direction of becoming "well-adjusted" and "productive" adults. The emergence of sexuality education as a broad national movement in the 1950s is also, perhaps not coincidentally, coextensive with the emergence of a youthful subculture that was rebellious and sexually less repressed, and a media industry that began to construct a new market of youthful consumers by appealing to their sexual desires. This, of course, was only a warning shot of what was to come in the 1960s, when the young would align themselves with a "sexual revolution" linked to a broader cultural revolution, and when the media industry would decide that there was more money to be made in desublimating than in sublimating sexual desire. Sexuality education, or "sex education" as it was most often called back then, was both a response to this revolution—an attempt to manage and control it—and also the result of the new openness about sexuality in popular culture. The "problem" of adolescent sexuality, it was argued, could only be addressed by bringing it out of the closet (so to speak) and into the bright light of the day, talking openly about it in schools and classrooms rather than pretending the problem did not exist and hoping it would go away. That problem, as it has been understood since the 1950s, has been organized around a set of interrelated subproblems, each calling into being its own interventions and pedagogical technologies: the problem of becoming "adjusted" to "normal" family life and gender roles, the problem of lack of information about "safe-sex" practices, the problem of the unwed teen mother, the problem of the homosexual and homosexuality, and the problem of sexually transmitted diseases (in recent decades HIV/AIDS). What emerges is a history of continuities and discontinuities, of a sexuality-education discourse that undergoes discursive shifts—creating new openings and possibilities—but whose governing problems and themes remain unchallenged. This, in itself, is one of the reasons why the era of sexuality education is drawing to an end, not with a bang but a whimper. If its battles have not all ended, there is less and less to do battle over, less and less reason to look to public schools and colleges to educate *eros*, at least without a fundamental rethinking of what such an education should entail in a society that aspires to be democratic.

The first and most influential framing of the problem of adolescent sexuality to emerge out of the post-World War II years was also the most generalizable. The problem was understood to be one of proper "adjustment" to "family life." The "normal" path of development was toward the goal of stable, heterosexual marriage and family life, consistent with modern (but still differentiated and unequal) gender roles. "Life-adjustment" education in the 1950s implied socializing young people into their expected functional roles in modern society, and that meant learning "healthy" boy–girl relations, dating, and courtship leading by adulthood to marriage. By the 1960s, the life-adjustment education movement had pretty well disappeared, to be replaced by a more competitive, math- and science-oriented reform movement—except in home economics and health education where "family-life" education integrated sexuality education within a curriculum that was all about adjustment, using a psychological discourse in which sexual desires, behaviors, and bodies were assessed as either symptomatic of maladjustment or of "proper" or "normal" adjustment. The modern, white, middle-class family was the standard of proper adjustment, and what made it modern was not so much the blurring of gender roles but rather a new frankness and openness between parents and children when it came to discussing sexuality. The imperative was to talk about sexuality, and, through a form of therapeutic dialogue, problems of adjustment were to surface and be dealt with openly in a supportive environment. Whether the problem was promiscuity, frigidity and fear of sex, or homosexuality, talking about a problem was part of the cure, and students with persistent problems could be referred to counselors for one-on-one analysis and treatment. This family-life discourse continues to be influential in defining and responding to the problem of adolescent sexuality, although the health and home-economics fields keep shrinking in size. Today, family-life education recognizes a broader range of "normal" families, and does not represent homosexuality as a maladjustment, but it continues to be about proper adjustment in a rather narrow social-functionalist language, a language that sees the problem of education as one of making the individual fit into society and its normative structure, to fulfill his or her "functions." It lacks a critical language that would deconstruct this functionalist ideology and consequently has not generally served to advance democratic progressive projects. By limiting sexuality to "family life," in an age when the family is still by law defined as a heterosexual family in most places in the nation, family-life education also works to make homosexuality, and lesbian, gay, bisexual, transgender, and otherwise queer (LGBTQ) issues and concerns largely irrelevant, for they supposedly fall outside the realm of the family.

The social-functionalist sexuality education of the 1950s began to be challenged in the 1960s by a more liberal movement of professional educators who defined the problem somewhat differently. The problem of adolescent sexuality was not primarily one of adjustment from the perspective of this new discourse, but rather a lack of accurate information on sexual behavior, including information on how young people can engage in "safe-sex" practices to protect themselves from unwanted pregnancies and sexually transmitted diseases (STDs). Scientific "facts" and "evidence" were to be the core of the sexuality curriculum, and, armed with these facts, young people were to be trusted to make responsible choices—although learning how to make "responsible" choices was also to be part of the curriculum. The Sexual Information and Education Council of the United States (SIECUS) was the first vehicle for such a discourse, and it remains the most influential today. Its liberalism consisted of support for young people's rights, as individuals, to make their own informed choices, and also their rights to be exposed to a "value-neutral" curriculum, one that did not (for example) condemn homosexuality as a maladjustment or an immorality. In this case, they followed in the footsteps of Alfred Kinsey, whose groundbreaking studies of human sexual behavior in the human male and female shook the foundations of "life-adjustment" sexuality education in the late 1940s and early 1950s, although the cracks only became visible in the 1960s when SIECUS was organized. But SIECUS, like family-life education, was primarily a movement within health education, and it would find common ground in defense of sexuality education against its right-wing critics. In the first major battle of the cultural wars over sexuality education, in Anaheim, California, public schools in 1968 and 1969, SIECUS and family-life educators came together in defense of that district's comprehensive sexuality curriculum which contained elements of both approaches. By "winning" that battle, they ushered in a period in which comprehensive sexuality education would expand its reach and enter its heyday.

These two generic problems, of adjustment to "responsible" adult family, work, and citizen roles, and of information—countering "misinformation" that adolescents received from peers and the media with accurate, unbiased, value-neutral scientific information—were applied to a series of more specific problems of adolescent sexuality. First and foremost among these was the problem or "crisis" of the unwed teen mother, and, even more specifically, the unwed teen mother on welfare. The existence of welfare, in the form of Aid to Families with Dependent Children (AFDC), legitimated the state's intrusion into the "private" sexual lives of welfare mothers. But calculations were also made of the economic costs of young welfare mothers who could not finish high school or continue their education to become "productive" members of the labor force. Then there was a concern with the family structure encouraged by welfare dependency, which, because it was "abnormal," without a breadwinner male "head" of the family, was presumed to cause maladjustments in the young. The poor, black, female-led families of welfare recipients came in for special attention in the influential Moynihan Report of the Johnson administration in 1965, and the "pathologies" and "dysfunctions" of the black family were blamed for the continuation of welfare dependency. A bit later, in the Nixon administration, the Rockefeller Report of 1972 would frame the problem as one of "population control," specifically population control of poor, dependent populations of black and Hispanic Americans who were supposedly out-breeding whites. Within this framing of the problem, abortion became one of the several technologies of population control. These concerns with population control link Nixonian sexuality-education policies with the early 20th century eugenics or racial-hygiene movement, which demonstrates that abortion rights have not just been about individual rights to privacy in the doctor–patient relationship, as the Supreme Court said they were in 1973 in

Roe v. Wade. Deployed within a discourse and technology designed to manage the population of "inferior" or "unproductive" classes and groups, abortion can become a tool of racism and fascism. The real question is how abortion gets "framed," in relation to what uses and abuses, under whose control. Roe v. Wade framed abortion within a rights discourse, and the women's movement has fought to keep abortion about a women's right to choose. As such, abortion rights advance a democratic project of choice and control over women's own bodies, and the battle has been with those on the Christian right who want to restrict these rights. But concerns with population control of dependent populations in the U.S., and of people in the "developing world," has not gone away entirely either. Foucault used the word "biopower" to refer to the discourse and practice of governmentality designed to manage subpopulations of Others to make them more "productive" and "healthy," but also to control the growth of these subpopulations, and it is clear that concerns with biopower have been behind much state discourse on sexuality education and the "problem" of the unwed teen mother since the 1960s.[2]

The "problem" of homosexuality and the homosexual has received far less attention in sexuality education, and this is at least partially because, from a biopower perspective, the homosexual stands outside a direct interest in population management and control, and thus with unwanted teen pregnancies—the central problem that has mobilized the field of sexuality education. Even over the past two decades, the age of battles between comprehensive sexuality education and abstinence-only sexuality education, the battle has been between opposing approaches to responding to the "crisis" of teen pregnancy and, to a lesser extent STDs. Homosexuality and the homosexual are made irrelevant, beyond the concern of sexuality educators. But homosexuality was not, initially (in the 1950s), so completely irrelevant to the debate. For family-life and life-adjustment discourse understood homosexuality, and even more specifically a "stable" homosexual identity, as a threat to the proper adjustment of all young people toward their expected roles in a monogamous heterosexual marriage. A distinction was made between adolescent homosexual experiences, which were to be considered "normal," and a pattern of homosexual behavior which was not, between latent homosexual desires and the homosexual "lifestyle." The best way of insuring that young people developed "normally" was to protect them from known homosexuals, who might push latent homosexuals over the line toward a "permanent" homosexual identity. Conservative religious leaders found little to fault in such a family-life-perspective on homosexuality, except that they preferred homosexuality not be talked about at all in schools, since talk might give young people ideas. Better to keep them ignorant and thus innocent of this "dark side of life." This all began to change with the emergence of a lesbian and gay rights movement in the late 1960s, which led to the declassification of homosexuality as a disorder by the American Psychiatric Association in 1973 and the American Psychological Association in 1975. Suddenly, the old "truths" about homosexuality were recognized as "myths," and new truths were established in the profession. Homosexuality was recognized as a "normal" human sexual response, homosexuals were recognized as being just as well adjusted on the whole as heterosexuals, and the problem was that they suffered from prejudice and discrimination. The problem was with the homophobic culture, not the homosexual. This suggests the power of "coming out" as a technology that changed public perceptions in fundamental ways, although it certainly did not do away with homophobia and what queer theorists would later call "heteronormativity," the assumption that everyone is "straight" or ought to be. However, the fact that the establishment in sexuality education continued up through the mid-1970s to preach the supposedly scientific "truth" that homosexuality was a psychological disorder, but one that could be treated if detected early enough, indicates just how much science and psychiatry were involved in producing "evidence" to sustain commonsense homophobic and het-eronormative beliefs. This is the result of privileging scientific evidence in educational policy over ethical reasoning and democratic dialogue, when in fact scientific evidence has never been neutral or disinterested. And homosexuals remained a "problem" population, requiring now special interventions in order to keep them from being harassed and bullied in schools.

They became a problem population again in another sense in the 1980s as the AIDS epidemic ravaged urban, gay, male communities across the U.S., and as fears spread of the virus "leaking" into the "normal," heterosexual community. Fear of contagion was a new manifestation of an old fear, that fear of the homosexual as a threat to the health of the body politic. When the virus spread to poor black and Latino/a urban communities, it only seemed to confirm that these "minorities" all engaged in unhealthy and unclean sexual practices that now threatened the health of good, middle-class, heterosexual, white folk. The fear of contagion initially motivated the state response to the AIDS epidemic through AIDS education, along with the fear that the epidemic would put a severe strain and economic burden on the nation's health-care system. Under the Reagan administration, when the AIDS epidemic appeared to be contained within these "minority" communities, AIDS education was not a policy priority and the President would articulate a discourse of silence in the face of the epidemic and its victims, symbolized by his refusal to speak the word "AIDS." Silence was a response that spoke volumes, and it did nothing to counter the victim blaming and fear mongering of those who saw AIDS as a sign of moral condemnation, somehow linked to the moral condemnation of the homosexual—a sign that homosexuality was a dangerous, risky, and ultimately deadly "lifestyle." But as the gay community, which was the hardest hit, endured the effects of the plague and the stigmatization of those who would judge it with a voice of moral condemnation, the AIDS epidemic also created the conditions for a coming together within that community, and a new sense of political activism tied to a language of social justice—as in groups such as ACT UP.[3] The Gay Men's Health Crisis (GMHC) in New York began to develop the core elements of a new model of sexuality education, one that employed workshops facilitated by volunteers who were also persons with AIDS or who were HIV positive, and they helped men talk openly about their sexual lives in ways that recuperated the positive, life-affirming sense of *eros*. For men with low self-esteem, having risky, casual sex was often one of the responses, so the workshops were aimed at helping them respond in ways that are consistent with what Foucault called "care of the self." Such workshops, using the men's own sexual language rather than a clinical language, provided one model of an alternative, community-based sexuality education, linked to a discourse of civil rights and social justice, that would spread and develop differently in many different community contexts over the next two decades. Along the way, these responses would bring new voices into HIV/AIDS education and reconstruct it as a democratic practice of and for the people being educated. As the public school sexuality curriculum continued to largely ignore HIV/AIDS, except in chapters on STDs, and as federal policy shifted toward abstinence-only sexuality education, these community-based and community-supported education initiatives have emerged to meet people's needs. They remind us that empowering forms of education always are developed out of grassroots movements, and that a democratic state educational policy on sexuality education must work through such movements. A second lesson learned out of the AIDS crisis was that a progressive sexuality education must help young people develop critical media literacies, so that they can critique and deconstruct the representation of AIDS in popular culture as part of a broader study of how social stigmatization and moral judgment gets represented in the media. In the 1980s, for example, a dominant media narrative distinguished between the "innocent victims" (such as Ryan White) and the supposedly non-innocent victims (gay men, intravenous drug users, and all those who were supposed to be sexually "dirty").

The AIDS epidemic of the 1980s and 1990s, when fear of the virus was like fear of the plague, also was a time when the Christian right gained in strength as it had in medieval Europe in the time of plagues. Its brand of moral zealotry, warnings of the judgment day approaching, call for a return to sexual stoicism and abstinence, and for the quarantine of the infected, all seemed more reasonable in the time of the new plague. By the mid-1990s the Christian right was strong enough politically to ensure that its brand of sexuality education—"abstinence in preparation for marriage"—became federal law, through the Welfare Reform Act of 1996. Progressives and liberals fought back with an "abstinence-plus" discourse of sexuality education that was about "getting real" by acknowledging that adolescents didn't always do what was best for them, and they needed information on condoms and "safe sex" when they fell off the wagon of abstinence. The battle narrowed to the question of which was the best approach to reaching the goal of abstinence until marriage—abstinence only or abstinence plus. Since the mid-1990s, "evidence" has been marshaled and interpreted by both sides to prove their approach "works" best to reduce unwanted teen pregnancies and lower STD rates, and to delay the onset of sexual activity. Under the Obama administration, funds have been made available for programs based on both approaches. Meanwhile, the Christian right has been constructing its own media-savvy sexuality curriculum, delivered through faith-based communities and movements, and modeled after youth-oriented popular culture texts such as music videos, television shows, and movies. This curriculum, in turn, is connected to powerful rituals, such as "virginity pledges" and "chastity balls," that solidify bonds of identification with the movement for abstinence before marriage. This too provides a model of a sexuality education that takes popular culture seriously, and that speaks to and with young people in their language. In doing so it reveals the underlying failure of mainstream sexuality education to "reach" young people and affect their sexual lives, even if its messages are socially conservative, moralistic, sexist, and homophobic. Democratic progressives can learn something from the Christian right when it comes to reaching young people, even if their message would need to be somewhat different. I say somewhat because the debate over abstinence-only education cannot be framed in terms of two opposing "virtues": total abstinence or its opposite unbridled *eros*. As a care of the self, abstinence may be a useful strategy, at least for a time, and as a way of focusing energies on other pressing matters. The question comes down to who chooses abstinence, for what purposes, and within which context.

Sexuality education as a movement in health education began to reach its discursive limits by the turn of the 21st century, and consequently proved unable to think itself out of its own box of predictable "problems" and responses. At the same time new community-based, social justice, and human rights discourses of sexuality education were emerging that had democratic potential, and these were loosely coupled with a "cultural studies" movement in the academy. By the 1990s, cultural-studies perspectives were already beginning to influence the way questions were raised in sexuality education and the language used to raise them, and by doing do so they have opened new ways of thinking about sexuality education that are potentially quite radical and transformative in their implications. While the impact of cultural studies remains quite limited with regard to state educational policy and school practice, and understandably so given that cultural studies is primarily a critical discourse, it has had a more significant impact on scholarship and on teaching about sexuality and culture in higher education. Indeed, this book may be positioned in the cultural studies of education, so when I discuss the historical emergence of cultural-studies discourses of sexuality education, I am discussing texts that have influenced my own writing of this history. Most importantly, I have been influenced by Foucault's three volume *The History of Sexuality*, which is the subject of Chapter 7. Foucault offers a compelling if sketchy history of sexuality in Western culture—from the early "Victorian" era in Europe, then returning to ancient Greece and pre-Christian Rome to develop the idea of an ethic and practice of "care of the self." But Foucault's history is also historical in that its reception in the 1980s and 1990s was a cultural phenomenon, fundamentally reframing the question of sexuality education in ways that moved it beyond its discursive stuck points. He did this first of all by rethinking history as "genealogy," a term he borrowed from Nietzsche to refer to a history of the production of "truth." For Foucault and for social constructionists more generally, "truth" is not already out there waiting to be "discovered," it is an active production of discourse, or language in use, and, like language, its production is always part of a power/knowledge nexus.

The questions are then no longer about what is the truth about the problem of adolescent sexuality, and what is the truth about how to respond to this problem most effectively. Instead, the question is about how has power produced certain truths about adolescent sexuality, and what are the effects of these truths on the production of the adolescent body as a body of desire in contemporary culture. Foucault argued that the modern project had been to discipline sexuality more than repress it, and discipline it within a utilitarian discourse on the docility and pro-ductivity of bodies and populations. He identified this as an aspect of "governmentality," in this case establishing the "truth games" for governing subordinated groups. Disciplinary power and governmentality worked to transfer power to the new social and human sciences, and to cadres of health, education, and medical professionals. So when he points to disciplinary power as undemo-cratic, it is this form of disciplinary power in which the human and social-science "disciplines" are called into being in order to serve as the new agents of discipline in the production of docile citizen and worker bodies. Sexuality education enters the picture for Foucault as an aspect of this disciplinary discourse, and hence as an agent of surveillance over adolescent bodies, and the production of certain "truths" about how to manage more effectively their desires within the authority structures and norms of the dominant culture. Problems, from this perspective, are produced by particular discourses, and they are produced in dominant discourses consistent with seeing subordinated or marginalized groups as the problem. W.E.B. Dubois famously remarked, "how does it feel to be a problem?", in reference to the emergence of a social-science discourse in the early 20th century on the "problem" of the Negro.[4] Adolescents in general are a problem from the perspective of dis-ciplinary power, and more particularly subpopulations of adolescents: the unwed welfare mother, the homosexual, and the delinquent. Problems, in this sense, are not necessarily constructed to be solved or resolved, since that would alleviate the need for continuing disciplinary power over adolescent bodies. Rather, it makes more sense to speak of problems as coextensive with interventions meant to manage the problem, to bring it under a regulatory gaze of power. The democratic alter-native, according to Foucault, is to be found not in doing away with disciplinary power, but rather in articulating it with a new mode of governmentality in which people govern themselves, primarily through a set of ethical claims that are not prescriptive or prohibitive, but rather educate *eros* in the skills of a self-disciplining "care of the self."

It is hard to overestimate the effect of Foucault's work on the emerging movement that I have called cultural studies (perhaps overunifying rather diverse movements). In Chapter 8, I provide an overview of several important currents in cultural studies that have developed out of or alongside Foucault's work and that have begun to effect discourse and practice in sexuality education—especially over the past decade. These currents include a feminist performance theory of gender, a theory of hegemonic masculinity in the new field of masculinity studies, a queer theory, and a theory of critical media literacy and critical pedagogy. If gender, as Judith Butler and other "poststructural" feminists argue, has no essential or given meaning, then it is a performance, albeit one that is repeated so many times people forget they are performing. Within disciplinary and regulatory discourses of power/knowledge, including those that are patriarchal and phallocentric, rather rigid norms are established for the "normal" performance of gender, and this involves the establishment of categories of abnormality and pathology. This has helped refocus educational attention on how young men and women learn to perform their sense of a gendered self in relation to popular culture and youth culture. In order for young women, for example, to take back control of their sexuality, they need to learn new ways of performing femininity. In a similar vein, Patricia Hill-Collins has written about the "controlling images" of black femininity designed to keep black women in their place as "mammies." By the 1990s, masculinity studies was beginning to open up space to turn the gaze on masculinity as a performance, to deconstruct the performance of the "real man" as an effect of power. Within masculinity studies, R.W. Connell's notion of "hegemonic masculinity" has been influential, referring to forms of masculinity that ensure that white, heterosexual, middle-class males maintain power over both women and other men, including gay men and gender non-conforming men, as well as men of lower socioeconomic classes and differing racial and ethnic backgrounds. Finally, queer theory emerged in the 1990s—heavily influenced by both Foucault and Butler—as a discourse that "troubled" the hegemonic binary oppositional sexual identity categories "straight" and "gay," suggesting these categories had been socially constructed as a way of granting privileges to the former and stigmatizing the latter as the abnormal sexual "Other." They certainly do not reflect the diversity of sexual responses Kinsey found in his studies of sexual behavior among males and females in post-World War II America, when this history begins, and the poststructural project has been to "queer" or destabilize all oppositional identity categories constructed through the disavowal of elements of the self onto an alter ego, an opposite Other. The queering of sexual and gender identities is just beginning and must be the subject of a future history. But it points democratic progressivism in a new direction, toward recognizing a proliferation of sexualities and sexual responses, no longer tied to normalizing performances of gender.

By bringing critical and radical democratic social theory to bear on the problem of adolescent sexuality and the project of sexuality education, cultural studies has helped bring a cultural politics to a field that never acknowledged it had a politics. Along with a critical, philosophical, and social theory that draws upon Hegel and Marx as well as Nietzsche, cultural studies has been grounded or anchored in a critical psychoanalytic theory that goes back to Freud and the questions he posed in *Civilization and Its Discontents* and *Beyond the Pleasure Principle*. In 1956, Herbert Marcuse published *Eros and Civilization* as a response to Freud, and, as I indicate in Chapter 1, that book looked forward to a sexual revolution that would "liberate" not only sexuality from the unnatural constraints and disciplines of capitalist society, but also the creative, life-affirming forces repressed along with sexuality. In more recent years, poststructural psychoanalytic theorists influenced by Jacques Lacan have argued for a sexual politics that is less "reactive," less about constructing a socialist or democratic progressive alternative in the mirror of the repressed society as its opposite, and more about deconstructing the repression–liberation binary. The true liberation of disempowered and oppressed groups comes, and here Foucault would agree, when they refuse to play the role of the "slave" anymore—in overtly sexual performances and also in metaphorically sexual performances. The trick is to introject the disavowed "master" as an element of the self, and thereby learn self-mastery as a practice of freedom and care of the self.

1

CONSTRUCTING THE "NORMAL" ADOLESCENT

The 1950s and 1960s

The U.S. entered the second half of the 20th century with a bang—the publication within several years of each other of two books by Alfred Kinsey and his associates, at the Institute for Sexual Research at Indiana University—*Sexual Behavior in the Human Male*, published in 1948, and *Sexual Behavior in the Human Female*, published five years later.[1] These two books would herald the beginning of a new way of framing and talking about sexuality in popular culture and public debate. But nothing is ever entirely new, for the books were written, read, and talked about using the frameworks that were available at the time. Both conservatives and progressives in the field of sex education tended to take for granted a perspective on sexuality that had been influential throughout the modern era and that found expression in the psychoanalytic movement and its "founding father" Sigmund Freud. In two short books written a decade apart—*Beyond the Pleasure Principle* in 1920 and *Civilization and Its Discontents* in 1930—Freud sought to situate psychoanalysis within a much broader theory of cultural development.[2] At the same time he sought to talk to a broader public audience about the implications of psychoanalysis in social and educational reform. In both these short volumes, Freud argued that "civilization"—which he presumed had reached its most fully developed form in contemporary Western European culture—had only been possible because of a good deal of repression of sexual desire and sexual behavior. Civilization demands of people that they subordinate their immediate desires and impulses to the authority of the boss, the demands of the work routine, and to the controlling influence of reason—Freud's "ego." Why, Freud asks, would people agree to give up their desires, and the object of their desires, to live a highly repressive and disciplined public life and work life. Of course, at the outset Freud assumes that people have made this choice themselves, rather than having it foisted upon them through the industrialization process. His response is another variation on the theme of the social contract of Hobbes, Locke, and others. People agree to authority and disciplined labor—and thus the disciplining and repression of most sexual desire—in exchange for security, increased material wealth, and the other advantages of living in the modern, "civilized" world.

Freud identified the psychic organizing principle of the child and "primitive" peoples as the "pleasure principle," which aims "on the one hand, at an absence of pain and unpleasure, and, on the other, at the experiencing of strong feelings of pleasure."[3] Notice that pleasure is undifferentiated at some point in the young child (corresponding to the age of "savagery"), and that sexual pleasure simply is one specialized form of bodily pleasure that develops over time. This is an important point, for Freud implies that sexuality and sexual desire cannot totally be separated from other desires, and from a basic undifferentiated desire that takes on many culturally specific forms. Sex is not just sex, in other words. It is part of the life force that lies behind all creative, expressive, spontaneous play, so it cannot and should not, according to Freud, be overly repressed, for that can lead to neurosis and psychosis, both individual and collective. But it cannot be given free reign either. It must be subordinated to the "reality principle" in modern culture. For one thing, when given free reign, the pleasure principle leads toward "polymorphous perversity"—finding sexual pleasure in many different forms—which Freud believed threatened the stability of the marriage and patriarchal family. The reality principle was not, for Freud, to be associated with the abandonment of desires so much as the deferment of the fulfillment of desire. The reality principle, he wrote, does not abandon the intention of "ultimately obtaining pleasure" but rather carries out "the postponement of satisfaction, the abandonment of a number of possibilities of gaining satisfaction and the temporary tolerance of unpleasure as a step on the long indirect road to pleasure."[4] This theme of the postponement of pleasure would, of course, become very important in sex education for adolescents, and Freud clearly is getting at the notion that while young people may have to postpone desire, at the very time when their sexual desires are at a peak, that they must be convinced it is in their long-term interests to do so, that repression and denial now will lead to more pleasure later, in the form of a more mature married life. He found himself dismayed, consequently, by claims by some that "our civilization is largely responsible for our misery, and that we should be much happier if we gave it up and returned to primitive conditions."[5]

Surely one of the reasons why Freud became so influential, even if he stayed controversial, was that much of what he had to say was consistent with the commonsense wisdom of the day. He took for granted an existing middle class, Eurocentric, and colonial narrative about the evolution of "civilization" out of "savagery." Freud and his followers then applied this narrative to the upbringing of the modern, Western child. Cast in these terms, the child is understood to be a savage, much like the "backward" races of the world, and education is about "civilizing savages."[6] Education is a developmental process that moves the impulsive child toward the rational, responsible adult. In the first half of the 20th century, no one had really questioned this basic narrative—from health educators, to developmental psychologists like Granville Stanley Hall who coined the term "adolescence," to teachers and school administrators, and even to young people and their parents. Still, this development is not about totally vanquishing and subduing the pleasure principle, and (by implication) adolescent sexual desire and behavior, but rather bringing the pleasure principle under the control of reason and long-run interests. Freud's own psychoanalytic case studies of upper middle-class Austrians had convinced him that most of their neuroses were the result of overrepression rather than underrepression—the kind of overrepression typically associated with a moralistic attitude that sexuality was shameful, "dirty," and immoral. He argued that sexual temptations "are merely increased by constant frustration, whereas an occasional satisfaction of them causes them to diminish, at least for the time being."[7] Freud could be interpreted by conservative and mainstream progressives as supporting their views. But he also clearly provided the basis for a quite radical and subversive theory of sexual repression and the sublimation of desire in modern industrial capitalism. He could be invoked to support the teaching of deferred gratification by adolescents, but also to support the teaching of a less-alienating balance between the reality and the pleasure principles. He would even be invoked by the mid-1960s to support a radical cultural politics of "desublimation" of long-repressed desire, as America began to undergo what in popular culture was called (not inaccurately I think) a "sexual revolution." The "revolution," however, was understood within the framework that Freud had left, as Freud was taken up by those on the political left, including most prominently Herbert Marcuse—a German cultural theorist who had emigrated to the U.S. when the Nazis came to power and became a U.S. citizen. In Germany, he had been affiliated with the Frankfurt Institute for Social Research, which brought Marxist categories to the critique of contemporary popular culture and everyday life in advanced capitalism.

In 1955 Marcuse published *Eros and Civilization*, which consisted of his own reading and response to Freud's *Civilization and Its Discontents*, bringing Marxism and the psychoanalytic tradition into dialogue. While Marcuse is critical of Freud's argument about the importance of keeping the pleasure principle under a tight disciplinary reign, his criticism is measured. He means to argue that if Freud may have been right for his day, the day is arriving when we no longer have to be so repressed, when *eros*, with all of its creativity and spontaneity, its joy in living, can have its day. While a great deal of repression of desire (and thus sexuality) had been necessary to build "civilization" to its current advanced state, it was wrong to suppose that the subordination of the pleasure principle to the reality principle had to continue indefinitely, or that one principle had to be set off against the other. Instead, "the very achievements of repressive civilization seem to create the preconditions for the gradual abolition of repression."[8] Marcuse was willing to acknowledge that some repression of *eros* was necessary in civilization since people had to provide for the basic necessities of life through their labor. However, advanced capitalist society was characterized by a "surplus repression," beyond that needed to provide for the necessities of life, and beyond that required to get work done. This surplus repression is "necessitated by social domination." In other words, there is no real, tangible need for so much repression of the pleasure principle, beyond the need to dominate people. There is no real, tangible need for the continuation of alienated labor now that machines can do much of the "dirty work" of producing commodities. People can, for the first time in their long history, begin to reap the reward of so much repression and denial. Marcuse thus links the subversive reassertion of the pleasure principle to a radical cultural politics, and he envisions a sexual revolution that is inseparable from a broader cultural revolution. The body, no longer used as an instrument of alienated labor would be resexualized and re-eroticized, and this would be accompanied by a "reactivation of all erotogenic zones" and a return to a polymorphous view of sexuality that is no longer genital centered and orgasm centered. The whole body would become "an instrument of pleasure."[9] This imagined society, that Marcuse argued was becoming possible, was to be characterized by "an enlargement of the meaning of sexuality itself." Work would become creative and expressive, and thus "libidinal and erotic."[10]

Marcuse's words could have been written by Alfred Kinsey, although he probably would have used a somewhat different language. And while Marcuse would have a great impact in the academy and within a growing counterculture movement among white, middle-class youth, Kinsey received much greater attention from the popular media and generated a lively public debate—partially because he avoided lofty theoretical arguments and stuck to a scientific presentation of "the facts." There is something very American about the idea that we should begin with the facts about sexual behavior, supposedly free of any bias, and from those facts try to shape a public response—as if the facts could ever be separated completely from bias and attitude. Surely, Kinsey had his biases, his sexual politics, but these had to do with facing facts and accepting human sexuality in a multitude of forms and expressions without moral judgment or psychological diagnosis. He maintained that society should, quite properly, "attempt to control sexual relations which are secured through the use of force or undue intimidation," but otherwise interfere as little as possible in the affairs of individuals.[11] This is often labeled "libertarianism" in the U.S., and is in some ways not very consistent with progressive approaches to sexuality education, which understands the individual as produced by, and acting within, a cultural context. Neither Freud nor Marcuse would have argued that sexuality is merely an individual affair, and no one else's business. For them, like it or not, our sexuality is produced and regulated within a cultural context, and cannot be understood apart from those broader cultural politics. Still, there was a cultural politics to the call for a return to a more natural, less-tightly regulated, sexual development and for accepting as natural a broad range of sexual behaviors. His research was untainted by any romanticization or moral judgment when it came to sexuality. Critics attacked his conclusions by calling into question the representativeness of his sample of interview subjects and his analysis of the statistical data, but his studies remain to this day the most sophisticated and complete study of sexual behavior in the U.S. These studies, framed as they were in the language of the natural sciences rather than cultural studies, were presented as studies of sexuality in the "human" male and female, as if people were the same everywhere when it came to sexuality. While there may be some truth to this, it is also a central premise of this book that sexuality is produced culturally, and Kinsey's studies tell us something about how a sample of Americans expressed and talked about their sexual behaviors at a particular point in history.

Perhaps the most striking finding to emerge from these studies is that there is a much wider range of "normal" sexual behavior—among both men and women— than was typically acknowledged in public. This, in itself, was subversive, for it challenged the whole ideology of normality. Kinsey classified six forms of sexual response among men and women: masturbation, nocturnal orgasms and sexual dreams, heterosexual "petting," heterosexual intercourse, homosexual relations, and bestiality. All these he treated without judgment, as forms of sexual activity that resulted (or could result) in a common physiological response: sexual "output" or orgasm. It is impossible to scientifically distinguish one orgasm from another, even male and female orgasms, since "all orgasms appear to be physiologically similar quantities, whether they are derived from masturbation, heterosexual, homosexual, or others sorts of activities."[12] By far the most common form of sexual activity among both males and females, according to Kinsey, was masturbation, and that of every possible type of sexual activity, "masturbation ... is the one in which the female most frequently reaches orgasm."[13] Heterosexual intercourse was thus dethroned as the most erotic or even preferred form of sexual activity. Furthermore, Kinsey noted, "we have recognized exceedingly few cases, if any outside of a few psychotics, in which either physical or mental damage has resulted from masturbatory activity."[14] In this one sentence, Kinsey effectively demolished the rationale sex educators had used for decades in arguing against masturbation as "unhealthy," as weakening the system, and even leading to insanity. Furthermore, in recognizing the clitoris rather than the vagina as the focus of female sexual arousal, and arguing that the clitoris was most fully aroused in masturbation, Kinsey encouraged a view of women as more than passive sexual objects waiting to be used for men's pleasure.

At the same time, Kinsey's reduction of sexual behavior to the achievement of sexual "output" took for granted a particularly masculine construction of sexuality, with attention focused on the most efficient and effective means of achieving that end. Kinsey's sexual champion, in this regard, was the adolescent male—both because the adolescent male's sexual "output" was greatest, and because adolescent males appeared least inhibited sexually. He idealizes them as sexual athletes, with the "strongest" winning the race for sexual conquests over their "weak" peers. These "strong" adolescent males are clearly a version of the "alpha male," and Kinsey reports that they have higher sex drives and mature sexually at an earlier age than "weak" boys—and they continue to outperform (at least sexually) their peers as they move into adulthood. He writes: "these early-adolescent males are more often the more alert, energetic, vivacious, spontaneous, physically active, socially extroverted, and/or aggressive individuals in the population." In contrast, late-blooming boys are typically "slow, quiet, mild in manner, [and] without force."[15] This all reinforced a social Darwinism that presumed "strong" boys were superior and should be held up as standards of masculinity, while "weak" boys should be weeded out. The football team, and try-outs for the football team, thus became a primary mechanism for "weeding out" the "weak" boys and selecting the "strong" boys. Of course, bullying is another mechanism for sorting the weak from the strong and that is perhaps one reason why it has been such a persistent and hard-to-eradicate practice in our schools and playgrounds; and why the harassment and even rape of adolescent girls by "strong" adolescent boys continues to be sanctioned. Strong boys are just being strong boys. Kinsey never acknowledges any of this sexual and gender politics, and, as the scientist, his interest is with the "strong" boys, as specimens of heightened masculinity and sexual potency—which are presumed to be inseparable.

In separating "weak" from "strong" boys, Kinsey did break with conventional wisdom on one important point. He was not able to establish any relationship between these two types and exclusive heterosexuality and homosexuality. In fact, he found that most males and females were not exclusively either heterosexual or homosexual, thus seeming to confirm Freud's theory of natural bisexuality—with a heterosexual preference among most people. Kinsey's findings have often been cited to suggest that approximately ten percent of the population is exclusively homosexual or gay. But Kinsey himself avoided labeling people homosexual or heterosexual, gay or straight. Instead, his interview data led him to reject the sexual identity binary of the modern era as reflecting the reality of people's sexual lives. He found that 46% of his male subjects had "reacted" sexually to both males and females as adults, and 37% had a least one homosexual experience. Almost 12% of males were rated as being equally heterosexual and homosexual in their experiences and responses; and about ten percent were "more or less exclusively homosexual for at least three years."[16] For females, seven percent were rated equally hetero–homo in behaviors and responses, and somewhere between two and six percent were exclusively homosexual.[17] It is hard to underestimate the effect of these statistics on homosexual behavior among males and females. As I noted earlier, the gay rights movement that began to coalesce in the U.S. by the late 1960s cited Kinsey to the effect that ten percent of the population was gay, and that, as a sizable minority, gay people needed to be taken into account and their struggles for equality and social justice taken seriously by the majority "straight" population. But Kinsey also revealed a great diversity of sexualities of the middle that did not fit neatly into the straight–gay identity option, and in this way he is consistent with the contemporary movement among some youth to "queer" sexual identity and thereby disrupt binary identity formation. What was clear, and could not easily be avoided, was that homosexuality was a "normal" part of many "normal" peoples' lives, and that exclusive homosexuals also seemed well adjusted and happy.

In spite of the considerable differences between Marcuse's radical rereading of Freud, and Kinsey's empirical, scientific observations, they both led in the same direction, the separation of sexuality from any moral condemnation (in direct defiance of church doctrine), and the acknowledgement and even celebration of sexual diversity—including homosexuality, again in defiance of church dogma and in opposition to the rather overt homophobia and heterosexism of American culture in the 1950s. The "new" right had found itself two great Antichrists, around whose images it would begin, ever so slowly, to wage a cultural battle: Freud and Kinsey. If Freud was, ironically, a social conservative in so many ways, he also had spawned a radical democratic movement, which Marcuse moved within, that was quite subversive of conventional sexual mores and norms. Kinsey himself had developed quite a reputation for being a sexual libertine, and in the public media Freud and Kinsey were two faces of a common threat, or salvation, depending on your point of view. For conservatives, sex educators were radical progressives, out to teach sexual relativism and perversion to the nation's youth. When *Sexual Behavior in the Human Female* was released, the *New York Times* asked the highly respected cultural anthropologist, Clyde Kluckhohn to review it. His was the voice of a fellow scientist of human behavior, and he admitted to finding it "alarming" that so many people were attacking Kinsey and the report who had not read it, or, if they had read it, lacked the background specialized knowledge that other scientists had. This cannot help, however, establish a cultural divide that separates an educated elite who can understand Kinsey and have freed themselves from traditional norms, and the common folk who are still too bound to outdated cultural traditions to appreciate Kinsey, or even read him. It hardly goes without saying that this cultural divide, which (somewhat ironically) positions progressives as cultural elites with libertine sexual values against "common" Americans who uphold traditional "family values," has been hard to bridge in the decades since, and the cultural divide has only widened. Kluckhohn wrote that he had "no patience with the prudery ... and the anti-scientific, anti-rational attitudes" expressed by cultural and religious conservatives who opposed teaching young people the facts about sexuality.[18] Sadly, scientific knowledge has not yet "penetrated beneath the surface" of even the most "educated minds." But the scientific attitude would prevail ultimately. The only real fault Kluckhohn could find with Kinsey's study is that it failed to take culture into account. The "pretentiousness" of the term "human sexual behavior" is that it claims to take in the world, while Kluckhohn concluded that the study should more aptly be titled "Some Aspects of Sexual Behavior in American Females (Primarily Educated, Protestant, Regionally Localized, Adolescent through Middle-Aged)."[19] Cultural anthropologists like Kluckhohn were in some important ways precursors of the contemporary cultural-studies movement in the academy, and Kluckhohn was already turning an anthropologist's eye on American culture, to ask what gets taken for "human" in a particular cultural context.

Kinsey's "human," as Kluckhohn observed, just so happened to be very white and middle class. Kinsey "controlled" for race by including his small sample of African Americans in the general pool.[20] This can be taken as an attempt to erase race in the analysis, to make it invisible or irrelevant to an analysis of sexual behavior within a culture. Kluckhohn argued that Kinsey could have at least been up front about who got included in the category of the "human." This would also discourage using the studies to making sweeping, universalizing claims—the kind of claims that go with the language of the "human" as opposed to the cultural and historical. By thinking sexuality through the eyes of a cultural anthropologist, Kluckhohn was able to make a fundamental conceptual leap: sexuality was a cultural production and it needed to be understood within a cultural context. This is, from a cultural studies standpoint, one of the major criticisms of the Kinsey reports. At the same time, it is important to recognize that the language of the "human" can be used in a particular cultural and historical context to bring people together across racial, gender, and other identity divides. When Kinsey and his associates decided to include the few African Americans in their sample within the general sample pool, leadership in the black community heaved a collective sigh of relief. They had been fearful that whites might use any racialized analysis of the data to associate them with promiscuity and deviance—as they historically had been represented in the white media and popular culture. If the few African Americans in the sample were even somewhat more sexually active and less puritanical than the majority of middle-class whites in the sample, that could be used as ammunition to blame "Negroes" for spreading sexually transmitted diseases (STDs), promoting immoral behavior, and in other ways undermining "traditional" moral virtues.[21] Like homosexuals, they could be represented as a threat or danger to the "normal," white, middle-class population. In the context of the early 1950s, Kinsey's decision to use a universalizing language of "human" sexuality may also be read as an attempt to emphasize an underlying humanness and humanity in an age in which people of color and homosexuals were stigmatized as sexually deviant and promiscuous. Kinsey sought to reveal just how little these categories of oppositional sexuality—linked to race and sexual-orientation identity—reflected the reality of people's lives. Interestingly, one instance in which Kinsey did explicitly compare "Negro" and white sexuality is his analysis of data on the length of the penis in males, and in this case it is in the interests of dispelling the popular mythology of black, male sexuality, organized around the controlling images of the sexual stud, the breeding stock with a huge penis. Kinsey reported that his team could find no significant differences in the average length of the penis by racial background. Kinsey thus exhibited a willingness to make race visible, and even focus his gaze upon race, when it served to dispel the controlling images of race in America. At other times he chose to make race invisible, since making it visible could be read as confirming the deviancy of the racial Other. It was always Kinsey's aim, in either case, to challenge conventional wisdom and make people face facts. In this regard, the most direct implication of the reports was that even most white, middle-class, heterosexually identified mid-Westerners were not leading "normal" sexual lives by the standards of conventional middle-class morality. Which raised the question of what it means to be normal.

It goes without saying that "facing facts," "facing reality," and questioning what it means to be "normal" is a subversive act in the eyes of the keepers of the official mythology—including politicians. On August 30, 1953, Representative

Louis Heller, a Democrat, of Brooklyn, introduced a resolution calling on Congress to ban the distribution of Kinsey's study of female sexuality through the U.S. mail, and to set up a House of Representatives committee to undertake an investigation, the aim of which would be to ascertain the "value of such studies, if any." Particularly troubling to Representative Heller, and to other vocal critics of the Kinsey reports, was what they had to say or implied about the sexual behavior of white women. Dr Kinsey was "accusing the bulk of American womanhood of having sinned before or after marriage," according to Heller. "Under the pretense of making a great contribution to scientific research," Kinsey was "hurling the insult of the century against our mothers, wives, daughters, and sisters." The studies had the effect, Heller concluded, of "contributing to the depravity of a whole generation, to the loss of faith in human dignity and human decency, [and] to the spread of juvenile delinquency."[22] He called for the classification of the Kinsey reports as obscene, lewd, lascivious, and pornographic. Heller and others couched their outrage at the report in terms of protecting the good image of the married, white woman, who (as in the Old South) is to be placed on a pedestal as a model of virtue. Kinsey's report on female sexuality is to be banned because even imagining white women having sexual relations outside marriage, or through masturbation, is (on the one hand) an appalling affront to their virtue, and (on the other) erotically appealing and thus pornographic.

In 1955, when Marcuse's mentor Erich Fromm was asked to assess the contributions of Kinsey's work to psychoanalysis for a volume on *Sexual Behavior in American Society*, he began his essay by urging his psychoanalytic colleagues not to be so dismissive of Kinsey, even if his methods were different from theirs. He urged them to remember that Freud's theory of sexuality, when it was presented to the public, "was a challenge to a generation which still had an unshaken belief in the sex taboos of the Victorian age." Like Kinsey, Freud had shown that moralistic stigmatization and overrepression of sexuality could lead to neuroses and lack of adjustment. Both Freud and Kinsey also demonstrated that "deviations from the so-called normal sexual behavior were not rare monstrosities."[23] Both were progressives, and ahead of their day in some ways, whose job was to shake things up. Only when people's commonsense beliefs about sexuality could be "shaken up," as Fromm wrote, would they be open to seeing the potential of sexuality in developing people's fuller potential as human beings. Sexuality ethics thus need to be disassociated from "sexual morality and virtue" and from "obedience to the sexual taboos postulated by the culture."[24] In retrospect, it becomes possible to see that, by questioning "so-called normal" sexuality, Fromm and other progressives were taking on a battle that would not be resolved over the next six decades. There is some evidence to claim that, since the 1950s, reason and enlightened thinking have more often than not prevailed over a traditional moral discourse of sin, and over commonsense discourses of "normal" versus "abnormal" sexuality. But it is also true that conservatives and those on the new political right have been able to effectively mobilize and gain political strength by campaigning against Freud and Kinsey and the new progressive approaches to sexuality that began to enter public dialogue in the U.S. in the 1950s. The failure of progressives was related to their optimistic assessment that reason and enlightened thinking would win out, that progress was being made, and that we could expect progress to continue. They simultaneously underestimated the commonsense appeal of discourses of the moral and the normal.

The radical Freud—the Freud who situated sexuality within culture and linked it to cultural systems of power such as patriarchy, and the Freud who viewed most of the neuroses of modern life as the result of overrepression of sexuality and thus the life force—was embraced by progressives on the political left in the U.S., but never by mainstream progressives, the progressives who controlled public education at mid-century. These mainstream progressives drew heavily upon a more conventional reading of Freud in which adolescent sexuality was tied to notions of "normal development" and a "well-adjusted" personality. They understood the problem of adolescent sexuality in terms of adjustment, and in terms of what could go wrong in a "normal" path of development. Neither moralistic nor strictly repressive, mainstream progressives sought to produce well-adjusted individuals, who fit in to the norms of family and community life. This language even entered into the major reform movement in public education in the post-World War II years— "life-adjustment education".[25] It would be difficult to imagine a more powerful group of allies than those aligned behind life-adjustment education by the early 1950s. The U.S. Office of Education, the National Education Association, the Progressive Education Association, and the National Association of Secondary School Principals all gave their support to overhauling the nation's high schools around a life-adjustment curriculum, in which the curriculum would all revolve around making a "normal adjustment" to adult roles and responsibilities, including those in the family, the community, and the workplace. This all merged with the dominant functionalist sociology of the day, in which various institutions like the school were seen as functioning—performing their specialized roles—to sustain the social system as a whole. One leading supporter wrote that, reduced to its simplest terms, life-adjustment education "stands for an adequate program of secondary education for fairly complete preparation for all the areas of living in which life adjustment must be made, particularly home living, vocational life, civic life, leisure time, and physical and mental health."[26] In the hands of life-adjustment progressives, the language of a student-centered, or experience-centered curriculum, was adapted to an education designed to fit young people into existing social roles and norms for the performance of gendered identity. It lacked entirely a critical, socially reconstructive aim. Lester Kirkendall, perhaps the leading sex educator of the pre- and post-World War II era, summed up the progressive perspective in a 1951 article in the *NEA Journal* "Sexual misconduct and maladjustment is the consequence of emotional and personality maladjustments rather than too much or too little information." Kirkendall went on to say that factual knowledge is important in sex education, but that "objective knowledge ... seldom leads to marked changes in patterns of sexual conduct." There is in this statement a frank acknowledgement that sex education is more therapy than factual instruction, and it is a therapy in which young people are expected to reveal intimate details of their lives so that the educator can help them with their "adjustment problems." He writes of recently talking with a "boy" whose family had kept him ignorant of sex, who—when he was in the armed forces—"accepted the warped ideas about sex which his buddies had." Here a young man is transformed into a boy to make him appear more needy of guidance and protection, and his buddies become his worst enemies, promoting "warped" ideas about sex which, because he has not had a responsible adult to counter them, have made him maladjusted. Kirkendall recounts that "I discussed the facts of sex with him and tried to put sex in its proper place." This "proper place" is within the context of a loving, romantic relationship, leading toward a happy marriage and family life, with sex becoming a "normal," non-obsessive part of life. "As the boy left," he writes, "I had a feeling that for the first time the boy had a real understanding of the subject and a proper and mature attitude toward it."[27] Once more, the word "boy" is repeated twice to refer to a young man already out of the armed forces, and words like "real understanding," "proper," and "mature attitude" all carry a very normalizing meaning.

When it came to adolescent sexuality, life-adjustment education was synonymous with family-life education, a movement that developed out of health education and was closely linked to home economics. Family-life education was based on the belief that educators should take a "modern" and non-moralistic, but not "permissive," approach to adolescent sexuality. Some "petting" and even masturbation were typically viewed as healthy, or at least not as dangerous and morally corrupting. Family-life education tried to reconcile restricting adolescents' natural sexuality with a realistic awareness of the limits of trying to do so. So long as sexual expression was leading in the right direction—monogamous heterosexual dating leading to marriage after high school—educators were encouraged to accept some adolescent "premarital" sexual behavior. But there were only two intelligible forms of sexuality: premarital and marital, with the former leading to the latter. Because family-life education was all about normalizing adolescent sexuality for the family, many family-life supporters urged teachers and other educators to develop a much closer working relationship with parents; and an effort was made to re-educate parents, to help them talk to their children about sex. In 1954 the prestigious Child Study Association, one of the major progressive education associations in the nation with a long history dating back to the early 20th century, published a book aimed at parents titled *What to Tell Your Children About Sex,* in which parents themselves were brought under the gaze of professional experts on family-life and sex education. Most parents, according to the medical doctor who wrote the foreword, realize the vital importance of adequate sex education. "They are aware of its influence on the child's normal development, his later adjustment to the opposite sex, and his ultimate happiness." Everything is at stake, it would appear, in making sure nothing goes wrong in "his" (referring to both boys' and girls') "normal" psychosexual development. The problem is that parents, raised in an earlier era, "feel strangely uncomfortable, hesitant and inhibited when speaking of sex." Because "sex talk was taboo" when they were growing up, they need help in negotiating a new social reality. "What about masturbation? ... What about necking and petting? What about crushes?"[28] These were among the questions that parents supposedly lacked the language, knowledge, and confidence to answer adequately.

The book was organized developmentally, as a "handy reference manual" from preschool, to elementary age, to junior high or "preadolescence," to teenagers. Overall, the book was designed to help parents prepare their children to become "healthy, normal adults with a wholesome, comfortable feeling for sex and a capacity to love."[29] This was the new purpose of sex education: healthy, normal, wholesome, comfortable, young people. Each of these words came with its own history of meaning and usage, but when they were woven together they were meant to convey a thoroughly modern, secular, "non-Victorian" attitude toward sexuality, one attuned to a changing American family in which it was no longer possible (or desirable) to hide sexuality and censor sexual talk. Kinsey had pretty well ended an era in which it was not "polite" or acceptable to talk about sex in public, and Hollywood was no longer censoring sexuality like it used to. Parents were admonished to talk about sexuality with their children, so that, together, parents and professional educators could more effectively ensure that young people developed in "normal" directions. The book begins with a definition of sex as "being male or female," then immediately adds that it is "differences in body structure that separate male from female," and also "the attraction that draws male and female together." Then sex is defined in terms of intercourse, pregnancy, and childbirth, which depend on, and result from, sexual relations between males and females. All this hints at the enormity of the task that confronted sex educators in even defining what they meant by "sex." It is simultaneously gender, body structure, heterosexual desire or "sex appeal," and certain acts related to the continued existence of the human species: that is, reproduction. Gender gets named (as male or female) but not named as gender, but rather as "sex," suggesting that the inner essence of gender is to be found in different sexual organs and hormones, and different assigned roles in the reproduction process and child upbringing. Finally, sex is linked to "love, the desire to find meaning and worth in another person," which is necessary for human happiness. Outside love, according to the text, sex is about "humanness" (as in the human animal), but not "humanity." This is a framing of sexuality that is comprehensive, if also heteronormative and sexist. It refuses to reduce sex to body parts and STDs, but rather seeks to provide a basis for a positive, "well-adjusted" sexuality as part of human development to "normal" adulthood. Indeed, sex is not to be separated from "joy, pride, torment, wonder, grief, or greatness."

If parents were not doing an adequate job of talking with their children about sex, according to the text it was because they were not "up to date." They didn't know the basic facts about sex established by modern science, and they had not kept up with changing sexual mores. "We like and admire the sexy glamour boys and girls of our movies, TV, and books, and yet we disapprove of youngsters ... who behave the same way in 'real life.'"[30] Note that already, at this early date, it becomes necessary to place "real life" in quotes, for the line between the real and the unreal or virtual world was beginning to destabilize in a TV age. In a sense, the text was calling on parents to catch up to the images of youth in popular culture, to become more "up to date" and not so old-fashioned. Parents not only needed more information, they needed to get over their prudishness in talking openly about sex. As for "teenagers," the Child Study Association text for parents restated the conventional wisdom of developmental psychology that this long period, between 14 and 19, is "perhaps most vital" to normal development, and "most difficult" to negotiate. It then turned to address a series of crucial adolescent questions, including: "Should teenagers go steady? ... Should teenagers neck or pet? ... What about premarital intercourse? ... Is masturbation harmful in adolescence?" In a general sense, the text steered away from easy answers to these questions. Even "necking" and "petting"—handholding, kissing, and simple caressing—might provide an opportunity to develop deep emotional bonds useful in the development to maturity. On the other hand, young people need to know that "while there may be a temptation to be swept away by the passions of the hour," in "cooler moments" they can learn to seek a "balance between their long-range goals and their immediate desires." This restatement of Freud's basic argument in support of the reality principle (with its capacity to defer present gratification to get more in the long run) offered a way of framing adolescent sexuality that did not call for either moral indoctrination or abstinence until marriage, but that nevertheless embraced a conventional "family-values" discourse on sex. Premarital intercourse, while not explicitly condemned, is presented as giving in to the pleasure principle, to the immediate "desire and opportunity to have sex relations," with long-term negative consequences. Not only does "our society" have a "basic moral objection to inter-course out of wedlock," premarital intercourse also exposes young people to many risks, including STDs, unwanted pregnancies, and relationships they are not ready for. It concluded with a "fact" parents could use to help convince their children not to engage in intercourse. "So far, we have no proof that premarital intercourse makes either person a better sexual partner in marriage." Interestingly, no proof existed to the contrary either. For girls in particular "loss of virginity ... may be deeply regretted later on." Of course, there is truth to this, given that young women had the choice of being either a "good girl" or a "bad girl," and boys liked to "play around" with the latter and marry the former. Still, this distinction between "good girls" and "bad girls" is not questioned in the text as a patriarchal binary, but rather naturalized, as something girls had to adjust to. Once married, young people could experience intercourse or coitus as part of a happy family life. "The male usually leads [in coitus], but, despite the old wives' tales, there is no reason for the female to be inactive." The tradition-bound past is one of "one wives' tales" in which women are supposed to be sexually passive. This hardly seems a "tale" that wives would tell and might more aptly be called an "old husband's tale," but that would be to question a patriarchal framing of the issue that is taken for granted, a framing which claims, however, to be modern and up to date, recognizing as it does that women may be something more than "inactive" in intercourse—if still not really active. "The pressure of the penis against the clitoris and other sensitive tissues brings the female to a climax or orgasm," according to the text, although the male frequently reaches orgasm before the female. Parents are advised to tell their adolescent boys and girls that, after marital coitus, both partners experience an "afterglow of contentment and relaxation."[31]

Near the end of the chapter on teenagers in this authoritative text published by the Child Study Association—presented as the unified voice of the professional educational establishment—are two relatively brief sections on "sexual disturbances" (sterility, impotence, and frigidity), and "problems" (homosexuality, prostitution, venereal disease, and abortion). Of abortion, parents are advised to tell their adolescent children that "it is a desperate solution to a difficult but not hopeless problem." But there are many local organizations "ready and willing to help without asking questions or placing blame" as the unwed pregnant teen seeks help in "bearing, caring for, or adoption of her baby." For an unwed teen to even consider abortion "must mean that she is filled with tremendous fear, guilt, and loneliness."[32] While this discourse does not morally condemn or blame the unwed, pregnant teen for her sad condition, it does position anyone who even considers an abortion as a sad, neurotic, desperate soul. Clearly, there is something wrong with such girls, something wrong in their upbringing and family life, that can hopefully be corrected if parents can have frank discussions with their teenagers—in cooperation with public-school professionals and doctors. All are to speak with a common voice and work as allies in raising "healthy," "normal," young people. Unfortunately, the text warns, "natural human sexual functions are sometimes perverted," and homosexuality and the homosexual were the primary signs of perversion among adolescents and adults. It is with great difficulty, one senses, that the anonymous authors of the text write about this "problem." They would rather not, but feel compelled, as modern, scientific professionals, to speak openly about a delicate subject, one that should not have to be talked about at all if all children were brought up in well-adjusted homes, homes in which gender roles were clearly defined and gender role models firmly established so that the sex impulse does not get perverted from its normal function. The "problem" of homosexuality persisted, but it was better to confront this problem outright with young people than to pretend it did not exist. "No longer is discussion of this subject taboo in the modern home." It is still okay for parents to be disapproving of homosexuals and homosexuality, but, by understanding the problem better, parents can lessen fears about "the problems of the seamy side of life."[33] Parents are advised that except for those homosexuals "who parade their problem in public, you can't identify a homosexual on sight." This would seem to increase fear that almost anyone could be a homosexual and you wouldn't know it, even a son or daughter who appears "normal." But this fear is countered with the comforting message that "it is not very likely" that one or more of your children will be homosexuals. Even "episodic" homosexuality among adolescents, or same-sex crushes, do not necessarily mean young people will develop into homosexuals. Finally, the text encourages parents to view homosexuals as "unfortunate" individuals, rather than morally condemning them, who can be "cured"—although "the homosexual person must want to change." Some, apparently are not willing or able to move beyond "emotional immaturity" to "normal contact with the opposite sex."[34] The truth about the homosexual and homosexuality could no longer be hidden, and, besides, it was better not to hide the "seamy side of life" from young people. It needed, rather, to be confronted head-on and without either fear or shame.

In the 1950s, the homosexual and homosexuality were just beginning to emerge from the shadows of popular culture and public discourse, and when they did emerge, they no longer seemed so fearful. They were pathetic people, sad, neurotic, not really to be blamed for their fate, but not really something that normal Americans had to spend much time worrying about. Their emotional immaturity was only a threat to themselves, not "normal society," and besides there were only a few "committed" homosexuals out there. It was truly sad that homosexuals lived such meaningless and lonely lives, locked outside the normal family, but at least the normal family was safe within the protective environment of the school, home, and church. This had become the conventional wisdom, the commonsense knowledge of Americans in all walks of life in the 1950s, reinforced by medical doctors, psychologists and counselors, and sex educators. It is perhaps not really possible to say who had the most influence in shaping this image of homosexuality and the homosexual—whether it was popular culture, professional experts, or just represented a slow evolution in beliefs among many Americans about homosexuality, moving away from moral condemnation to a more medical (and thus less controversial and supposedly objective and neutral) pronouncement of the "problem of the homosexual." But in this shift, there were continuities with the past to be sure. It was just that, in modern society, social mores had to be validated by scientific inquiry and expertise, and framed in a secular language of maladjustment rather than a religious language of sin. Homosexuality could be more carefully regulated and controlled, even possibly eliminated, through scientific understanding and sympathy rather than moral censure. The modern, enlightened parent, like the modern, enlightened, professional educator, is to understand homosexuality very much like he or she views other psychological problems, that is, as a problem of emotional immaturity and developmental retardation.

In a 1959 text, *New Ways in Sex Education: A Guide for Parents and Teachers*, by noted sex educator Dorothy Baruch, a list of people who "stopped in their growing up" includes: "the henpecked husband, the baby doll, the frigid wife, the impotent husband, the homosexual, the gallant bachelor, the man or woman who marries and divorces repeatedly."[35] A whole popular history of the language of being "henpecked" could be written, and also of the language of the frigid wife, and the impotent husband whose problem is related back to his wife's frigidity; and all of this gets repeated now in the language of science and clinical psychology—along with the history of the homosexual as the feminized male and masculinized female, and the child-like narcissist. But because sexual identity has not yet been reconstituted around a "straight"–"gay" binary, because sexual identity is not yet naturalized but assumed to be constructed in the context of the healthy or unhealthy family and community, there is a third space recognized between the pure homosexual and the pure heterosexual: the "latent homosexual." This was a condition that resulted when "so much of the person's emotions stay focused unconsciously on the same sex that not enough of the sex urge is free to attach itself to members of the opposite sex."[36] Like Brick in Tennessee Williams' *Cat on a Hot Tin Roof* who was still so emotionally attached to a buddy from high school that he was unable to consummate his relationship with his wife, Maggie the Cat, latent homosexuals were presumably not conscious of their same-sex attachments as erotic because they had repressed them so much. Later, gay rights advocates would say that "latent" homosexuals are really homosexuals too afraid to come out of the closet, or even acknowledge to themselves who they "really" are. Certainly it is the case that "latent" homosexuality was a product of the time, when homoerotic desire was often channeled through homosocial bonding between "buddies" and "girl friends" that was not considered by the participants or others as homosexual. Today, the language of the "latent homosexual" has given way to the language of the "closeted homosexual," although the two convey a distinctively different meaning. The closeted homosexual lives in a post-gay rights movement era, in which sexual identity has been naturalized in a straight–gay binary and made visible in the public. One is either straight or gay, and to be "closeted" is to be gay but to try to hide that fact in public, to "act straight." To be a latent homosexual in the 1950s was something quite different. It was to be so repressed, so much in denial, so ashamed of her or his sexuality that to acknowledge a homosexual identity was almost unthinkable, and unimaginable. Self-denial went hand in hand with social denial. As attitudes slowly changed, and as homosexuality was in the early 1970s declassified as a psychological disorder, the language of the latent homosexual began to vanish rather quickly both from professional discourse and from public discourse broadly.

But in some important ways, the "new ways" in sex education and in public discourse on adolescent sexuality were not that different than the "old ways" from which they sought to distance themselves. The "new way" was that of honesty, of no longer seeking to hide that which earlier generations supposedly had hidden, with deleterious effects for both the individual and society. Talking about sex honestly was to be the solution to the "problems" of sexuality in 1950s America. Parents were encouraged to become educated about sex and to produce a "frank" and "open" discourse of sex education in the home, with the aim of keeping the focus on the family and marriage. "Being Married is Part of Sex Education," according to the title of the first chapter in *New Ways in Sex Education*. Normal sexual development, like normal psychological development, was understood to lead in one direction, to one destination—monogamous heterosexual coupling, marriage, and children. Those who went a different developmental path were "abnormal" in the strong sense of being degenerates, perverts, and deviants, the unfortunate result of stunted development. This was the dominant discursive or linguistic frame that family-life educators used to understand sex education issues by the end of the 1950s. So long as the family-life progressives were in charge, what young people learned in school and in church or synagogue was not really in conflict—even if the school spoke in a secular, scientific voice and the church in a religious, moralistic voice. Church leaders sometimes called for greater emphasis on abstinence before marriage, and they accused progressives in family-life education of being "permissive." Nevertheless, both family-life progressives and religious leaders were concerned about socializing young people into expected social and gender norms, and both were concerned about how to respond more effectively to the "problem" of homosexuality and abortions. The claim of those who supported the "new way" of sex education was that they were not about "prescriptions," but rather "facts," which made their prescriptive discourse sound nonprescriptive and neutral, and thus all the more powerful. They clothed themselves as experts, not preachers, although mainstream preachers could agree with much of what they had to say. Religious leaders and family-life educators could agree, most importantly, that sex education should focus on the family. When in 1953 a supporter of life-adjustment education wrote an article on sex education in the widely read professional educational journal *Phi Delta Kappan*, he chose a rather provocative, almost antireligious title: "A Curriculum Not for Celibates." But the article itself was a call for the infusion of "family values" throughout every part of the curriculum and the school program. Sex education for life adjustment needed to be modern, and that meant being "realistic," recognizing that adolescents are already negotiating "changing relationships with parents, boy–girl friendships, and personal sex standards." It would not do to teach young people to be asexual, to deny their "intimate problems." Again, being modern is associated with taking a more reasoned approach to adolescent sexual behavior, rather than simply refusing to acknowledge it or moralistically condemn it. The important point was that adolescents learn to view their sexuality within the context of a growing national concern with "superior family living through the schools." This enhancement in "family values" reflects the "temper of our times." Indeed, Olsen argued that "the integrity of the family as the basic social unit to a democracy" was essential to the nation's strength and future growth. Sex education was a necessary part of a three-pronged life-adjustment curriculum program that focused on: "(1) harmonious family relationships, (2) intelligent sex adjustment, [and] (3) efficient home management."[37]

So long as adolescent sexual behavior was leading in these directions, and so long as young people learned how to rationally think about the consequences of sexual behavior, it was best for educators and parents not to overly moralize or attempt to stop it completely. Olsen's title, "A Curriculum Not for Celibates," referred back to an essay written in 1859 by Herbert Spencer, one of the first of those who brought newer evolutionary theories of society to education and a precursor of progressivism in his concern with an education that was useful or practical in improving personal and social life. Spencer had imagined a time traveler from some distant future returning to the mid-19th century. Upon examining a pile of school books and some student examinations, the time traveler is amazed to find no indication that the students were ever likely to be parents. Nothing at all was in the texts about sexual relations and reproduction or the role of parents, so he concludes that "[t]his must be the curriculum for the celibates," for young people bound for "one of their monastic orders."[38] The modern, progressive school would not be modeled on the monastery, but rather the nuclear family and the immediate community in which the family was embedded. Young people had to be guided through the difficult waters of adolescence toward responsible, moral, normal family life not by making sexuality a taboo topic of conversation in the home and school, but rather just the opposite, by inciting a whole discourse on sexuality on the assumption that talking about something was better than keeping it hidden and not naming it. Young people also needed to be guided through adolescence in "realistic" ways, that allowed for limited sexual fulfillment—given that young people were not being educated for a monastic order.

This family-life approach to sex education, forged out of the post-World War II life adjustment movement, had not changed in significant ways by the mid-1960s, when Helen Manley, executive director of the Social Health Association of Greater St Louis and a leading figure in health education, published a curriculum guide for sex education aimed at teachers and principals. The aim of sex education, she wrote, is to provide young people with an understanding of "their responsibility in using their sex powers wisely and with consideration for others." Ideally, sex education should extend from infancy to maturity, "which is planned and executed to produce socially and morally desirable attitudes, practices, and personal behavior."[39] The entire life of the young, up to "maturity" (marriage and responsible parenting), is to be brought under the gaze of the health professional, and the social-welfare professional. Their aim, furthermore, is not to develop young people's capacity to think critically about sexuality in contemporary culture—to explore changing sexual norms and mores, or think about how sexuality is racialized, classed, and gendered in popular culture and youth culture. The aim is that of disciplining the body and its desires, and moving the disciplined student body through a developmental path, planned and executed to produce the body as a normal, responsible, mature body. The language is that of teaching "responsibility" for using one's "sex power" wisely, and the word "wisely" clearly means consistent with conventional norms for each "sex." Sex education, Manley wrote, is thus really about "what good citizenship demands in sex control and self-discipline." The citizen has a responsibility to the nation not to squander his or her sex power unwisely, although the basis for such a responsibility remains unstated in her text. Being a good citizen is understood also to mean being a good member of a nuclear family, with society built from the bottom up on the strength of the "normal" family. In supporting the normal family,

Manley believed sex education could play an important role by countering the "persuasive, sex-oriented beckonings in the mass media and the wholly inadequate adult examples of good values in living."[40] The complaint here is that both the media and adult role models are "inadequate" and that only health professionals can insure that young people get a well-adjusted start in life. By the 1960s there is some recognition that homosexuals and homosexuality have been unduly stigmatized in the populace, and that this stigmatization should be reduced. "There is a growing feeling," she noted, "that the homosexual has been mistreated socially and legally." But what is the alternative, modern, enlightened approach to the "problem" of the homosexual? Manley claims that "much homosexuality can be prevented and cured and that information about it is essential." Rather than stigmatize homosexuals, they are to be cured. "It" can be prevented from becoming a fixed disorder. It is the school's responsibility to "contribute to the prevention of homosexuality" by allowing open and objective discussion, providing adequate sex education to both parents and students so that "the homosexual can understand himself [sic] and the community can free itself of its punitive attitudes," and providing family counseling and child-guidance services designed to "promote healthy family life." The objective is to catch these children when they "show early signs of developmental difficulties, before those become fixed."[41] This discourse of the normal family, while seemingly so secure and consensual—protected as it was by the combined power of health and social-welfare professionals—would not remain so secure, so hegemonic, much longer. For Americans were changing, and youth in particular, in ways that could not be fully contained within the discourse of the normal family. As the U.S. entered an era of culture wars from which it has not yet emerged, the ideas of the well-adjusted adolescent and the normal family, that were so taken for granted in the 1950s, would no longer be so taken for granted, so uncontested.

2

SIECUS, "VALUE-NEUTRAL" SEX EDUCATION, AND THE BATTLE IN ANAHEIM

The psychoanalytic discourse of adolescent sexual adjustment and maladjustment, grounded, if only loosely, by a Freudian tradition of interpretive psychology which stressed the importance of adolescents talking about their personal problems and fears, was clearly very influential among sex and health educators through the 1950s and into the 1960s. It positioned the professional health educator as psychoanalyst and put the student on the sofa, so to speak. The legitimacy and authority of the Freudian psychoanalytic tradition was well established in the public mind. Alfred Hitchcock's 1945 movie *Spellbound*, starring Ingrid Bergman and Gregory Peck, pays tribute to that authority and the power of psychoanalysis in curing psychological disorders. The hero of that movie is an aging, father-figure psychiatrist who risks his professional authority in an attempt to cure an accused murderer who has amnesia, and, in the process, prove his innocence. How different times were by the late 1960s, when Ken Kesey's 1962 book *One Flew Over the Cuckoo's Nest* suddenly became popular. In this case, the mental institute, ostensibly about curing patients, is actually a prison and its psychiatric overseers are prison wardens and normalizers— trying to make all the patients good, docile, well behaved. The so-called "counterculture" that Kesey represented and spoke for rejected the psychoanalytic model as one that sought to "adjust" people to docility and control; and it is wise to remember that the counterculture became the baby boomers, and so the anti-Freud, antipsychoanalytic reaction to the conforming interpretation of Freud's work in the 1950s has been passed down through the decades ever since. There is reason to believe this overreactive reaction, this dismissal of Freudian and psychoanalytic approaches to sexuality and adolescent development, may be coming to an end. A popular 2010 movie, *Shutter Island*, offers a more balanced treatment of the field, acknowledging both its authoritarian history of adjusting people to docility and discipline, and also the humanistic efforts of some psychoanalysts to help people who are suffering and in despair, to help them face reality rather than escape into illusion.

While a growing segment of the public was turning its back on the psycho-analytic discourse of adjustment and maladjustment, so too was a younger generation of professional sex educators. In place of a mainstream progressive discourse of sex education as adjustment, and as family-life education, they began to articulate a liberal-humanist discourse on sex education more attuned to the cultural context of the 1960s and 1970s. In the 1960s, liberal humanism emerged as the most viable and active force for the democratic reconstruction of culture in the U.S. Liberal humanism was built on a belief that the individual rather than the family is the basic unit of society, and that each individual should be as free as possible to define who they are and decide how they want to live their lives—so long as it does not involve oppressing others. Liberal humanists re-emphasized human rights, including the right to challenge traditional roles that kept people in their place at the margins and that thus effectively "dehumanized" and denied them basic human rights as citizens. Finally, liberal humanism in the 1960s reasserted the humanistic virtues of respect for others and tolerance for difference. To reassert the rights of individuals to control their own bodies and make choices for themselves, and to reassert the right to difference—these were radically subversive ideas in the 1950s, but they began to be thinkable and imaginable in the 1960s as the nation went through what can only be described as a cultural revolution. The sexual revolution was part of a broader transformative movement toward human freedom that was in many ways antithetical to the conformist, normalizing brand of progressivism that gripped American education under the "life-adjustment" movement. The liberal-humanist discourse on sexuality also provided a way out of the binary opposition established between "normal" and "abnormal" sexuality and sexual development. In place of a discourse of the normal and the abnormal, liberal humanists would insert a discourse of difference—the okayness of difference, the right to be different, and the "normalness" of difference. The reawakening of liberal humanism meant a reassertion of a politics of individual rights, legal redress, and individual choice, along with humanistic social norms of respect or tolerance for difference—including sexual difference. It meant linking sex education to equity agendas, particularly women's equity. And it meant endorsing sex education as the provision of information, the "facts" of sexuality, and then shifting more responsibility to adolescents to use these "facts" to inform their own sexual decision making. The facts of the new sex-education movement had to do with birth control, abortion, STDs, and homosexuality. And they were to be ascertained through value-free scientific research involving quantitative analysis of data, not through the interpretive and normative psychoanalytic method.

The first shots in the cultural battle over sex education were thus fired by two opposing groups of sex educators—those who supported a family-life approach that continued to be about "adjusting" adolescents to gender norms of family life, and those who supported a fact-based, ostensibly value-neutral, scientific approach. Being value neutral here meant, in fact, teaching young people about condom usage and how to avoid both STDs and unwanted pregnancies, and, later, about abortion as an option. This was a sex education for a consumer society of adolescents who wanted to know the facts in order for them to make better choices as sexual consumers, and for their parents who wanted to know that their children were protected and knew how to "stay out of trouble" sexually. To be fair, most of the advocates for the new sex education were also concerned that adolescents develop intimate, caring relationships between equal adults, and that they live a balanced and "healthy" life, but the emphasis was on giving them the facts they needed to make their own choices, and not to moralistically condemn any choices that are consensual and nonexploitive—including the choice to engage in homosexual behavior or a homosexual "lifestyle." From the beginning, this new group of sex educators insisted that homosexuality be recognized as a normal sexual response, not as deviant, or a disorder. While the dispute between sex educators committed to a "family-life" approach and a "facts" approach was substantial and involved significant philosophical and political differences, it should not be overstated. For they agreed on the importance of being more open, honest, and frank with adolescents about sexuality, on the importance of talking about sex in public schools, and on the importance of understanding changes going on in youth culture. By the early 1970s, they would begin to find common ground and understand themselves as on the same side against a new army on the battlefield, that of the Christian right.

One group in particular embodied the new sex-education discourse, and it served to build bridges of support among health professionals and family-life educators as social conservatives and Christian fundamentalists began to attack sex education and sex educators. The Sexual Information and Education Council of the U.S. (SIECUS) brought together a power block of "human-service" professionals, including those in the fields of marriage counseling, sociology, family life, psychiatry, religion, education, and preventive medicine. Mary Calderone, its first leader, was a health educator who had become a tireless lobbyist for sex education at Planned Parenthood. With the help of generous grants from the U.S. Department of Health, Education, and Welfare (HEW) in the Johnson administration era, she helped SIECUS become a major source for information and resource materials on how to implement a sex-education program in local schools, and how to involve parents and community groups. When, in 1964, she was invited to contribute an article to a special issue of *Phi Delta Kappan* on "The School's Responsibility for Moral Behavior," she reframed the debate over sex education in terms of a question of to whom the school is responsible to, and what the school is responsible for—avoiding entirely a language of morality. Instead, she invoked a humanist language of sexuality as part of a "vital, creative" force that everyone has a natural right to—including adolescents. Moralist approaches to sex education too often were "negative" in their view of sexuality, and it was thus imperative that sex educators join with those forces being unleashed in the culture that believed it was not too late to "change the 'set' of our country from negative to positive with regard to sex and the part it could and should play for individuals, for families, and for society."[1] Calderone turned to no less a figure than the popular historian of Western civilization and the rise and decline of civilizations to support her contention that unless there was a change in the "set" of Americans regarding adolescent sexuality and sex education, American civilization might be in decline. Arnold Toynbee had written an opinion piece for the *New York Times Magazine* on May 10, 1964, on "Why I Dislike Western Civilization," in which, among other things, he had argued that contemporary Western culture was more and more contradictory when it came to young people and sex. On the one hand, he wrote, through popular culture "we drive them [young people] to a premature awareness of sex even before physical puberty has overtaken them." This early development of a "sex consciousness" in American young people—presumably through their exposure to Hollywood movies, television, and popular music—had, Toynbee feared, spread to Britain, and "who knows how many other Western countries." This is basically a conservative argument about the decline of Western civilization wrapped in the language of liberalism—that is, of young people's human rights. "We deprive our children of the human right of having a childhood," he wrote, when we expect them to grow up too quickly, and when the mass media and the public expect young people to be sexually active at an earlier age. "This forcing of sex consciousness" at an ever earlier age, this lowering of "the age of sexual awareness and frequently the age of sexual experience" in the U.S. was, Toynbee argued, making the U.S. "closer to the Asian than the European," making adolescents sexual beings "to a veritably Hindu degree." While this "Hindu course" is more and more the American way, it is in conflict with another American trend, to prolong the formal education of young people and postpone marriage, perhaps until after higher education.

What Toynbee proposes is a theory of Western civilization, and its decline and fall relative to other civilizations (here Asian civilization and the Hindu course) that is thoroughly colonial, yet is folded within a liberal-humanist discourse on modern sex education for adolescents in the U.S. The decline and fall of Western civilization as the highest, most civilized of the civilizations of the world, is linked to the Western capacity to defer gratification of sexual desire. This is supposedly one of the things that made the colonial European subject superior to, and more powerful than, the sexually more "primitive" colonial subject. And, of course, all colonial subjects, all subjugated races, are represented with a universalizing brush. The Asian Other is also the Hindu, as if Islam and Buddhism could be all reduced to a sexual Hinduism in which even children are expected to have sex lives, with no room for an age of "childhood innocence." But Toynbee then turns to acknowledge this Hinduization of U.S. youth culture to argue that we have to face facts. Young people could not be expected to postpone sexual fulfillment while pursuing 16 or more years of education and then a few more years of job hunting before marriage. There was even evidence, Toynbee suggested, that social stigmas against adolescents having any kind of sexual life "may be one very important cause of so-called feminine frigidity." This concern with "frigidity" is a very masculinist, and heteronormative concern. But feminists and women's rights advocates were also emphasizing the importance of a sexually fulfilling sex life for women in a society that had taught women that their sexuality was bad, and that they only existed to give pleasure to men. Sex education had to address what Toynbee called "psychosexual inhibitions" programmed into the personality.[2] To Toynbee, as for Mary Calderone, this meant a focus on sex education to counter "psychosocial inhibitions," and to encourage some limited fulfillment of sexual desire on the way to marriage—preferably through masturbation (that practice which had so long been discouraged by sex educators, including many family-life educators), and through sexual intercourse (when passion rules the moment) with the use of condoms and other forms of birth control. Calderone called for a form of sex education that treated adolescents as "persons on the way to becoming adults," which meant according them rights we wish for ourselves, "especially as relates to information about sex as a vital, creative force."[3]

SIECUS was a decisive break from the past in a number of important ways. It opposed the use of the labels "normal" and "abnormal" to refer to sexual orientation, it called for a recognition of female sexual pleasure through means other than coitus, it encouraged providing adolescents with condoms and information on condom use, and it promoted masturbation as perhaps the most effective method of controlling and managing adolescent sexual behavior outside marriage.[4] There was even room in SIECUS for those who thought too much emphasis had been placed on married life, given that so many young people were not growing up in traditional families anymore. Behind these specific concerns, SIECUS challenged the idea that young people were clay to be molded by the state in a predetermined image of good citizens and good family members, that they had rights to a sexual life as they slowly matured toward full rights as adults, and that they had a right to factual, unbiased information about sexuality. Ira Reiss, an affiliate of SIECUS, observed in 1968 that there were two basic forms of education, one aimed at "teaching people how to think and not what to think," and the other a form of "indoctrination." What young people needed was the facts, and the fostering of a capacity "to think calmly and rationally in this area and thereby better handle whatever problems may arise."[5] Furthermore, as Reiss so astutely put it, "when we resort to moralizing, the student's typical reaction is to tune out the teacher." Of course, there are some obvious problems with the idea of a "value-free," "objective," sexuality curriculum, in which students are not taught what to think but only how to think, as if there was ever a thinking which did not involve some level of persuasion—something even Reiss finally admitted. But the values in the SIECUS discourse that favored an "objective stance" did at least allow room for a critique of sex education as a kind of indoctrination that often preached at young people moralistically, and in which their typical reaction is to "tune out the teacher."[6]

Some of the new sex educators accused mainstream family-life educators of moralizing to young people in the guise of helping to "adjust" them. Behind the professional-sounding, psychoanalytic language, they claimed that family-life education was promoting very traditional family values and gender roles, and also an antihomosexual bias. John Gagnon, senior research sociologist at the Institute for Sex Research at Indiana University, charged that family-life education was based on a "castrated Freud," a reading of Freud that reduced what he had to say to "social adjustment" and "mental health" understood in a very conventional way. Family-life educators did promote some good ideas, he observed. For example, family-life curricula teach that "not only is sex a positive force in life but managed correctly ... it can result in better marriages, better mental health, and greater productivity." But this is all conventional wisdom, Gagnon argued, and it gets tied to the conventional wisdom of family-life sex educators: "only have coitus before marriage if you are in love, and perhaps it would be better if you waited; do not masturbate excessively."[7] To suggest that family-life education was grounded on a "castrated Freud" is obviously to invoke a patriarchal metaphor. Still, the implication is that Freud was a radical thinker when it came to sexuality and society, but that his ideas and the psycho-analytic method no longer threatened power in any way. To castrate Freud is to rob him of his radical power, his libidinal power, to transform society. And by the mid-1960s, young people were turning away from a castrated Freud to embrace the sexual revolution. SIECUS argued that educators needed to come to grips with a new reality. One of those to acknowledge this new reality, and endorse the SIECUS position on sex education, was Lester Kirkendall, the most influential figure in the field, and in family-life education more generally, since the early 1950s. In the 1950s, Kirkendall had been a mainstream progressive sex educator, committed to the notion that sex education should be about counseling and adjusting the individual to the norms of middle-class family life. By the mid-1960s, however, he was beginning to have a change of heart. In an article in *Phi Delta Kappan* in 1964, Kirkendall presented the profession with a choice. Either changes in adolescent sexuality would occur "through a war of attrition, a sort of guerrilla in-fighting, with youths engaged in a kind of civil disobedience campaign" against adults who sought to deny them sexual rights, or educators would begin to under-stand sex as "integrated along with the rest of our capacities in a genuinely humane concept of life and its purposes."[8] Kirkendall was a bit vague about what a "genuinely humane concept of life and its purposes" means. But what is clear is that his attitude toward the "youth problem" of the 1960s had been influenced by the civil rights and civil disobedience language of the day, and even the language of a guerilla war borrowed from the war in Vietnam. Kirkendall warned that if family-life educators stood in the way of the sexual revolution among adolescents, they would no longer have credibility with young people, and, once that was gone, they would only become obstacles to change, engaged in a war against young people that they could not win.

The new SIECUS sex educators were deeply suspicious of family-life education for these reasons, but, as I said earlier, they began to form an alliance of professional sex and health educators in the face of the attack from the political right that came by the late 1960s. In that attack, the right did not distinguish much between different approaches to sex education. Rather, the attack was on sex education, and all sex educators were lumped together as un–American and anti-Christian. One of the first, symbolic battles of the long cultural wars over sex education took place in Anaheim, California, in 1968, and SIECUS would play its part, although the battle itself was about much more than SIECUS. The most popular and detailed description of the Anaheim battle over sex education was written by a journalist who lived through it and took meticulous notes. Mary Breasted's *Oh! Sex Education* (1970) attracted a fairly large public audience, and it framed the battle over sex education through a new cultural, even countercultural, lens, associated with the *Village Voice* and *Rolling Stone* magazines. Breasted represented a new open-minded generation, and she spoke from outside the professional health education establishment. She represented the new cosmopolitanism of progressivism in the U.S., embracing sexual freedoms and sexual differences that would have been unheard of—because they were unthinkable—a few generations before. *Rolling Stone* had its eye on Anaheim in the late 1960s, along with the *Village Voice*. In April, 1967, the *Village Voice* had sent a reporter to see what the battle over sex education was all about. When he returned he wrote that "the Anaheim School Board, located in the country of John Birch and Mickey Mouse," is today giving its school children the "most intelligent, realistic, honest, and complete course in sex education anywhere in the United States." He concluded that the path taken in Anaheim since 1965 "is almost certainly the way the American sex-education boom is going to go."[9] That in itself helped alert conservative Christian groups, and by the time that Breasted arrived on the scene as a reporter for *Rolling Stone* in the early autumn of 1969, Anaheim had been transformed into the scene of a national battle, complete with the media. Breasted was interested in the scene of this particular battle, for she saw it as symbolic of the broader cultural war. The Christian crusade was being mobilized to fight sex education, with the help of the older more established John Birch Society and other antistate groups on the right. She had arrived right before the Reverend Billy Graham came to town for a crusade, a bit worried that word might have gotten out from an earlier article she had written that she was after the "right-wingers." But no one seemed to have read the *Village Voice* in Anaheim. This was Disneyland, the "family capital of the world," even if the reality did not live up to the image. Divorce rates were high and many individuals and families who had come to Anaheim looking for jobs in the new tourist industry were just moving through on their way to, hopefully, a fancier suburb, or another military base somewhere in the world. In Orange County in the late 1960s, sex education was linked to both the communist menace and attacks on religious values and morality. Communism was still the great evil Other used to construct a national American identity, and those on the right used it effectively as a signifier of anti-Americanism that could be linked to the new sex education, and more particularly to the new acceptance of homosexuality and the homosexual as "normal." Those on the political right, Breasted wrote, had fallen victim to the "grand-design" theory of society, according to which events are part of some powerful, integrated conspiracy to undermine the nation's moral strength. Some of those on the political left, she acknowledged, also unfortunately adhered to grand-design theories of history, but the right seemed obsessed with grand-design conspiracies. In this case, the Anaheim Family Life and Sex Education (FLSE) program was represented as part of a conspiracy by "the SIECUS crowd," as one critic labeled them, to undermine the moral fabric of Anaheim young people.

What Breasted found was a sex-education program in the Anaheim schools that was much less radical than she had expected it to be, a program that was still at its core about family-life education, but with the addition of scientific, objective, value-neutral language borrowed from SIECUS. It was, in other words, a hybrid curriculum full of tensions and even contradictions. The sex-education unit in FLSE, for each of the secondary grades, spanned four weeks, covering reproduction, pregnancy, birth, and physical changes during puberty. As Breasted observes, "everything about the FSLE program had been designed to produce good family members."[10] It was explicitly aimed at adjusting students to expected roles in the family, and encouraging "healthy" boy–girl relations that developed toward marriage and "healthy" families. The curriculum guide contained excerpts from popular advice-to-teenagers books written by "experts" in adolescent development, medicine, and clinical psychology, all of which contained cautionary warnings on premarital intercourse. The section on masturbation, for example, noted that while masturbation is no longer considered physically harmful, "a boy or girl should carefully consider his [sic] other feelings and religious beliefs before practicing masturbation." The contemporary reader is left to wonder whether the authors of the guide made a Freudian slip in using a masculine pronoun to refer to masturbation by boys and girls, or whether the universalization of the masculine pronoun was just part of the language of the day, or both. Certainly, masturbation was primarily framed as a masculine problem, in spite of the evidence from Kinsey and in spite of SIECUS' promotion of a more sex-equitable approach to masturbation. In short, Breasted reported, "the FLSE curriculum had been designed to prepare the Anaheim student for a family life that was like none you or I had ever seen." How could this be considered so subversive, so threatening to conservative Christian and anti-communist groups? Breasted concluded it was little more than the conventional morality articulated in *Ladies Home Journal* and *House and Garden*. It presented a romanticized conception of an ideal American family, without any of the "real anguish that has kept our divorce rate up so high that we might as well stop marrying each other to save ourselves the legal fees." Furthermore, the "mature person," as represented in the curriculum guides, excluded "just about every rebel, heretic, or revolutionary leader who shaped our culture, our religion, and our politics."[11]

As for why conservative critics would take aim at a program so nonthreatening to the status quo, Breasted concluded that three factors seemed to be at work. First, critics objected to what they saw as an overemphasis upon "raw sex," or the "vivid details" of sex, which they thought was unnecessary and morally objectionable.

"Raw sex" was sex stripped of its romantic idealism and religious sanctity within the family, sex presented only in a scientific, detached, detailed manner—as when a sex-education teacher was encouraged to demonstrate the proper use of a condom on a plastic penis, or discuss in detail the biology of sexual arousal and climax. Conservatives, particularly religious conservatives, were fairly comfortable with the family-life, clinical-psychology approach to sex education, in which "normal" adjustment leads toward sexual fulfillment only in marriage and in which sexuality is never separate from emotional commitment and love. But these critics were not comfortable with the new scientific language of sexuality, which was impersonal and seemed to reduce human sexuality to animal behavior. Indeed, SIECUS was receptive to this criticism. From the beginning SIECUS had been associated with a liberal-humanist movement in the mainstream Christian churches, and with family-life professionals, and the movement had been built around a commitment to a positive view of sexuality, one that was consistent with the fuller development of the "human spirit" and "self-fulfillment." But SIECUS came to be known more for the scientific discourse of sexuality than the ethical discourse; and its curriculum program guidelines were, by the late 1960s, framed in the language of scientific "facts" of sexuality and what scientists tell us, without judgment or moral consideration. The tension between a family-life discourse of "adjustment" and a scientific discourse of "facts" was considerable, and it was a scientific "just-the-facts" approach to sexuality that conservative critics found most threatening. For they saw in the scientific refusal to judge or condemn some sexuality and valorize other sexuality, in other words to view all sexuality as equally "raw" and animalistic, a set of values of tolerance and acceptance, of letting young people decide what they want to do once they are armed with the "facts." This was the ideology of liberalism, they complained, and indeed it was.

A second and related argument of conservative critics of the FLSE curriculum was that it presented homosexuality and other "perversions" as acceptable lifestyles. This was, once more, only partially true as the curriculum had stitched together family-life and SIECUS perspectives in ways that were often contradictory. Thus, according to the ninth-grade unit on "sexual deviations," students were to learn that homosexuality had existed throughout human history and in all societies. Homosexuality was not to be "approved" or "condoned," although "occasional sexual interest in others of the same sex" was reported as typical among adolescents and did not mean they would "become homosexuals in adult life." At once, homosexuality is relegated and assigned to the status of other "deviations," including rape and exhibitionism, but also acknowledged as existing throughout history—that is, as part of a natural human sexuality. Homosexuality is not to be feared—even occasional homosexual relations in adolescence are no cause for alarm. But the hope is that this will not lead to that which is still to be feared: becoming a full-fledged homosexual. Sex education is needed, according to one ninth-grade curriculum guide, so that "the homosexual can know himself better" and so that the community "can free itself of its punitive attitudes toward all sexuality."[12] Yet, the only representation of the homosexual in the ninth-grade FLSE was in a section on "sexual deviations," and students watched a ten-minute instructional movie, *Boys Beware*, that depicted a middle-aged homosexual on the prowl for adolescent boys. How was the homosexual to know himself if not as a "pervert," a threat, as something "normal" boys had to beware of? Still, even acknowledging the existence of such "deviant" behavior was going too far for some on the Christian right. As one local critic told Breasted, FLSE was going into the "vivid details" of "all kinds of perversions right into the how-to-do-it."[13]

A third criticism of the FLSE program had to do with its pedagogy or instructional style. Classes typically were organized around group discussions, role playing, and values-clarification activities, with the teacher as a facilitator of group dialogue. These methods were suspect among religious and social conservatives, who supported a much more directive, authoritative, and moralistic approach to instruction. As Breasted noted there were elements of what critics called "sensitivity training" in the organization of classes, with circular seating, students role playing situations where they might have to assert their rights to say no to sexual advances, or practicing the right kinds of thing to do and say on a first date. The class even sanctioned "group decisions" about hypothetical situations under discussion. To conservative critics, this was another example of the counterculture endorsement of "group encounters" and "group touch-ins," which they claimed were designed to "brainwash" young people into endorsing radical sexual beliefs and values. Those involved in the program represented these teaching methods as proven to be more effective in producing "morally responsible" students than "an extensive use of precepts or moralizing."[14] In other words, the professional educators argued, and with some conviction, that their aims were the same as their critics—a "morally responsible" student. They just had a more effective way of producing the morally responsible student, a way which alleviated much of the resistance students had often shown in the past toward overt moralizing. If there was truth to this assertion, it is also the case that the morally responsible adolescent—from the perspective of the FLSE curriculum—was one who was a bit more tolerant of difference, and a bit more willing to recognize that individuals may make different choices. This was not a great difference perhaps, but as it was exaggerated, the conservative right—increasingly the Christian evangelical right—would make it the basis for a cultural crusade against sex education that has not ceased since. Who can be said to have won the battle over sex education in Anaheim? After the battle had waged off and on in various forms over several years, a compromise was finally negotiated. Professional educators would be able to continue to control the context and pedagogical style of FLSE. But a state law was passed in 1969 that required school districts to notify parents about sex-education classes so that they could exercise an opt-out option. Family-life educators could claim they won the battle in Anaheim in that their professional expertise had been upheld. However, opt-out options for sex education were institutionalized in school systems throughout the nation in the following decades. While this probably served to defuse some of the anger on the political right and among religious conservatives over sex education, it did not make that anger and organized resistance disappear.

It was also becoming clear to everyone that what happened in Anaheim was going to happen elsewhere, and that a well-organized and funded assault was being made on both sex education (in any form) and sex educators. The assault on sex education was tied to a new conservative politics of resentment—at gains made by women and the growing movement for abortion rights, at the growing recognition of the "normality" of homosexuality and homosexuals, and at the "sex revolution" that was being led by the young, in which sexuality was uncoupled from conventional norms and moral obligations, and recognized as (in the language of the day) revolutionary. The revolution of 1968 and 1969 in the U.S. was a revolution of long-repressed desire, and the youth would lead this revolution. The result was a reawakening of a puritanical, fundamentalist, and evangelical Christian right, seeking a return to a safe and secure sense of what is morally right and wrong, and what it means to be a woman and what it means to be a man. In returning to fundamentalist Christian understandings of sexuality, social conservatives also challenged the authority of the health-education profession to establish the sex-education curriculum, and they wanted sex education out of the schools. This was a challenge that health professionals were not well prepared, at least at first, to take up. They did not have a political language to frame a response since their professionalism was grounded on their claims to objectivity, scientific knowledge, and political neutrality. But they did begin to find a voice to respond to the assault on their field, one that understood that professionals could not sit on the sidelines in a cultural war that now threatened them. Health professionals were still a fairly powerful group in the formulation of government policy and the sex-education curriculum, and some up-and-coming leaders in the field, whose consciousness was forged out of the 1960s, were beginning to push the field toward an activist politics of engagement.

When the annual convention of the American School Health Association was held in Philadelphia in November 1969, the atmosphere was different than it had been in the previous 42 conventions. This was a year in which revolution was in the air, and in which language—even professional language—became impassioned. In a speech at the convention, Gere Fulton, a professor of health education at Trenton State College in New Jersey, began by quoting a passage of which he said the circumstances were different but the sentiment applicable: "If a vocal minority, however fervent the cause, prevails over reason and the will of the majority, this nation has no future as a free society."[15] The quote was from a television address on November 4 by President Nixon, on the situation in Vietnam, in which he made the claim that dissent by a vocal minority at home should not block continuation of a war supposedly supported by the majority. If Nixon's claim that a majority of Americans supported an "unpopular war" was hard to sustain, his point—according to Fulton—was a good one when applied to the "radical right," which suddenly had "discovered sex!" This naming of a movement as the "radical right" was a decisive discursive shift, for it positioned the movement as out of the mainstream of American politics. Fulton noted that the education director of the Christian Crusade, Dr Gordon Drake, in his "classic exposé" *Is the Schoolhouse the Proper Place to Teach Raw Sex?* also supported campaigns against water fluoridation and the theory of evolution, claimed that "being homosexual means you don't believe in God," and that "birth-control chemicals can be legislated into the drinking water"; and he even believed "that if God meant us to be nudists, He would have created us with fur, or at least feathers." By placing the attack on sex education within the context of these ridiculous claims by a few "crazy" people, Fulton both made fun of critics and belittled the seriousness of the threat. This was perhaps not the best thing to do, since it implied not worrying about the attacks on sex education and dismissing them—or at least having confidence that "the facts" would prevail over "extremism" and the "propaganda mills of the Christian Crusade and the John Birth Society." Fulton linked both these groups with a number of committees: Mothers Organized for Moral Stability (MOMS), Movement to Restore Decency (MOTOREDE), Parents Opposed to Sex Education (POSE), and even the Committee to Halt Indoctrination and Demoralization in Education (CHIDE). For Fulton, all these groups and committees on the radical right were characterized by an "aura of self-righteous piety and super-patriotism," and had appointed themselves "guardians of public morality." Brandishing the Bible and the flag, they "desecrate both in their efforts to destroy all that they represent."[16]

In the rest of his talk, Fulton identified and commented upon four codes that the radical right used to discredit sex education: sex education as a communist plot, sex in Sweden, sex and children, and sex and sin. Sex education as a communist plot is a theme that harkened back to the late 1940s and early 1950s McCarthy era, when communists were represented as being everywhere, undermining the strength of the nation from within and preying on impressionable young people. Fulton cited a story circulated by some radical-right groups that claimed to be a true account of a Soviet document found near the end of World War II by Allied Military Intelligence agents titled *Communist Rules for Revolution*. At the very top of the list, revolutionaries were called upon to "corrupt the young, get them away from religion. Get them interested in sex." While Fulton noted that the authenticity of the document was highly dubious, that did not seem to matter. Once it was distributed and promoted as true, it was taken by many as true. Those on the radical right who were of a "conspiratorial orientation" had recently reported to the press that Dr Isadore Rubin, a leader of SIECUS, had been "identified" as a member of the Communist Party before the House Committee on Un-American Activities. To be "identified" is thus, Fulton argued, equated with being "confirmed" as a communist, when, in fact, Dr Rubin had taken the Fifth Amendment in the early 1950s when she had been asked if she was or ever had been a member of the Communist Party. She did so, according to Fulton, as a way of protesting "the un-American activities of these committees." To refuse to answer their questions was the only honorable choice many people called before the committees could make. Another accusation against sex education by groups on the political right was that it would lead to the kind of "decadence" exhibited in Sweden. In this case, critics of sex education in the U.S. made much of a 1967 book by Birgitta Linner, *Sex and Society in Sweden*.[17] Fulton observes that the use of this highly regarded, scholarly work by the Christian right exemplified the tactics of extremists—"the glib lie, innuendo, out-of-context quotations, and the ubiquitous *non-sequitur*."[18] Inferences were drawn from evidence that could not be substantiated, and even contradicted the interpretations of the scholars cited. Sweden was represented by antisex-education crusaders as a "decadent" space, with high rates of divorce and promiscuity, STDs, use of pornography, and suicide—and all the result of sex education in the schools, which had been mandatory since 1956. What got unsaid, Fulton said, is that these rates were comparable or lower than in the U.S. and other developed countries. As for pornography, he agreed that "sex censorship seems to be quite limited in Sweden, but they are much concerned about obscenity of another type—violence. Strange people those Swedes."[19] The attempt by the radical right to turn Sweden into a "strange," "decadent" country is here countered by the ironic use of the word "strange." Who after all is strange, and from whose perspective?

The argument about "sex and children" on the right, according to Fulton, had to do with the fear that exposing children to sex education would encourage them to "experiment." Coupled with this was an assumption that if the schools did not tell young people about sex, they would not know anything about it and would not therefore "experiment." Then there is the argument that children (including adolescents, from the right's perspective) are not ready for the "raw" language of sex. "I would suggest," Fulton responded, "that it is not the children who aren't ready for the words, but rather the adults who refuse to recognize the existence of childhood sexuality." Finally, to characterize the theme of "sex and sin," Fulton quoted from a popular evangelical talk-show preacher in New Jersey, "The teaching of sex without the teaching of sin is the work of Satan!" But this moralistic stance of sex education refused to acknowledge that the question the nation's educators faced was "Whose morals shall be taught?" Indeed, many more moderate and mainstream religious groups had endorsed sex education. Health-education professionals had an obligation, Fulton said, to endorse a secular democratic ethics based on principles of "self-respect, respect for the rights of others, and a concern for developing good interpersonal relations."[20] Slowly, across the next decade, health educators like Fulton would begin to understand their role more politically, if only because the Christian right had politicized sex education. The professional discourse of sex education would shift from a narrow concern with "adjustment" and "normal development" to concerns with "getting real" about adolescent sexual behavior, providing adolescents with the "facts" they needed to protect themselves, and advancing an antibias and equity curriculum. To be sure, the concern with "normal" adjustment never really disappeared in sex education, for schools have been and continue to be very "normalizing" institutions. That is, they have been organized in ways that teach a "hidden curriculum" of conformity to dominant norms for the performance of gender, race, class, and sexual identities. The widespread acceptance of bullying practices in public schools in the U.S., for example, teaches a hidden curriculum of adjusting to dominant norms for the performance of gender. Those who do not normalize themselves, which is to say act like "normal" males or females, get targeted for bullying and harassment practices. But at least the formal sex-education curriculum, and professional health educators began to create a space in schools for challenging some of this hidden curriculum of schooling, a space in which tolerance, if not full acceptance of homosexuality and the homosexual, was the official curriculum. Even family-life education no longer preached that homosexuality was a disorder after the 1970s and began to develop a more inclusive and expansive view of the changing American family—although the emphasis in family life continued to be about understanding adolescent sexuality as preparation for heterosexual marriage.

Some like to think of the 1970s as the golden age of sex education in the U.S., when sex education received more attention in family-life and home economics courses, and in health and physical-education classes in high schools across the nation. The liberal-humanist approach associated with SIECUS was the most popular model of sex education, although elements of life-adjustment progressivism continued to be found in family-life courses. But there were problems with this narrative of the success of sex education. As I have already said, it put sex educators and the sex-education curriculum in conflict with a hidden curriculum of schooling that still was not friendly to either female, homosexual, or gender-nonconforming students. Outside the sex-education curriculum, the school remained a hostile place for sexual and gender difference. So long as the discourse on gender, sexuality, and homosexuality could be contained to a few lessons in health classes, it posed no broader threat to the hidden curriculum of inequity and intolerance. This suggests the importance of moving beyond the fight for a safe space to talk about sexuality in the curriculum to viewing sexuality education as a resource and agent for change in the overall ethos of a school. Another problem with the narrative of the "success" of sex education was that health educators developed a fact-based curriculum that almost completely ignored popular culture and youth culture. It is ironic that as professional educators debated about how best to talk about sex and sexuality with adolescents, young people were tuning in each week to *Peyton Place* on primetime network television, and this was a powerful new sexuality curriculum which professional health educators were ill-prepared for and unwilling to engage in. Youth were talking about sex and sexuality, but their texts and their language were not represented in the sex-education curriculum. In fact, the Christian right would prove to be far more effective than professional health educators were in presenting their message in the media and in the language of youth culture. Finally, the apparent success and growth of sex education in the U.S. after the "victory" against the Christian right in Anaheim has to be balanced by the fact that the Christian right was not going away, and would continue to mobilize power at local and state levels until it was able to take on the professional health–education establishment on a somewhat more equal footing. Professional health educators pursued a strategy of belittling and poking fun at social-conservative and Christian-right opponents of sex education by representing them as on the political, lunatic "fringe" and as outright "liars" when it came to the "facts" about sexuality. But throughout the 1970s the Christian right would continue to grow at local, state, and national levels. It would forcefully enter the battle again in the 1980s with a Republican administration in power that was beholden to it. Christian-right and social-conservative movements would move from being fringe groups, to a major power bloc in the Republican base.

3

THE "PROBLEM" OF TEEN PREGNANCY AND THE WELFARE MOTHER

The 1960s and 1970s

The problem of the unwed teenage mother and of unwanted teenage pregnancies have been perennial problems in sexuality education, and it is no exaggeration to say that these related "problems" called the field of sexuality education into existence, for it would have no life and history without them. As perennial problems, they have been articulated across a broad spectrum of social classes and racial and ethnic groups. But it is also true that poor black and Latina, teenage, welfare mothers have been made to represent the crisis of teenage pregnancy in its extreme, and that they, more than white, middle-class, pregnant teens, for example, have been defined as a problem population—a population whose sexuality is to be explained as the effect of a dysfunctional family structure and a vicious cycle of poverty and welfare dependency. When this new interest in the welfare mother and her sexuality began to surface in the mid-1960s, it was cloaked in a language that was ostensibly liberal, that offered help for those stuck in the vicious cycle of poverty and welfare dependency. But, as its critics were quick to point out, it blamed the victim and made them—both individually and as members of racial minority communities—responsible for healing themselves by developing "normal," white, middle-class sexual mores, tied to two-parent family structures and normative gender roles. That would supposedly solve the problem of unwanted pregnancies and the problem of welfare dependency at the same time. The "problem" of the adolescent welfare mother, and the larger "Negro problem" were linked in these ways in federal policy for the first time in the Johnson administration, and they found expression in particular in the 1965 Moynihan Report, released by the U.S. Department of Labor as *The Negro Family: The Case for National Action*.[1] The report located the source of the problem of poverty in the Negro family, which had been broken up during and after slavery. The rise in the number of welfare-dependent, single, black mothers that the report decried was only a sign of a larger problem that was holding "Negro society" back. "At the heart of the deterioration of the fabric of Negro society is the deterioration of the Negro family," the report began. This in turn was producing a "weakness" in the Negro community, since the family was so important in "shaping character." The problem, according to the report, was more specific than the Negro family—it was the lower-class, lower-socioeconomic, Negro family that was the problem. The middle-class Negro family was emulating its white counterpart, which "had achieved a high degree of stability and is maintaining that stability."[2] Interestingly, the white middle-class family that was experiencing high divorce rates is still the model of the stable family, the family that shapes the "character and ability" of young people in ways that lead to high levels of achievement and success in school and life. By contrast, the family structure of the "lower class Negro is highly unstable, and in many urban areas is approaching complete breakdown." One of the results was that a quarter of all "Negro births are now illegitimate." Just as bad, "almost one-fourth of Negro families are headed by females." Note as well that while Moynihan goes out of his way to point out that the problem is with "lower-class Negroes," the statistics are for Negroes as a whole versus whites as a whole. Differences are recognized in the black community only to have those differences ignored and erased through an analysis that focuses on race. The problem is reduced to one-dimensional racial analysis of differences between "stable," white families and "unstable," black families. Finally, this "Negro problem," situated in the instability of the Negro family, is shown to have a direct state cost in "a startling increase in Welfare dependency."[3] The contradiction of such a conclusion is that the Johnson administration had overseen a massive extension of the federal welfare program through Aid for Families with Dependent Children (AFDC), and was in this sense actively involved in promoting welfare dependency. But now that welfare costs were no longer so affordable, what with a war to fight in Vietnam, the report announced that a long history of Negro dependency upon the support of whites needed to come to an end, that Negroes had to become self-supporting, and that required rebuilding strong, patriarchal families that supported achievement and economic advancement. The Negro problem is thus to be solved through new means, with more and more responsibility shifted to Negroes to solve the problem for themselves rather than having to continue to rely on others to support them.

Perhaps it should not surprise us now that social scientists and political leaders and other supporters of the Moynihan Report were surprised by the intensity of the reaction from the black community when the report was issued. Moynihan and his associates spoke from the unquestioned perspective of a white, cultural elite, and part of that perspective was imagining that they were actually representing an objective, neutral, sociological analysis of the "problem." When African Americans spoke and wrote and researched about "the Negro problem," they presumably did so from a biased standpoint and thus what they had to say had to be understood and appreciated for what it was—their perspective. But when social scientists and political leaders, who just happened to be white, spoke and wrote and researched the "problem," they presumably did so from the perspective of reason and science alone, and, thus, what they had to say could be trusted. They certainly could not be accused of being racist. Quite the contrary, they maintained. They took an enlightened, social-science perspective on race in America, one that acknowledged the crippling effects of slavery and then the Jim Crow era in the South, as well as the crushing impact of generational poverty, on the "problem" the nation faced. How could "Negroes" have any problem with that? In fact, one of the key attributes of the culture of whiteness in the 1950s and 1960s was this pervasive positioning of social-science analysis by white, middle-class males as objective and unbiased. Black Americans, as the object of this white research and policy gaze, could see it for what it was—a discourse that legitimated the continuation of racial inequality in the U.S. by "blaming the victim," as one of the report's major critics within the social-science community—William Ryan—so aptly labeled it.[4] The deficit theory of poverty and racial inequality had been woven together into a unifying narrative that explained why people were poor, why they tended to stay poor, and why African Americans in particular tended to be characterized by a pathological "culture of poverty." A subtle but nonetheless significant shift had occurred in the way the civil-rights struggle was being framed. Whereas it once had been a battle for equality before the law, now it was to become a battle to normalize the Negro family, certainly with the support of some African Americans who held positions of power. When President Johnson went to Howard University, a historically black institution serving an African American elite, on June 4, 1965, to introduce the overall argument of the Moynihan Report and to announce an upcoming White House conference of social scientists, political leaders, and "outstanding Negro leaders" to address the problem of the Negro family, he got polite applause, but not the reception he expected. Later that fall, when the conference was held, it was a site of intense conflict among invited civil-rights leaders and administration officials.

We can almost mark the date of a shift in thinking and speaking that occurred within the black community in the U.S. and among civil-rights leaders as the time of the Watts Riots in Los Angeles in the summer of 1965. The civil-rights victories had not changed much about race in America, and the ghettoes were places of unemployment, abandoned dreams, street gangs, drugs, and hopelessness—mixed in with intense existential and visceral anger at the injustice of racial oppression, overseen by a watchful police force, in the "land of the free." That summer, a growing realization surfaced and began to take shape among civil-rights leaders: the realization that the struggle had to take on a new form, and that this next battle would be against institutional and systemic racism and the commonsense beliefs that supported institutional and systemic racism. That meant civil-rights leaders would have to take on the white liberal ideology of colorblindness, which, in fact, hid a pernicious form of white racism, one less easy to fight than overt racism because it claimed to be scientific, a form of racism that sought to normalize racial Others, to help them overcome their "pathologies" and their linguistic and "skill deficits." In this new context, they were increasingly unhappy with "social-work" and welfare-state approaches to overcoming the "problem" of the Negro family, but also the new conservative approaches associated with Moynihan that advanced the argument that the problem of illegitimacy and instability in the Negro family could not be successfully addressed through more welfare programs, but rather had to be addressed through a change in attitude among Negroes. Both positions were variations on a theme of blaming the victims of racial oppression. At the November 1965 conference on the problem of the Negro family, the convening papers were revised to make them more palatable to civil-rights leaders, with some papers countering Moynihan's view that the Negro family was undergoing "massive deterioration" and was in effect "crumbling." Instead, these authors argued for a "plateau" theory of the Negro family that suggested illegitimacy rates in the Negro community had stabilized since 1957, but still at a far higher rate than for whites.[5] One witness remembered a civil-rights leader commenting that "it was intolerable that the government had all these white men sitting around discussing 'our problem.'"[6] The black community wanted the government to do something about enforcing civil-rights laws now that they were on the book, and they wanted job-training programs, and they wanted an economic policy that created more good jobs. But most of all they were tired of being the problem and wanted whites to acknowledge who owned the problem, and who had to change their thinking in order to overcome it.

One of those to criticize the Moynihan Report and reframe the "problem" it addressed was Martin Luther King. In an address delivered on October 29, 1965, King played with the language of the "Negro problem," reinscribing it as the "Negro's problem," and thereby shifting the gaze to white racism as the cause.[7] He began by affirming the importance of stable families "consisting of mother, father, and child" as the "main educational agency of mankind." An individual's capacity to love was determined by "family life." He recited the then already-familiar statistics from the report—the high divorce rates, the substantially higher illegitimacy rates for Negroes, the number of Negro families headed by women, and the high proportion of Negro children who as a consequence were recipients of public aid. The problem was real, and the nation had to "meet it as other disasters are met with an adequacy of resources." But there was a danger, he warned, "that the problems will be attributed to innate Negro weaknesses and used to justify neglect and rationalize oppression." He dared to use the word "oppression," a word the Moynihan Report avoided like the plague, to refer to the current condition of African Americans living in Northern urban slums and ghettoes, not just to the condition of African Americans in the era of slavery, or the Jim Crow era in the South. At the same time, he situated the current condition of the Negro in this American history, this "ghastly background." Marriage among slaves was forbidden on plantations. "There were polygamous relationships, fragile, monogamous relationships, illegitimacies, abandonment, and, most of all, the tearing apart of families." Masters and their sons felt free to use female slaves to "satisfy their spontaneous lust or, when a more humane attitude prevailed, as concubines." King pointed to Virginia, "which we sentimentally call the state of presidents," as among the worst slave states, where slaves were bred for sale "in a vast breeding program which produced enormous wealth for slave owners." This history of treating African Americans as a "breeding stock" for a vast, racialized underclass had not disappeared. Rather, it had taken on new forms. The problem was in an oppressive white mindset, and if black families had suffered greatly because of this mindset, if too many were broken and unable to sustain themselves against the forces of racism, there should be no mistake who and what were responsible for a "tragedy that utterly defies any attempt to portray it in terms the human mind can comprehend." As for the matriarchal character of many black families, King once more framed this as the result of the "Negro's problem." Matriarchy had been established under slavery, and later it continued in Northern cities where women could find work as domestic servants at low wages. "The woman became the support of the household, and the matriarchy was reinforced." The Negro male, meanwhile, was often disabled by "rage and torment" that turned inward, "because if it gained outward expression its consequences would have been fatal." King attributed much domestic violence and spousal abuse in the black community on this black male rage and torment at their treatment in society. "In short, the larger society is not at this time a constructive educational force for the Negro." The larger society, more than the Negro family, was "psychopathic" to the extent that it did not recognize these truths. King also called on the white community to stop "mocking" the Negro community for its unstable families, and to remember that "severe strains are assailing white family life" as well, although they had a greater impact on the Negro family. The Negro family, King concluded, is "working against greater odds than perhaps any other family experienced in all civilized history. But it is winning."

King's words were meant to be conciliatory rather than inflammatory, but to address the very real anger many in the black community felt because an administration that had championed civil rights seemed to be blaming the victim for continuing racial inequalities in America. James Farmer, president of the Congress of Racial Equality (CORE) was not so conciliatory in his syndicated newspaper column. He argued that the report, though no doubt well intentioned, "provides the fuel for a new racism" built on the analysis of "Negro mental health." Nowhere, Farmer observed, did the report speak about the mental health of a white family structure that is "weaned on race hatred and passes the word 'nigger' from generation to generation." Nowhere in the report was there any understanding of how high illegitimacy rates in the black community are related to the fact that birth-control information and covert abortions are "by and large the exclusive property of the white man." Farmer wrote that he was angry, and that those in power needed to know that the "cocktail hour on the 'Negro Question' is over," that blacks were "sick unto death of being analyzed, mesmerized, bought, sold, and slobbered over while the same evils that are the ingredients of our oppression go unattended."[8] The white, male, power elite that had produced the Moynihan Report heard this message, but it heard it as perspectival discourse, in this case as representative of the perspective of a relatively small group of civil-rights activists whose anger and attitude was understandable, but hardly rational or scientific. Under the Johnson administration, what civil-rights leaders said could not be ignored or dismissed, for the Democratic Party was heavily dependent upon a high turnout among "Negro" Americans. But white political leadership was also more dependent upon the white vote, and that meant that "standing up" to black activists and civil-rights leaders helped them among white voters. The "culture-of-poverty" discourse that emerged out of the Moynihan Report attempted to hold this fragile racial alliance together, one in which whites showed sympathy for the victims of white racism, while at the same time blaming them and calling upon them to be more responsible and less impulsive sexually. This was a secular "family-values" discourse that represented the heterosexual, middle-class, "nuclear" family as the stable grounding for social order and a public morality—the "normal" family—at a time when the white, middle-class family was itself "collapsing." At least it affirmed for white, middle-class voters that their family type was still the cultural norm and standard, even if that norm bore little relationship to the reality it claimed to represent. For many African Americans, particularly middle-class African Americans, the culture-of-poverty rationale played into a desire to distance themselves culturally and spatially from the ghetto and the poor black masses living in poverty there, and to establish a fragile alliance with the white middle class around "family values" and "family life."

President Nixon's election in the fall of 1968 was interpreted as a decisive shift in American cultural politics toward the political right, and in many ways it was the beginning of a new ruling coalition and power bloc—the so-called "silent majority" of conservative, white, working-class and middle-class voters. This power bloc believed that "law and order," along with moral standards, had collapsed in the 1960s, that "welfare mothers" were getting all the help and attention from the government while "responsible," "law-abiding" "hard-working" citizens were paying for it, and that white people were increasingly victims of "reverse discrimination." At the same time, the new administration was more pragmatic and utilitarian than ideological, and decidedly centrist in its politics. Indeed, in the areas of sex education and family planning, the Nixon administration was more liberal than any administration before or since—although I want to argue that this apparent liberalism was linked to a "racial hygiene" perspective that historically was quite conservative and even racist. The consensus, pragmatic politics of the Nixon administration was reflected in his appointment of Moynihan, a Democrat and close advisor to the last president, as his Counselor on Urban Affairs. Under Moynihan's renewed leadership in urban policy, the Nixon administration began to follow through on one of the major conclusions of the 1965 Moynihan Report—that the welfare system was actually helping to produce the problem of welfare dependency and keep welfare mothers in a "vicious cycle of poverty." Under Moynihan's direction, the Nixon administration proposed the most radical overhaul of the welfare system ever proposed, and one that went far beyond what liberal Democrats proposed. The Family Assistance Plan (FAP) proposed to Congress by the administration would have ended the welfare system as we know it and replaced it with a federally guaranteed income for needy families with dependent children, paired with a requirement that recipients work, except for mothers with children under the age of three. Recipients were to be allowed to keep a portion of the wages they earned in addition to the guaranteed annual income. While never enacted, Nixon's welfare-reform proposal did establish a model for a system that would become popular in many states over the next several decades, combining work requirements with income support.

To help counter criticism that they proposed vastly expanding the role and scope of public aid to dependent children, Moynihan and Nixon countered with a strategy for reducing the need for public assistance by reducing the number of children born into poverty through family planning. This is where the sexuality of the welfare mother enters the picture again. The problem of a mushrooming welfare caseload was, in effect, to be managed by controlling the population of welfare-dependent children—through abortions, genetic screening, and voluntary sterilization. To reduce or eliminate welfare dependency, Nixon and Moynihan proposed a strategy of fighting for the rights of poor welfare-dependent mothers and unwed teenagers to have unrestricted access to family-planning services, just like middle-class and upper-class women had. They explicitly had Planned Parenthood in mind as an exemplary model of family-planning services. Founded in 1921 in Brooklyn, New York, by Margaret Sanger to bring birth-control advise to the urban poor, Planned Parenthood was, by the late 1960s, providing adults and adolescents with information and advice on birth-control options—including abortion in states where it was legal, like New York and California. After the 1973 Roe v. Wade decision by the U.S. Supreme Court legalizing a woman's right to choose, Planned Parenthood grew to become the nation's leading provider of family-planning services, and Nixon and Moynihan looked to it as a model of the type of program that would be needed to respond to what they identified as the most pressing social problem of our times—the problem of population growth. This was the subject of President Nixon's special address to Congress on July 18, 1969. In that address, Nixon modified the framing of issues in the Moynihan Report. He would choose to ignore race entirely in his address, and instead focus on the problem of high birthrates among "low income women of childbearing age" within the U.S., and upon U.S. responsibility to respond to the problem of high birthrates and over-population within "developing" nations.[9] He began his remarks by speaking of the global challenge of overpopulation, and of the need to regulate population so that it does not outstrip economic growth within the population. The current problem, consequently, was attributable to an imbalance between population growth and economic growth. High birthrates among the poorest of the world's peoples, Nixon said, were "in large measure a consequence of rising health standards and economic progress" that allowed people to live longer and reduced the infant mortality rate. The "developed" world had, in effect, helped create this problem by promoting "social progress" through economic development in the "underdeveloped" world, and now the U.S. and other developed nations had a responsibility, the President said, to help lift the "burden of population growth" from those nations undergoing development. If "economic development falls behind population growth," he warned, " [the] quality of life actually worsens." He thus had directed the Agency for International Development (AID) to give population control and family planning high priorities, and also directed the secretaries of Commerce and Health, Education, and Welfare and the director of the Peace Corps and the United States Information Agency "to give close attention to population matters." With birthrates remaining high and death rates dropping, the U.S., he said, would stand ready to "provide assistance to countries which seek our help in reducing high birthrates." This assistance, he added, "can be freely accepted or rejected" by the individuals and nations that receive it. This was to be the stipulation: that no one would be forced to use birth control against their will or in opposition to their own religious beliefs. But the U.S. would actively support making family planning and birth control more widely available in the developing world. This would be done because people in developing countries, who shared a "common humanity," had a right to birth-control and reproductive-rights counseling, but also because high rates of population growth in the developing world "threaten international stability." When population increases outstrip economic development, the standard of living drops, and people can become more militant and even revolutionary in their demands—and thus presumably more open to communist propaganda. So birth control was a mechanism for stabilizing the global order, and allowing the development of undeveloped populations and lands to continue in an orderly manner that did not generate a revolutionary fervor. If the West was to win the Cold War with communism, it would have to make sure that the development of "undeveloped" lands and peoples occurred in ways that were not "destabilizing" of the current world order.

As for the problem of population growth within the U.S., Nixon's argument was in all ways the same. He called upon the Office of Economic Opportunity (OEO), the agency created by the Johnson administration to coordinate the "war on poverty," to shift its attention to family planning for the poor. Under the Johnson administration, OEO had been actively working for empowerment of the poor, and it hired many people of color to lead the "war." This militant activism, community-organized approach within OEO was now to be replaced with a more conventional family-planning approach, which saw high illegitimate birthrates among the urban poor as the cause of their problem, rather than as a symptom of their oppression. That cause would now be waged in the language of the right of low-income women to "adequate access to family-planning assistance." Nixon declared that "no American woman should be denied access to family-planning assistance because of her economic condition." By framing family planning in a rights discourse rather than a utilitarian, biopower discourse of social costs, Nixon appealed to deeply rooted American beliefs about freedom and equity. But he also raised the fear of instability among economically disadvantaged people in the U.S. if increases in population and large families kept them locked in poverty and deprived them of "quality of life," similar to people in the developing world. The 1972 report of President Nixon's Commission on Population Growth (more commonly known as the Rockefeller Commission Report), further developed themes Nixon had raised in his 1969 speech to Congress and moved them in the direction of specific policy recommendations. The report recommended public and private financing of all the costs of family-related health services, including contraception, voluntary sterilization, and the "safe termination of unwanted pregnancies." Released just one year before the U.S. Supreme Court Roe v. Wade decision, the report called for the repeal of all laws that restrict abortions so that they may be performed (as in New York state) "on request by duly licensed physicians under conditions of medical safety." As for the decision to have or not have an abortion, the report said that "should be left to the conscience of the individual concerned ... with the admonition that abortion not be considered a primary means of birthrate control." Under the category of research, the report called for the study of genetically related disorders and the development of effective screening techniques to identify genetic disorders. This would all be linked to a network of genetic-counseling services, supposedly to offer advice to prospective parents as to whether a fetus is genetically defective so that they might choose to abort it, or choose not to have a child given their own genetic profiles. In public schools, the report called for the elimination of legal restrictions on young peoples' access to contraceptive and prophylactic services, and also the adoption of affirmative laws permitting minors to receive sex-education instruction without parental consent. Finally, woven throughout the report was the language of "sex equity." Sex-education and family-planning agencies were to encourage young women to "choose attractive roles in place of or supplementary to motherhood," and they should be free to "develop as individuals rather than being molded to fit some sexual stereotype" (Rockefeller Commission Report).

Nixon had appointed the commission and its chairperson, and charged them with their task; and it seems likely that they came up with pretty much what he expected them to come up with, which is to say a report that completely ignored traditional religious teaching. But even in 1972, it was not possible to completely ignore the Christian right or its growing influence in the Republican Party. So in accepting the report, Nixon made a public statement that, "I do not support the unrestricted distribution of family-planning services and devices to minors. Such measures would do nothing to preserve and strengthen close family relations."[10] Much could hinge, of course, on what the president meant by "unrestricted." Nixon appeared to be affirming "family values," yet his words in support of the report seemed to contradict "family values," at least as that term was beginning to be used by Christian conservatives. This rhetorical strategy, designed to placate those on the Christian right even as the President ignored them in the formulation of policy, was a hallmark of the Nixon administration. If it were still possible to, for the most part, ignore the Christian right in 1972, it would not be possible for later Republican, and even Democratic, presidents to do so. It is also possible that Nixon's strategy backfired to the extent that it made the Christian right more cynical and suspicious of the Republican Party and its leadership, and more certain that a new leadership in the party would be needed in order to realize "God's agenda" for America. Nixon would not be their man. By framing the "population problem" in terms of a woman's right, and more specifically the rights of poor women in the U.S. and abroad, and by affirming a woman's right to choice with regard to abortion, Nixon won the support of women's rights and reproductive rights groups. Susan Gustavus, writing in a special issue of the *Social Science Quarterly* on the Rockefeller Commission Report, summed up the attitude of most women, from low-income welfare mothers to suburban professionals, that the recommendations made by the report on contraceptives, abortion, and role alternatives for women "are certainly not new recommendations to … anyone who has heard of Women's Liberation."[11] At the same time, she expressed hope that because these recommendations were part of a government report, "they are likely to get wider exposure, gain greater respectability, and stimulate even more discussion." Women's liberation used a more "provocative" and less academic voice, but agreed on many of the same points. Gustavus did raise one concern. With all the report's emphasis on choice and freedom to choose among women and adolescents, "what would we do if, given these freedoms, women still preferred the motherhood role and preferred to engage in sexual relations without the benefit of contraception?" Her point was that the report valued some choices over others. For example, the report suggested that in a family-life sex-education course in high school, girls could study the economic costs and lost-opportunity costs of bearing each child, which the report estimated at $59,000. This rather "startling" figure, Gustavus observed, is designed to "cause some girls to reflect past the immediate hospital bills or baby furniture fees," and its manifest aim is to reduce the birthrate.[12] But no moralistic appeals were to be made and the stigma of illegitimacy was to be removed. The only fault she could find with the report's recommendations on abortion were that they carried several qualifiers, including the admonition that abortion not be considered as the primary means of birth control. That, she predicted, would run into resistance from some of the "more vehement" women in the movement, while the overall report would be "welcomed by groups currently lobbying for women's right."[13]

In this special issue of *Social Science Quarterly*, Ozzie Edwards wrote the article on "The Commission's Recommendations from the Standpoint of Minorities." It is noteworthy that minorities' standpoints are acknowledged in a social-science journal, where researchers had previously always spoken just as researchers, looking at things objectively and scientifically. Now, suddenly, in 1972, a top-tier, social-science journal includes essays from a woman's standpoint and the standpoint of minorities (as if they could be lumped together under one standpoint). If these two standpoints do not adequately reflect the diversity of standpoints and identities in the U.S., they are a beginning, and they do seem to acknowledge that standpoint or perspective matters. Edwards carries the burden of speaking for all "minorities," and thus sees it as his responsibility to raise objections to the report's primary recommendations. "Were these advanced in another context," he notes, "the effort might be applauded as reinforcement for a worthy cause." Yet, given the nation's history, "America's minorities," he concludes, have reason to question the merit of "national birthrate control programs."[14] What goes unspoken, but is clearly implied in Edwards' comments, is the fear of a resurfacing of a "eugenics" and "racial-hygiene" movement aimed at eliminating genetically defective individuals from the gene pool.[15] In the early 20th century in the U.S., the eugenics movement represented racial minorities and the poor as genetically defective. This led to state legislation in support of eugenics marriages—between individuals certified by the state to be of "good" genetic stock. It also led to laws banning interracial marriage in an effort to maintain the "purity" of the white race, and to the sterilization of welfare recipients and those institutionalized for mental illness and "retardation." Why, Edwards wondered, was the government so concerned about slowing population growth among the poor and racial minorities? Why did the report link crime reduction in the inner city to population control? The effect was to deflect attention away from the real causes of poverty and crime. "This time it is fertility. A decade ago it was breakdown in the family structure. Tomorrow ... who knows?" In each case, the problem is located in minorities, and the minority "problem" is to be solved by lowering their fertility levels. Edwards proposes a novel alternative as a way of making his point. The report had recommended that birthrates among various racial minorities should be adjusted to maintain the current racial ratios in the population. Why should we make the assumption that the current racial ratios are ideal? "Is it not plausible," he writes, "that marked increases in the proportions of blacks, Chicanos, and Indians would do much to promote harmonious race relations?"[16] Why not support a program to control white fertility and increase fertility rates among minorities until various groups are more equally represented in the population? Williams knows that these questions will strike the white reader as ludicrous, and that they are politically unfeasible. But he makes his point, that the "population problem" among the poor and minorities is a problem constructed from a white, Eurocentric standpoint.

Finally, the special issue of *Social Science Quarterly* contained an essay by Arthur Dyck on "ethical assumptions and implications" of the report. Dyck was Professor of Population Ethics at Harvard Divinity School, and he brought a rather orthodox, Christian perspective to an analysis of the report. For him, the report placed altogether too much emphasis upon individual freedom, and even extended this freedom to those as young as 12 and 13, who could exercise their rights to procure and use contraceptives, and even have an abortion, as a matter of individual choice, without regard for parental permission or social consequences. According to Dyck, "minors appear to have been given total reproductive freedom," by the report's recommendations. The report did not explicitly distinguish between minors of 12 and 13 living at home, and older adolescents and adults living on their own. In effect, the whole idea that adolescence was a special phase of life, and that adolescents needed to be encouraged to delay sexual fulfillment until marriage was giving way, he argued, to an age in which "sex is not a familial matter at all," only something for individuals (regardless of age) to make choices about. Sterilization and abortion, Dyck noted, were irreversible choices which immature young people may make today but regret tomorrow. Then there was the very real possibility that "permissive abortion policies might undermine our regard for human life." He cited reports from New York of fetuses born living and left to die, and of physicians knowingly performing abortions past the legal 24 weeks. Dyck feared that the report would encourage people to think of freedom as "the removal of legal and administrative impediments," rather than a more positive freedom based on the establishment of conditions (such as the elimination of poverty) that make it possible for people to develop their fuller potential. The report explicitly did not recommend a continuation of the "war on poverty," claiming that it was inconsistent with American values of an unregulated, "free" economy, which required a small government. According to the report, "Imbedded in our traditions as to what constitutes the American way of life is freedom from public regulation, ... freedom to do as we please with what we own."

Consequently, rather than structural changes in the economy, "population control" was presented as the answer to the burden of poverty and as the means for the poor (particularly the black and Latino/a poor) to extricate themselves from the crippling cycle of poverty. As for sex roles, Dyck concluded, the report admirably advanced the cause of women's rights, but at the same time went too far in suggesting that women assume more "nontraditional" roles and even consider choosing not to become mothers. The report championed giving women and parents more freedom to choose different lifestyles, and "freedom in this report is always good in itself." The "welfare of children, and the quality of their development in their earliest years" also needed to be considered, and that might mean a mother at home to provide "warmth and security" to infants.[17] Dyck, as a social conservative, feared that a sexual and reproductive rights discourse would be applied to young adolescents as well as older adults, and that women's rights might be privileged over women's responsibilities as mothers. In the case of such criticism, women rights groups would rally around the report's recommendations. The report did appear liberal when it came to women's rights, reproductive rights, and the rights of poor women; and much of the report, as I have said, was framed in a language of rights. But it was also possible to see in the report, as some African Americans and Latino/a Americans did, a revival of the eugenics and racial-hygiene movements, part of a national strategy to keep minority populations in check. Which of these was the "real" report?

Both the emphasis on women's rights and adolescent rights (on the one hand) and population control (on the other) came together in a discourse that was about what Foucault called "biopower." Foucault used the term "biopower" to refer to this form of governmentality over populations and subpopulations to manage and control rates of fertility and invest in the health and productivity of the citizenry and labor force.[18] What was new by the late 1960s was that biopower was becoming a much more explicit and organized force in national policy, and new technologies of biopower were being developed. Biopower concerned itself with the financial and social burden of "unwanted children," and also with the economic productivity of welfare mothers and adolescent bodies. Populations and subpopulations become the subject of complex statistical analysis by social scientists, with intervention strategies targeted at both subgroups and individuals in these subgrounds (such as unwed welfare mothers). Is there anything wrong with this? There is, as I said earlier, something wrong with it when the aim is to control or "manage" the population of subordinate or oppressed groups in society as a way of insuring that their proportion of the total population does not rise. Then biopower becomes part of a system of racial domination. If many whites seemed unaware of this history of eugenics and "racial hygiene" in the U.S., racial minorities could not afford to be unaware. According to one study of social workers in Louisiana, black social workers assumed that population policy, certain economic policies, and programs for preventing adolescent pregnancy "are, in fact, a 'hidden agenda.'" In private interviews, "fears of genocide" were openly discussed. White social workers were aware of this attitude among their black colleagues and went to "elaborate lengths" to convince them that "genocide is not the population policy of either the U.S. government or the state of Louisiana."[19] Because biopower discourses of the problem of adolescent female sexuality are narrowly pragmatic and social functionalist, even if they invoke a language of women's rights and human rights, they have been open to criticism by social and religious conservatives who view them (rightly I think) as coldly rational and utilitarian, as well as racial minorities who associate them with a legacy of genocide and "racial hygiene" in the U.S. Nevertheless, throughout the 1970s both Republican and Democratic administrations would approach the "problem" of teenage pregnancy and motherhood with much the same pragmatic biopower perspective designed to control "overpopulation" among dependent populations. If this made sense to the power elites who helped shape welfare and population policy, it did not make sense to leaders of America's growing, racialized and gendered underclass, and it did not make sense to the growing ranks of Christian conservatives mobilized as a backlash movement on the political right. For these reasons, the Nixon administration was never able to follow through on population control legislation; and then the Watergate investigation began and everything was put on hold.

The U.S. Supreme Court's Roe v. Wade decision in 1973 would, however, succeed in carrying out the core element of Nixon's population control policy: unrestricted access to abortion and birth control for minors, without parental consent. Ironically, the legalization of abortion did not lead to a leveling off of the birthrate among the urban underclass in the U.S., nor did it lead to a decline in the birthrate among unwed adolescents. In the 1970s, for a number of reasons, a sexual revolution was going on among young people of all class and racial backgrounds. The availability of birth control and abortion on demand, along with wider accessibility of drugs to treat STDs, may have encouraged young people to be more sexually active with more partners, but it is also clear that the sexual revolution was a cultural production, and a direct outcome of the liberalizing of sexual mores in the 1960s. At the same time, sexual politics became less about social transformation and more about individual freedom and what the sociologist Christopher Lasch called a "culture of narcissism."[20] For all these reasons, by the late 1970s the nation faced what was being called an "epidemic" of teenage pregnancies. As Willard Richan has observed in his history of social-welfare policy in the U.S., 1978 was the year when teenage pregnancy suddenly became big news in the media, and it was precisely at this point that the word "epidemic" began to be used as a way of describing what was happening. Headlines blared: "TEEN-AGE PREGNANCY: GLOBAL EPIDEMIC, ... AMERICA'S TEEN PREGNANCY EPIDEMIC. ... THE TEENAGE PREG-NANCY EPIDEMIC." A Harvard University biologist claimed that the problem "has reached dimensions of a national disaster, comparable to a flood, epidemic, or famine."[21] Here, before the AIDS epidemic—which was just around the corner, a real epidemic involving the spread of a deadly contagious virus—we find the language of an epidemic entering the public and policy discourse on adolescent sexuality in the late 1970s. And the epidemic is not STDs, but pregnancies, as if the bodies of unwed young women were diseased when they became pregnant. Almost all commentators, of all political stripes, used the same language of an "epidemic" of teenage pregnancy, although they differed considerably in what they thought the nation should do about this "epidemic."

The Guttmacher Institute is generally given credit for coining the term "epidemic" to refer to teenage pregnancies in its 1976 report *Eleven Million Teenagers: What Can Be Done About the Epidemic of Adolescent Pregnancies in the United States.* Alan Guttmacher had been an active participant in the organization of SIECUS in the 1960s when he chaired the medical advisory committee of Planned Parenthood, and he had established a quasi-autonomous affiliate of Planned Parenthood—which he called the Guttmacher Institute—to conduct statistical research on unwanted pregnancies, sex education, and the availability and use of contraceptives and abortion. It continues to be a leading institute engaged in collecting and analyzing survey data in these areas of concern, and disseminating findings to policy makers. Its 1976 report was cited again and again in newspaper articles, magazine articles, and in congressional hearings, and stirred considerable public debate. Its conclusions were also stated in statistical form. The U.S. had one of the highest teenage birthrates in the world; more than half the nation's adolescents (11 million) were sexually active; a million teenage girls became pregnant each year (about five percent), and 600,000 gave birth.[22] For the Guttmacher Institute, the policy-level response needed was to make family-planning services, including abortion, more widely available to teenagers, particularly the poor. If there was an epidemic, as the Guttmacher Institute claimed, then it seemed reasonable to adopt a medical model for responding: through contraceptives and abortions. So the language of "epidemic" is not neutral. It already envisioned its own medical response. For others, however, the sexual epidemic called for a moral rather than medical prophylactic. Those on the Christian right argued that the epidemic of teenage pregnancy had been encouraged by "pro-choice" rather than "pro-life" policies and that sex-education programs were part of the problem. By the 1976 presidential election, the Christian right could no longer be ignored, and Jimmy Carter's victory was in no small part attributable to his ability to win favor with this constituency since he was a Southern Baptist and personally opposed to abortion. His choice of Joseph Califano as Secretary of Health, Education, and Welfare—a Roman Catholic who also had publicly spoken out against abortions—was a sign that the cultural tide was shifting. That this shift to the right on sexual policy was begun under a Democratic administration suggests that it was a fairly broad cultural shift, a reaction against a decade of sexual freedom and the celebration of adolescent sexuality in popular culture and youth culture. In 1977, while the U.S. Supreme Court was affirming that family-planning agencies could not require parental consent for abortions, Congress passed legislation restricting the use of public funds for abortions. In 1978, the Carter administration managed to push through Congress a policy response to the "epidemic" of teenage pregnancies: The Adolescent Health Services and Pregnancy Prevention and Care Act. The law was a compromise in most every way. It provided federal funds for sex education and birth control, and family-planning services that advised adolescents on the availability of abortions, but it also required these agencies (such as Planned Parenthood) to "encourage" adolescents to inform their parents or guardians before they chose to have an abortion.[23] Furthermore, family-planning agencies opposed to abortion were not required to indicate to adolescents where they might go if they wanted to consider abortion as an option.[24] Once passed, the bill was funded at a low level, so that its impact was minimal, and so that resistance from pro-life groups was muted.

Constance Nathanson, in her study of social policy and adolescent women's sexuality, writes of "the dangers that lie in advocating birth control (or abortion) on grounds other than as a means for enlarging the opportunities of women to gain control of their lives."[25] We might add control of their bodies. This was the basis for the Roe v. Wade Supreme Court decision of 1973, and it is useful to return to that decision at the end of this chapter to chart the course that the court steered and to see how it framed the issues. That decision is often viewed as a victory for women's right to choose, and it was. But the majority decision was also a finely crafted balancing act between a discourse of women's rights, over their bodies and their lives, and a discourse of "compelling state interests" in restricting a woman's right to choose an abortion. But even these "compelling state interests," according to the court, have to do with protecting a "potential" citizen's rights so that when a fetus becomes "viable," the state may legitimately restrict the mother's right to an abortion. At the same time, the mother's rights to health must at all times override the fetus' right to life, and if her life is threatened during delivery her doctor may elect to abort the fetus without her prior permission. The state is represented by the court as protecting the rights of women to "privacy," yet also "promoting its interest in the potentiality of human life." Instead of a clear, unambiguous decision, the court ended up acknowledging that competing claims had to be weighed and considered within a shifting cultural and historical context; and this left open the possibility that another Supreme Court, at some future time, might strike a different balance. For those who still think the Constitution "speaks for itself," the Supreme Court decision is a case study in the reality of legal discourse and argumentation, in which the Constitution is made to support very different, even contradictory, interpretations.

Justice Blackmun, in delivering the opinion of the court, began by acknowledging "the sensitive and emotional nature of the abortion controversy, ... the vigorous opposing views, even among physicians, and ... the deep and seemingly absolute convictions that the subject inspires." People's thinking about abortion, he noted, reflected their philosophy, experiences, "exposure to the raw edges of human existence," and religious training and family values. As for the state's response, talk of "population growth, pollution, poverty, and racial overtones tend to complicate and not to simplify the problem." This is clearly meant to refer back to the Johnson-era Moynihan Report, but also the Rockefeller Commission Report on population growth released in the previous year and the subject, as I have indicated, of much public controversy. What is called into question here is the attempt by the state to use abortion as a means of population control, particularly among the poor and racial minorities, and this, according to the court, "complicates" a problem which should be "simplified"—that is, understood in terms of legal rights of individual citizens versus "compelling" state reasons for restricting these legal rights. To "simplify" means to take race and poverty out of the picture and return to the framing of the issue in terms of individual rights to privacy. Finally, to "simplify" means, according to the court, to resolve the issue "free of emotion and of predilection." Yet to make a decision supposedly "free of emotion" the court had to reject its earlier argument, that people's thinking and feeling about abortion is a result of their experiences and values. The court had to assume that "it" could rise above "people's thinking" and make a purely rational judgment based on the law, while at the same time admitting that the law must reflect changing cultural values and practices. The court then proceeded to review the medical and legal history of abortion, to establish that abortions have been widely practiced throughout history in various cultures, including the U.S., and that legal restrictions on abortions were a relatively recent development, noting that they derive from statutory changes made, for the most part in the latter half of the 19th century. As for earlier times, "We are told that at the time of the Persian Empire abortifacients were known and that criminal abortions were severely punished." At the same time, the Greeks and Romans apparently practiced abortion without moral condemnation or legal restriction. Roman gynecologists regularly performed abortions for their women patients when their health was threatened, and were trained "to think first of the life of the mother." The Greeks, according to the court, were more conflicted over abortion, and it found in ancient Greek culture the basic tension it identified in contemporary American culture. On one side was the Pythagorean school of philosophy which held that "the embryo was animate from the moment of conception, and abortion meant destruction of a living being." The abortion clause of the Hippocratic Oath, in its various translations, echoes this Pythagorean doctrine: "I will give no deadly medicine to anyone if asked, nor suggest any such counsel; and in like manner I will not give to a woman a pessary to produce abortion." While the Hippocratic Oath was endorsed by the American Medical Association (AMA) and grounded many doctors' principled opposition to performing abortions, the court notes that "the Oath was not uncontested even in Hippocrates' day." Only those who followed the strict ethical codes of the Pythagorean school of philosophers condemned abortion, along with doctor-assisted suicide. For most other Greeks, including Plato and Aristotle, abortion was accepted as a form of birth control, at least before "viability." So the court would follow Plato rather than Pythagoras. If the Christians were neo-Platonic in their separation of the spirit and the material world, they were more Pythagorean in their attitude toward abortion, and certainly this had something to do with the mythology of an "immaculate conception," but also of a human soul that exists from the moment of conception. According to the court, "this, it seems to us, is a satisfactory and acceptable explanation of the Hippocratic Oath's apparent rigidity."

Yet the court did not find this same rigidity in the British common-law tradition in which decisions were made in reference to centuries of preceding decisions in which various competing claims are recognized. "Abortion performed before 'quickening'—the first recognizable movement of the fetus in utero, appearing usually from the 16th to the 18th week of pregnancy—was not an indictable offense." The notion of the "quickening" of the fetus, like the Greek notion of "viability," suggests a more complicated notion of when life begins than orthodox Christianity. The question of whether or not abortions were acceptable hinged on the point at which the fetus was "formed," or "recognizably human," or when it became a person "infused with a soul" and "animated." A consensus evolved in old English law, Blackmun wrote, that "these events occurred at some point between conception and live birth," a point referred to as that of "mediate animation." Both the church and the state agreed to fix this point at 40 days for a male and 80 days for a female—supposedly because males were more animated than females. This code of "mediate animation" was the basis for common-law decisions about abortion up until the 19th century, when the term "quickening" came into favor, in reference to St. Thomas Aquinas' use of that term to refer to the moment when the soul enters the fetus. Before that time, while abortion was a sin, it was not a mortal sin and so to be treated far differently from abortions performed after the "quickening." The term "quickening" found its way from English common law to colonial common law in America, when abortion of a "quick fetus" was a crime, but apparently a very minor one—"a lesser offense." When a woman "quick with child" had an abortion, it was an injustice, but not murder, and probably not even manslaughter. The court then proceeds to argue that "a recent review of the common-law precedents argues … that even postquickening abortion was never established as a common-law crime." At least, the court concluded, it is "still disputed" as to whether or not the abortion of a "quick fetus" was ever a felony under common law in either England or in the U.S. up through the mid-19th century. New York enacted one of the earliest antiabortion laws in 1828, making it a crime to abort either a quick or unquickened fetus—although making the latter only a misdemeanor. That law also included a provision for "therapeutic abortion" to preserve the life of the mother. Still, the court noted, it was not until after the Civil War that most states began to draft antiabortion legislation to replace common law. Like the New York law, however, most differentiated between the severity of the offense for prequickening and postquickening abortions. Gradually, toward the end of the 19th century, statutory laws against abortion dropped the "quickening" distinction in penalties. The court found that by the end of the 1950s, "a large majority of the jurisdictions [in the U.S.] banned abortion, however and whenever performed, unless done to save or preserve the life of the mother." It found as well that in recent years there had been a "trend toward liberalization of abortions statutes," making the laws less stringent.

All this led the court to its conclusion that "throughout the major portion of the 19th century, abortion was viewed with less disfavor than under most American statutes currently in effect." Put somewhat differently, throughout most of American history, "a woman enjoyed a substantially broader right to terminate a pregnancy than she does in most states today." The court observed that the rise of the criminalization of abortion in the 19th century was associated with the rise of the American Medical Association (AMA), which had been fighting for tough abortion laws since its Committee on Criminal Abortion was appointed in 1857. That committee, in one of its early reports, claimed that there was "widespread popular ignorance of the true character of the crime," a belief among many that the fetus was not alive until after quickening. With the backing of the committee, the AMA adopted a resolution "against such unwarrantable destruction of human life," and called upon state legislatures to enact antiabortion laws. The court quoted an 1871 report by the AMA which recommended that it "be unlawful and unprofessional for any physician to induce abortion or premature labor, without the concurrent opinion of at least one respectable consulting physician, and then always with a view to the safety of the child—if that be possible." The 1871 report also condemned the "perverted views of morality entertained by a large class of females— aye, and men also, on this important question." Without having to say so directly, the court makes the point that the AMA, as a male establishment, had attempted to act as the final authority over female bodies, and also that a century before Roe v. Wade women had been fighting for the right to choose an abortion. In 1967, the AMA's Committee on Human Reproduction affirmed opposition to "induced abortion," except when there is a threat to the health of the mother or evidence that the child "may be born with incapacitating physical deformity or mental deficiency," or that a pregnancy "resulting from legally established statutory or forcible rape or incest may constitute a threat to the mental or physical health of the patient." By 1970, another AMA report noted a growing polarization among doctors on the issue of abortion, and a cultural shift in thinking seemed to be occurring in favor of legalization. That year the AMA adopted resolutions supporting abortions when performed by medical doctors, in hospital or clinic conditions, and when an abortion was in "the best interests of the patient."

In looking back over this troubled history, the court briefly reviewed the reasons given in defense of antiabortion laws in the 19th century, so that it might then argue that while there may have been some good reasons to ban abortions a century earlier, these reasons were no longer applicable or relevant. First, in the 19th century, antiabortion laws had been justified as a way of discouraging "illicit sexual conduct," based on the presumption that if women had widespread access to an abortion it would encourage them to be more sexually promiscuous and less morally virtuous. The court notes that this rationale does not distinguish between married and single women (a married woman may need an abortion after monogamous sexual relations with her husband); and it also extends the state's interest beyond a "proper" level of concern with "private" matters between a woman and her doctor. A second reason given in the 19th century for antiabortion laws was medical in nature. In the mid-19th century, abortion was still a hazardous procedure, without recourse to antiseptic techniques or antibiotic medicines. The court observed that "modern medical techniques have altered this situation," so that mortality rates for women undergoing an abortion in the first trimester were as low or lower than rates for normal childbirth. Finally, 19th century antiabortion laws had been defended in terms of the state's interest in protecting prenatal life, from the moment of conception. The court argued that the state has a primary interest in the health of the mother, but that it also had a competing interest in the health of prenatal life. However, "a legitimate state interest in this area need not stand or fall on acceptance of the belief that life begins at conception." A "less rigid claim" would be based on the state asserting the interests of the pregnant woman, but also some limited claim to prenatal life once it became a "potential" human—so long as the claim of this potential life never overrode the health claims of an actual existing life, the mother. "Maternity, or additional offspring, may force upon the woman a distressful life and future." These factors needed to be discussed, the court concluded, by the pregnant woman and her physician in private consultation. The text of the court's decision thus had the ironic effect of both condemning the medical profession for its historic role in promoting antiabortion laws, and then turning to that profession to help women choose whether an abortion is right for them. The court's decision rested on medical evidence as well, on the safety of abortions when conducted under the right medical conditions, and by licensed physicians. Even the court's discussion of rights is medicalized by framing the discussion in terms of the right of women to privacy in their consultations with and treatment by physicians. The doctor is to become both counselor and surgeon, the dispenser of advice as well as treatment. The pregnant woman cannot abort a fetus on her own, or with a midwife, or in any way except through a doctor. If this seems rational, it is also wise to remember that the court's decision was part of a larger movement toward the medicalization of social problems. Through medicalization, the problem is removed from the realm of morality and religious discourses regarding when a fetus has a soul—although the court's language on when a fetus becomes a "potential" human life and citizen certainly affirmed in its own way the distinction made by Aquinas between a "quickened" and "unquickened" fetus. The medicalization of the social problem of unwanted pregnancies also has the effect of insuring that the state intervenes as little as possible in decisions to terminate a pregnancy. There was always the possibility, implied in the Moynihan and Rockefeller Reports, that the state might encourage abortions among unwed teenagers or welfare recipients—particularly if they were poor or women of color—as a means of population control. Roe v. Wade only mentioned this possibility in passing, but the decision was a clear signal that the state had no business either encouraging or discouraging abortions. If the state may assert some public interest over a fetus after it becomes viable, it is not to interfere unduly with a private, individualized decision made in the privacy of a doctor's office. In fact, this privatization and medicalization was another form of biopower, with power invested in the medical profession by the state, to consult, advise, and make decisions with pregnant women, and perform abortions. If this is not direct, state-controlled biopower, it is an intervention by the state in concert with the medical profession and the discipline and technology of medical science in ways designed to limit the number of unwanted pregnancies. Much hinged, of course, on the word "unwanted" and who did not want them. The individualization, privatization, and medicalization of the problem of unwanted pregnancies was an attempt at a resolution of a socially constructed problem that of course did not go away and was not resolved, but rather only intensified, in the years after Roe v. Wade. The discourse of private, individual rights is essentially liberal, and it has been used in this case to counter movements on the religious right to bring moralistic religious values into a secular democratic public, and also to counter movements within the state that would link abortion to control of population(s)—although nothing explicitly would prevent the state from encouraging abortions among welfare recipients and developmentally handicapped people for example, or among unwed adolescents. What was left unresolved by Roe v. Wade is perhaps unresolvable: the tension between private concerns and rights over one's own body, and public concerns with the consequences of unwanted births on both young women and the broader public. There is also the tension between absolute moral and ethical principles and the messiness of living in a world in which competing moral and ethical claims must be weighed in the balance. The court's decision in Roe v. Wade is most useful as a sexuality-education text when it reminds us of this.

By the end of the 1970s, sexuality educators and policy makers generally were in agreement that the problem of "adolescent female sexuality and fertility control" (as the authors of a National Council on Family Relations study put it) was finally beginning to be effectively addressed, even if the crisis continued.[26] Two months into the new Reagan administration, in March 1981, the Guttmacher Institute published a follow-up report, *Eleven Million Teenagers*, to its 1976 report, *Teenage Pregnancy: The Problem that Hasn't Gone Away*. According to the 1981 report, more teenagers were using contraceptives, but because an increasing number of them were sexually active, more were becoming pregnant. Teenagers accounted for three of every ten abortions in the 1970s, and the number of abortions performed on teenagers doubled in the first five years after the Roe v. Wade decision. As a result, there had been a slight overall decline in the birthrate among teenagers. Increases in sexual activity among teenagers, the Guttmacher report concluded, were erasing earlier distinctions between different socioeconomic and racial groups, with the most dramatic increase in sexual activity among white, middle-class youth. The report endorsed programs of sex education that have as their "highest priority" the delivery of "preventative services" to youth, before they reach junior high, with an emphasis on contraceptive methods, such as the use of condoms, "that are appropriate to the episodic relationships of teenagers."[27] This policy-level discourse on the problem of teenage pregnancies played a large part in shaping the sexuality curriculum in the 1970s. Even before the Nixon administration's Rockefeller Commission Report on population control, a widely used 1970 textbook in sex education, designed for teachers, encouraged teachers to combine the topics of "population explosion" and contraception. The students' study of the "population explosion" involves drawing humorous political cartoons that depict the problem, and, as an example, the text mentions a cartoon that depicted "a stork flying with a baby over a large city. As the stork reaches the city he sees a large sign projecting in the sky that reads 'Sorry, Full.'"[28] That this stork fly-by occurs over a large city is significant; for this is where the problem of overpopulation is symbolically located, in crowded inner-city neighborhoods where America's racialized underclass lives. But all students, even "normal," white, middle-class students, are to learn of the economic costs of bearing an "unwanted" child, both on the mother and the society. In coldly economic rather than in moralistic terms, they learn of the advantages of "planning ahead" and being prepared to use contraceptives. Instead of raising questions about why young people should stay abstinent until marriage, the text suggests raising questions about why young people do not use contraceptives more often, what inhibits their use of contraceptives, and how they can become more informed users of contraceptives.

These were still questions that framed the sex-education curriculum by the end of the 1970s, although sex-education texts increasingly embraced a position of "values clarification" in which there were no "official" answers. In a 1981 text for sex educators, controversial topics include premarital sexual intercourse, masturbation, homosexuality, adultery, and abortion. The text offers a hypothetical question from a student: Should abortions on demand be allowed? On the one hand, teachers are encouraged to be very clear about the law. Students need to know that the U.S. Supreme Court makes abortion legal, at least in the first trimester. On the other hand, the text advises that "decisions related to human sexuality need to be made after considering input from many sources." These include parents, clergy, philosophers, and others who have thoughts and ideas related to abortion.[29] But it becomes clear that clergy and parents are a more likely source of advice than philosophers, "since learners' basic values most likely reflect those of their family, friends, and clergy." These are the people who are to help students decide how they feel about abortion. The teacher is to stick to providing information "input" for that decision-making process of each separate student. By emphasizing the teacher as only a dispenser of information, without values attached, and by focusing on individual student decision making on all controversial topics, sex educators effectively got themselves off the hook. They would endorse neither contraceptives nor abortion, nor premarital sex, nor homosexuality, nor even masturbation. And by encouraging students to fall back on the advice of clergy and parents, sex-education teachers also risked turning them over to a very repressive, moralistic, sexist, and homophobic culture, with taken-for-granted beliefs about sexuality that do not get questioned. This, then, would become the way sex educators sought to negotiate a position in the "culture wars" that were deepening throughout the 1970s. They would endorse a "values-clarification" approach, and an "objective," just-the-facts approach, all in an attempt to stay above the fray and, one might add, out of trouble. In the battles waged sporadically throughout the 1970s in local school districts across the country, Christian conservatives would prove to be better organized than progressives, and they would demand the firing of any teacher who "preached" or attempted to "indoctrinate" their children with progressive values; and they even became suspicious of "values clarification," seeing it as a form of values relativism. They wanted teachers to be teaching values, just Christian conservative values not progressive values. When "values clarification" became suspect, teachers stopped teaching about controversial issues almost entirely.

As for the supposed "epidemic" of teen pregnancy and the "problem" of high birthrates among poor, black, Latino/a youth in inner-city neighborhoods, with all the individual and social costs of this epidemic and this problem, they were still being announced as problems when the Reagan administration took office in 1981. The only thing that would change—and that was arguably quite significant—was the rationale and the technology for controlling the problems. The 1980s would see a shift toward a "just say no" attitude towards premarital sex in the culture, but still for the same purposes. A 1980 article in the *Journal of School Health*, based on a survey of professional sex educators, found that they believed the number one goal of sex education was "the reduction of unwanted adolescent pregnancy." Almost everyone, regardless of how they might differ in achieving that goal, agreed that the goal was important and should provide the framework for thinking about sex-education programs. A second, although also highly valued, goal was "the facilitation of positive and fulfilling sexuality [among adolescents]."[30] This second goal, while clearly valued by sex-education professionals, was understood to have a lower priority, and to cause conflict with some parents and community groups. The "epidemic" of teenage pregnancies and unwanted childbirths could not be effectively contained, and the problem of the unwed, teenage, welfare mother would not go away either—and this is precisely because this epidemic and problem provides a rationale for intervening in the sexual lives of adolescents, to bring young people under the control of state agencies and institutions in close cooperation with the medical profession. The state has granted the young more sexual rights—to contraceptives, abortion services, and family-planning services for example—but these rights have brought them under the regulative gaze of a state medical apparatus of power designed to manage more effectively the adolescent body and its desires. The discourse that has produced the "problem of teenage pregnancies" also has deployed apparatus and technologies of control that have been especially oppressive to poor young women of color, and urban youth more generally. This suggests that the problem has served its purpose, and continues to serve its social purpose. It provides a rationale for interventions in population control. This is why, when the "problem" of the unwed, teenage, welfare mother took center stage again with the Welfare Reform Act of 1996, nothing much had changed in the way the problem was framed, and who was blamed.

4

FROM THE PROBLEM OF THE HOMOSEXUAL TO THE PROBLEM OF HOMOPHOBIA

In April, 2009, New York City tourism officials unveiled a new campaign titled "Rainbow Pilgrimage," targeted at gay and lesbian travelers and timed to coincide with the 40th anniversary of a defining moment in the history of gay rights, the Stonewall rebellion. The campaign promoted New York City as a "rite of passage" for gays and lesbians, implying that they needed to relive that passage from the oppressive pregay-rights era to the out and proud gay-rights era as a right of personal passage, as part of the development of a self-accepting and self-affirming lesbian or gay male identity. The Stonewall rebellion, in which patrons of a gay bar in Greenwich Village fought back when police raided the bar and started bullying people, has become the symbolic starting point of the gay and lesbian rights movement, and also of gay and lesbian identity—as something different from being a homosexual. It is also the symbolic beginning of an era of social acceptance for lesbians and gays, at least among many liberal and progressive Americans. The *New York Times* took the opportunity of reporting on the Rainbow Pilgrimage to reflect back on its own reporting on the "homosexual problem" and its effects on tourism in the city in the years right before Stonewall. In a 1963 article on the front page of the *Times* titled "Growth of Overt Homosexuality in City Provokes Wide Concern," the concern was that tourists, particularly parents with children, would stay away from the city because they did not want to have to be exposed to homosexuals who were being "overt." Looking back from the vantage point of 2009, the *Times* felt compelled to offer an apology of sorts. "The article's language, from sources and reporter alike, is outdated at best, derogatory at worst, and many of its assumptions and assertions are long discredited."[1] The *Times* acknowledged that its 1963 article drew heavily on a study of gay men by a Dr Irving Bieber, a leading psychoanalyst. Bieber was an "expert" on homosexuals and homosexuality who viewed homosexuality as an "illness" that with treatment by professionals might be "cured."

Bieber was quoted in the 1963 article to the effect that public acceptance of homosexuals was encouraged when, instead of taking a moralistic attitude of condemnation, people learned to think of "homosexuality as an illness." Indeed, he argued, moralistic condemnation might only encourage some rebellious youth to embrace the homosexual lifestyle, so that a reduction in "manifestations of hostility" toward homosexuals is likely to lead to "a gradual, important reduction in the incidence of homosexuality." Once understood as sick people who need medical help, "normal" people could begin to replace hostility with sympathy. Treatment for homosexuals, according to Bieber, must proceed from a scientific analysis of causation, and there was now strong evidence that "a constructive, supportive, warmly related father precludes the possibility of a homosexual son." What gets replayed and reworked here is the Freudian notion that sexual identity and gender identity are linked, and that both are established through a "successful" resolution of what Freud called the Oedipal Complex. According to this notion, the son's first identification is with the mother, and he desires to kill (or castrate—symbolically or literally) the father and replace him vis-à-vis the mother. However, Freud argued that a proper resolution of the Oedipal Complex involved boys shifting from a strong identification with their mother, protecting her and modeling her beliefs and attitudes, to accept an alliance with the father with the hope of someday getting the mother back in the form of a wife. All this does provide some basis for understanding gender-identity formation in a patriarchal culture—the need for boys and young men to disidentify with anything represented as feminine, and their simultaneous identification with symbols, images, and narratives of masculine power and privilege. The homosexual, according to psychoanalytic theory, was produced through identification with the feminine in the battle of the sexes. Afraid to use their penis as a weapon to dominate women, homosexual males turn to their "sex" (gender) to compensate. They were stuck at an immature stage of development, unable to successfully resolve the Oedipal Complex and thus unable to effectively fit into society as happy, well-adjusted people. The importance of the bond and alliance between father and son that successfully resolves the Oedipal Complex is then understood to successfully produce heterosexual sons, who have resisted the "seductive or close-binding attempts" of the mother.

Consequently, the homosexual, by definition, represents a failure in normal gender development. According to the 1963 *Times* article, while many homosexuals "dream of forming a permanent attachment" to one other person, to give them some sense of "social and emotional stability," the "emotional instability that is inherent in many homosexuals" makes this impossible. Homosexual relationships inevitably flounder on "jealousy and personality clashes." It becomes important to establish that the homosexual cannot be happy, for if that were possible, even thinkable, then the whole theory of the neurotic, developmentally stunted homosexual could be called into question. There can be no happiness for the homosexual, only fleeting acts of sexual pleasure. The *Times*' words are eerily similar to those used by Mike Wallace in an early 1970s segment on gay men on *60 Minutes*, in which he would report: "most Americans are repelled by the mere notion of homosexuality. ... The average homosexual is promiscuous and not interested in or capable of a lasting relationship like that of a heterosexual marriage. His love life consists of a series of chance encounters at the bars he inhabits." A psychiatrist is then asked if he thinks homosexuals can be happy and replies that "the fact that someone is a homosexual ... automatically rules out the possibility that he will remain happy for long." The unhappiness of homosexuals and other "deviates" is laid at their own feet. By linking the establishment of a "normal" heterosexual identity to the supposed resolution of the Oedipal Complex—anywhere from early childhood to late adolescence—the psychoanalytic and medical establishment emphasized the importance of catching "borderline" boys at an early stage, when they first exhibited homosexual tendencies and before they had a fixed homosexual identity by the end of adolescence. This made it all the more important to identify "borderline boys" for counseling, but also so that they could be kept from contact with those who might seduce them into a homosexual lifestyle. This is where the issue of protecting tourists in New York City was brought back into the picture. The *Times* editorialized in its 1963 article that "strict enforcement of the law against seduction of minors is important to protect borderline cases from adult influences that could swing them toward homosexual orientation when heterosexual adjustment was still possible." The article concluded by addressing the question of how tourists might minimize their contact with "overt" homosexuals (which, according to the article, are also known as "inverts" and "deviates") when visiting the city. According to the article, "inverts are to be found in every conceivable line of work," so it is difficult to avoid them entirely. But they are "most concentrated—or most noticeable" in the fields of the creative and performing arts and in industries serving "women's beauty and fashion needs." Furthermore, just as homosexuals claim they can identify each other through eye contact, so "most normal persons believe they have a similar facility in spotting deviates."

One might say that, aside from the police, the public schools were involved in policing "gayness" to keep it in its place—either in the closet (preferably) or, when it becomes necessary to speak of it, to speak of it as a "problem." The homosexual was a problem on a personal level, wracked by psychological disorders and insecurities of ambiguous origins, and a problem on a societal level. The homosexual was a "problem" for the tourist industry in New York City and the larger society, an embarrassment, something that "normal" people did not want to be exposed to, and that adolescents, whose sexual identities were presumably still fragile and open, should not be exposed to for their own good. Gay people thus became invisible within the heteronormative hidden curriculum of public schooling as well as the official curriculum—expect perhaps for sex education where they were treated as "deviants," "deviates," and "inverts." The *Times* press coverage of the "problem of the homosexual," thus reflected what young people were being taught about homosexuals and homosexuality in schools, and from doctors and psychiatrists. The attitudes and beliefs that we today would see as hopelessly naive, prejudicial, unscientific, and even mean spirited, were in the mid-1960s legitimated by drawing upon medical experts and scientific evidence. This only raises more troubling questions about who science serves—particularly a science that claims to be "objective" and "disinterested," terms which have no possible meaning in the real world. The homosexual and the problem of the homosexual was a production of a hegemonic "straight" culture, and the scientific disciplines were part of that hegemony, serving to legitimate attitudes and prejudices that were irrational and unjust as rational and just. If the scientific community now takes a diametrically opposed view of homosexuality and has repudiated its former views—much as the *Times* repudiated its earlier reporting, which was also supposedly objective—is it because the dominant culture has changed in its official view of homosexuals and homosexuality, and the medical and psychoanalytic "truth" about homosexuals has changed in response? I do not mean to suggest here that the old "truths" might be just as legitimate as the "new" truths. The old truths provided the basis for a disciplinary apparatus that oppressed, marginalized, excluded, and made invisible or neurotic the homosexual Other. The new truths not only are based on a return to a more natural, authentic understanding of human sexual diversity, they also are attached to democratic and social-justice values, that name the problem as homophobia and heteronormativity. What this does imply, I think, is that progressives look more to social-justice commitments and democratic values in constructing a sexuality curriculum than to "expert" psychoanalytic and medical authority—at least when that evidence is not the result of research aimed at freeing people from oppression, building inclusive democratic communities, and advancing social-justice agendas. We do not need more research guided by a framing of issues that turns people into problems to be studied, managed, kept under surveillance, normalized, and policed.

Given the mass-media representation of the problem of the homosexual, supported as it was by the scientific establishment, a good deal of attention was focused in New York City and other major cities in the nation on containing the problem through ghettoization, and through an oppressive policing of gay men to keep them in their place in bars where they could be hidden from public view—bars police periodically visited to receive pay-offs, and periodically raided, ostensibly looking for underage drinkers, beating up people in the process and calling them faggots. This policing of gayness, in ways similar to the policing of blackness, was and remains a visible reminder of hegemonic power exercised over subjugated people's bodies, but also over their consciousness. For, to submit to this beating, this dehumanization, takes its toll on the human subject. What happened in the summer of 1969, on a series of several hot summer nights of confrontation with police at the Stonewall bar, should thus not surprise us either. The subaltern, the subjugated, the oppressed begin at some point to organize a collective movement of resistance to take back their humanity and claim their rights as citizens and fellow human beings. The Stonewall rebellion sent shock waves throughout gay America. Someone had stood up, someone had resisted, someone had said enough is enough. The coming decade would be one of a great shift in thinking about homosexuality and of rapidly shifting public attitudes concerning homosexuals, who had cast off the psychiatric establishment's naming of them and renamed themselves gay people, or gay men and lesbians.

It is a testament to the times that the 1960s would produce the civil-rights movement and, a few years later, the gay and lesbian rights movement. Both were movements framed in terms of liberal agendas: recognition of basic civil and human rights, and tolerance of difference. But they were about more than equal rights under the law. They demanded that "normal," middle-class, white, heterosexual Americans face up to Others in their midst whom they preferred not to see. It is not coincidental that the age of black invisibility in popular culture is coextensive with the age of gay invisibility, and both African Americans and queer Americans began to make themselves visible, to speak out and resist their erasure in popular culture, their relegation to the margins, and (when they were made visible) their treatment as "deviants" and social "problems." What occurred is something like a fundamental reframing of issues within popular culture and public life in a few short years. Negroes became Afro-Americans and then African Americans, and that implied a shift in representational politics from an era in which whites would name blackness and define it in terms of stereotypes (the era of the Negro), to an era in which black people would engage in their own renaming as an act of resistance to stereotypes and controlling images and as an act of self-affirmation. A similar kind of renaming occurred in the shift from the "homosexual" (a psychiatric naming) to "gay" and "lesbian." It is hard to overestimate the magnitude of this shift, this rupture, that occurred in American culture in the 1960s. Obviously, racism and homophobia did not vanish, they just became less politically correct, less acceptable in public discourse, and officially condemned. Whereas blackness and gayness had been invisible in popular culture they were now made visible, and racist homophobes, like the television character Archie Bunker, would become the object of ridicule. At the same time, with the modern gay and lesbian rights movements, and out of the 1960s, the homosexual became "gay," and in the public eye "gay" was often used to refer to both gay men and lesbians, as the opposite of "straight." The age of gay identity politics had thus also ushered in the age of "straight" identity politics, both organized around unified, oppositional constructions of identity. In the 1950s, in an age still influenced by Freud and Kinsey's belief in the fluidity of sexuality, these new gay and straight identities were as yet unformed, or just beginning to gel. The gay rights era represents a fundamental shift that has been essential in advancing the rights agendas of sexual minorities, even as it has set "gays" up as the absolute Other, defined by their abnormality within the dominant culture. There are fundamental limits to the rights agendas of sexual minorities, so long as sexual minorities do not challenge the very categories that define some as "normal," and others as "minorities," who quite naturally have to have their rights protected since "normal" people (the moral majority) might understandably be biased against them and not want to recognize their existence.

But in the gay culture that erupted upon the scene after the Stonewall rebellion, the category "gay" was taken on positively by gay and lesbian activists and members of the gay community, and served (and still serves) to advance a needed civil-rights agenda. The word "gay," however, came with its own history and this history associated gay men, and to a lesser extent lesbians, with the "gay Nineties" and "gay Paris," and with the "gay" bohemianism of Greenwich Village. Gay identity thus was to some extent still tied to this history of representations in the late 1960s and 1970s. In popular culture and in gay culture, gayness was often associated with a flamboyant lifestyle organized around a night life of sex, drugs, and nonstop partying—all located in urban spaces. The word gay thus served to counter the perception that all homosexuals are depressed and suicidal, but at the expense of turning them into party animals and sex machines, as foreigners within "normal" society—the kind of images unfortunately reinforced in early gay-rights parades in New York City and San Francisco. This "gay lifestyle" would take its toll in the 1980s, as AIDS ravaged gay communities across the nation. And what has been the consequence of the renaming of the heterosexual as "straight"? It is worthy of note, in this regard, that in 1967 a *Time* magazine correspondent could write of the "hippy" phenomenon that "it has touched the imagination of the 'straight' society that gave it birth."[2] Straight society is conventional, and "normal," whereas hippies are unconventional, and abnormal. Here again the history of bohemianism comes into play; for in the "hip" Beat culture in the 1950s, and early 1960s, "straight" was a term used to refer, usually in a somewhat pejorative manner, to conventional, white, middle-class culture. Today, the word "straight," as a synonym for heterosexual, still carries some of this history of meaning. It refers to a normal, but also conventional sexuality—the one who is not flamboyant or angry, who performs gender according to expected norms. Gay identity, like hippy identity, is understood to be produced by, or birthed by, "straight" society, as its alter ego, and thus somehow necessary and not ultimately separable from "straight" society. The hippy, like the homosexual, touched the "straight" imagination, similar to the way that the "savage" touched the imagination of the European colonialist. Gay society would touch the imagination of straight society—offering it what it felt alienated from, which is to say its sexuality and its "gaiety." But what straight society desired from gay culture it would buy as commodified fashion images and a sexuality that was able to detach itself from procreation and family values. But as the imagination of "straight society" was touched by the exotic gay Other, it sought to keep gayness in its place in urban ghettoes. Gays and lesbians were still deviants to most straights, and not believed to be good role models for impressionable young people. Straight society would slowly learn to accept gayness so long as it was kept in its place and not "promoted" or treated as equal to straightness.

It would take a decade for sex-education professionals and the sex-education curriculum to begin to catch up with shifting public attitudes towards homosexuals and homosexuality, and the use of the terms gay and lesbian to refer to sexual identities. In a popular sex-education text, *Sex Education in the Schools* (1970) by

Frederick Kilander, the reader learns that even though sexuality is ideally and naturally linked to human reproduction and to marriage and family life, "at one extreme" sex is "immediate, selfish, and irrational," there is no "harmonious blending of the physical and the psychical, of the individual and the social." Selfish sex, according to the text, is associated with "masturbation, homosexuality, rape, promiscuity, illegitimacy, venereal disease, unhappy marriages, and divorce."[3] This is an ordering in which even masturbation and certainly homosexuality are grouped along with strange bedfellows, all understood as selfish, impulsive, and dangerous— that is, governed by a mainstream version of Freud's pleasure principle. This use of a mainstream, hegemonic version of Freudian theory had been around since the early 20th century progressive era, and it had not changed in substantial ways. The text, again following a predictable pattern, distinguishes between "transient" and "permanent" homosexuals. As for the "permanent" type, "he [sic] creates a social dilemma because he or she does not fit into the family pattern." The permanent homosexual also "gets involved in temporary relationships which dissolve in emotional and social chaos." Anyone who does not "fit" into the "normal" family pattern creates a "social dilemma." What does normal society do with its "deviates"? If their relationships may be prone to emotional conflict (as if heterosexual relationships were not), would that not be expected in a society that actively discourages, devalues, and marginalizes gay relationships? Causation becomes important in such a normalizing discourse. The precise or imprecise causes for this failure to develop properly must be identified. Only then can a "cure" be effected. So the text lists, among theories of causation, "inborn genetic disorder," "hormonal imbalance," "glandular disorder" and "arrested or distorted psychosexual development." This last category seemed the most important, according to the text, and included homosexuality that resulted from "hostility to mother," "hostility to father," "affection to mother is excessive," "affection to father is excessive," and "cultural pressures and opportunities." The reader learns that early homosexual experience plays a part in this "personality disorder," and that "rearing a child as a member of the opposite sex" could make them homosexual, as could "heterosexual frustration" for prolonged periods and "castration anxiety." Under the category of "prevention," the author suggests creating a "climate of opinion" in which homosexuality might be discussed "openly and intelligently." As for "treatment," psychotherapy is recommended as effective if the individual is "strongly motivated to overcome his problem." Other forms of treatment listed in the text include "shock therapy," "psychosurgical procedures," and "endocrine therapy." The problem with all these treatments, the text concludes, is that too many homosexuals "cling tenaciously to their deviant practices."[4] This is the modern, enlightened understanding of homosexuality and the problem of the homosexual that was being taught in many if not most sex-education programs and classes around the nation in the early 1970s. It is a sad commentary on the state of the field of health and sex education at that time to find a major text proposing that shock therapy might work in some cases to treat homosexuals, and that, at other times, hormonal treatment might be advised. The preferred treatment, however, was psychoanalytic counseling perhaps tied to some form of aversion therapy. The text thus frames the problem of the homosexual as one that requires proper medical treatment by doctors and psychiatrists equipped with a variety of possible options. At the same time, the text adheres to the notion that if potential homosexuals can be identified in adolescence, before they become "permanent" homosexuals, and if they could be kept protected from exposure to homosexual opportunities, there is a good chance they could be "cured". The sex-education curriculum is, in this case, part of the problem that needs to be addressed in a genuinely democratic sexuality education oriented toward social justice and human freedom. Rather than responding to homophobia as the problem, it played a part in legitimating and institutionalizing homophobia.

Also published in 1970, complete with lesson plans and illustrations for teachers to use, was a text written by health educators John Burt and Linda Brower, *Education for Sexuality*. The text's shift in language from sex education to sexuality education was new, but it did not signal anything new. It was used rather to argue that sex and reproduction are biological aspects of human life that need to be studied, but that sexuality education was about "more than just a course in biology—it must be education for love." What was being argued was the accepted family-life perspective that sex education had to involve a study of human relationships, the family, and gender roles. The authors note that for many centuries in the West, after the 12th century in particular, there was a great schism between love and marriage. "[I]t was finally the 20th century," according to the text, "that bravely claimed that sex was for pleasure as well as reproduction and that both aspects belonged within a marriage based on love." In the chapter on homosexuality, the authors discuss movements to remove "private sexual behavior between consenting adults" from the list of crimes, and suggest that "students can be appointed by the class to send a letter to their congressman expressing the views of the class." Homosexual acts, students are led to believe, should probably be decriminalized. But immediately, this discussion is followed by an activity "Preparing the future parent," in which students are asked to "play the roles of happy parents who are likely to bring up heterosexual children, … [and] parents who are likely to push their children toward homosexuality." What family dynamics are exactly at work are never made clear, but clearly the happy family produces heterosexual offspring. Students are then asked to discuss "Is homosexuality inherited? Is homosexuality an illness? What are the chances of a homosexual being happy?"[5] To ask such questions is, of course, to open up the very real probability that young people will conclude it is an illness and that homosexuals by definition cannot be happy. All this spills over into a discussion of masculinity and femininity as "patterns of behavior that are characteristic of males or females in a particular culture." The text concludes that "although men are mostly masculine and girls are mostly feminine, no person is entirely masculine or feminine."[6] Masculinity and femininity are both understood to be particular to cultures and simultaneously have an essential meaning. How else is it possible to conclude that while men are mostly masculine some are more feminine? Both "masculine" and "feminine" must have some stable, fixed meaning, and the homosexual can be understood as an overfeminized man or an overmasculinized woman. Students are to learn, according to the text, that homosexuals are chronically unhappy because of their own psychological disorders, and because they come from unhappy families. When students are asked to role play parents who are likely to push their children toward homosexuality, one can only imagine that students are expected to role play parents who are emotionally cold and distant, or emotionally overbearing and seductive, or who are unhappy with their sex roles and lives.[7] The not-so-subtle message is that women who equate "equality" with "sameness" and men who do not act masculine enough are pushing their children toward gender confusion and then, supposedly, the short step from gender confusion to homosexual identity.

This dominant sexual and gender identity mythology was challenged by the women's rights and gay-rights movements of the late 1960s and early 1970s. And as more homosexuals came out and renamed themselves as gay (in the process dropping the medical name that had defined them for almost a century), it became more difficult to sustain stereotypes as well as supposed medical evidence that homosexuals were mentally disordered and in need of treatment, or that they were pedophiles out to seduce "borderline" boys. Liberal Americans, at least at a rhetorical level, accepted gays and lesbians as equals, and began to see their struggle as similar to other struggles for civil rights and equality. In December 1973, the American Psychiatric Association (APA) declassified homosexuality as a mental disorder and, two years later, the American Psychological Association followed suit. In a vote of 13 to 0 with two abstentions, homosexuality was deleted as a disorder and replaced with "sexual orientation disturbance." According to the resolution, homosexuality "in and of itself" does not imply impairment of "judgment, stability, reliability, or vocational capacities." This was important. For only if a condition could be demonstrated to be disabling in some way, could it be identified and classified as a mental disorder, open to treatment by psychiatrists. Then, quickly, the resolution shifted to "deplore" all public and private discrimination against homosexuals, and to support civil-rights legislation to "ensure homosexual citizens the same protections now guaranteed to others." Finally, the APA resolution urged repeal of sodomy laws "making criminal offenses of sexual acts performed by consenting adults in private."[8] This had particular significance, of course, for those affiliated with health education, which staked its truth claims on evidence from medicine, but also—and more importantly—upon the medicine of the mind. The whole history of the "problem of homosexuality" in health and sex education had relied on notions of maladjustment and mental disorder borrowed from psychiatry and clinical psychology. The sex-education curriculum had always staked its legitimacy claims on medical evidence. Consequently, when that evidence changed, seemingly overnight, when what had been a perversion and an inversion became normal and natural, when the problem shifted from the homosexual to those who discriminated against homosexuals, sex-education texts had to radically rewrite what they had to say about homosexuality within a few years—somewhat like the radical revision of history in Russian public schools when the Soviet Union collapsed.

The old psychiatric establishment, particularly those invested in the lucrative business of treating homosexuals, put up a fight. And they might have held out longer if not for the influence of gay-rights activists who began to demand change by the APA, and who began to stage well-publicized protests at APA conventions several years before the declassification referendum was passed. Melvin Sabshin, who was medical director of the APA at the time, has called the 1970 APA annual convention in San Francisco "tumultuous," with gay-rights activists protesting outside the assembly hall and staging "guerrilla theater." At the 1972 conference, a gay psychiatrist spoke from the convention floor in support of declassifying homosexuality as a mental disorder. Yet there is great irony in the fact that he wore a mask to protect his identity from professional repercussions. If the "out" homosexual was allowed to speak in public, it would still have to be from behind the veil, as if something still needed to be hidden, something still not to be seen or recognized in a public space. By 1973, gay and lesbian psychiatrists had established organizations within the APA and had booths at the annual meeting, with a banner that read, "Gay, Proud, and Healthy"; and the masks had disappeared from gay presenters at the conference. The closet door had been opened.[9] As a scientific institution, the APA was obliged to frame its argument for declassification on the evidence, and that meant both reinterpreting and discrediting old evidence and drawing upon some new evidence. In Sabshin's view, the societal and political impetus for change was scientific evidence. The evidence had changed, and people changed their attitudes; so that science is seen as leading public opinion. This may give science a bit too much autonomy and influence in shaping public opinion on controversial matters since it is clear that the social and psychological sciences have incorporated commonsense biases and reflect shifts in the culture. Scientific evidence does, however, count in legitimizing public policy and practice, and so it mattered very much what the APA did. Its Committee on Nomenclature, in charge of the naming of classified disorders, was charged with reviewing numerous studies that were becoming available on nonpatient populations of homosexual people, and these studies revealed that most gay people were satisfied with their sexual orientation and not socially or psychologically impaired. This meant that the psychoanalytic developmental theory that understood homosexuality as an immature level of development could no longer be sustained either. According to Sabshin, this represented the triumph of a "rational approach to pathology" that did not assume someone was sick just because they were in a socially defined group. Of course, the psychoanalytic movement had for almost a century produced the homosexual as a class of people who shared a common mental disorder, so that it might be considered disingenuous to now claim that a "rational approach to pathology" (which the old psychoanalytic theory also claimed to be) could now be used to undo this pathologizing of homosexuality and homosexuals. In fact, the declassification of homosexuality was accompanied by the creation of a new category—"sexual orientation disturbance"—applied to people "who are either disturbed by, in conflict with, or wish to change their sexual orientation." This category, however, was also criticized by the increasingly active and vocal gay and lesbian organization in the APA and was dropped after the mid-1980s. For it suggested once more that homosexuals could be cured, when they and others needed to learn to accept homosexuality as natural and alright.

One of those who led the fight to preserve the classification of homosexuality as a mental disorder at the 1973 meeting of the APA was Irving Bieber, whom the *New York Times* had sought out as an expert on homosexuality for its 1963 article on the fear that "overt homosexuals" in the city might keep tourists away. Bieber had emerged as the leading spokesperson on the causes and treatment of homosexuality—someone the mass media relied on when they needed an expert to separate the facts from the myths. On a segment of *CBS Reports* on "The Homosexuals" that aired on March 7, 1967, Mike Wallace interviewed Bieber, who repeated a line he had used with variations many times before: "the fact that someone is a homosexual ... automatically rules out the possibility that he will remain happy for long." Homosexuals needed to be cured in order to be happy, and Bieber claimed that he had cured many in his years of psychotherapeutic practice. Yet in voicing his opposition to the APA declassification resolution, Bieber had taken a new tack. The APA had adopted a new set of criteria for defining psycho-logical disorders, so that a disorder now had to "regularly cause distress," and "interfere with social effectiveness." Since the APA could find no evidence that nonpatient homosexuals suffered from either of these conditions, it could then argue that homosexuality should be declassified as a disorder. After years of arguing that homosexuals, by definition, could not be happy, Bieber argued that it did not matter whether they were happy or not. "Psychopathology" could exist without apparent symptoms or adjustment problems. He pointed to other conditions classi-fied as disorders that did not apparently cause "distress and social disability," including voyeurism, fetishism, and sadomasochism. Bieber thus shifted the terrain of the argument. He acknowledged that homosexuals can be happy, but wondered about the social effects of legitimizing deviant sexual behavior by groups who seem to "find their conditions normalized."[10] He also wondered whether he would be able to treat homosexuals as patients anymore. The answer to that question was "no," at least as a practicing psychiatrist. But Bieber and others would continue their practice through affiliation with such groups as the National Association for Research and Therapy on Homosexuality, which gives a veneer of legitimacy to the business of "curing" homosexuals—although they are discredited by the medical community.

Michel Foucault has argued that the homosexual was a production of the psychiatric profession in the late 19th century. Before that time, homosexuality was recognized, but not a whole class of people defined as homosexuals, subject to treatment. An analysis of the declassification of homosexuality by the APA in the

early 1970s suggests that it might be more accurate to think of the psychiatric profession as legitimating changes already underway in culture rather than playing a
leading role in initiating changes in culture. The "homosexual" might have been a
medical category, but it was also a social category of stigmatization. When homosexuals renamed themselves gays and lesbians, it was an act of self-affirmation, pride,
and normality. At the same time, the new categories (gay and straight) carried much
of the same meaning as the old categories (homosexual and heterosexual) within
popular culture. Only very gradually has the term "homosexual" fallen into disfavor
because of its historical association with a clinical discourse of sickness. But when
the APA declassified homosexuality as a disorder, and when the term "gay and
lesbian" began to replace the term "homosexual," one thing did not change. The
APA did not invoke Kinsey's groundbreaking research on human sexual diversity
to argue that homosexual behavior could best be understood when placed on a
continuum, with exclusive homosexual behavior on one end and exclusive
heterosexual desire on the other, but with many if not most people in between
for substantial periods of their lives. Kinsey's more fluid understanding of sexual
orientation and preference was invoked in the 1970s to suggest that approximately
ten percent of the male population was gay, and a somewhat smaller proportion
of the female population was lesbian. But this was only the percentage Kinsey
associated with exclusive or primary homosexuality, and the idea of a fixed sexual
identity as either heterosexual or homosexual seemed foreign to him. Perhaps
Kinsey had been too threatening to mainstream culture in his argument that
homosexual and bisexual behavior was far more common than exclusive
homosexual or heterosexual behavior. At any rate, the battle for gay and lesbian
rights would not threaten the reigning categories of oppositional sexual
identity, each totally excluding its Other, and each given at birth. Kinsey and
Foucault would be ignored until the 1990s, when queer theorists revived their
argument.

While the APA became embroiled in conflict over its classification and then
declassification of homosexuality as a disorder, sexuality educators were paying close
attention and doing their best to read the shifting signs. Until things were settled,
many supported "fact-based" and "values-clarification" approaches to sex education.
According to a 1973 article in *Phi Delta Kappan*, sex educators could avoid conflict
if they saw themselves as purveyors of "sex information" who dispel "sex misinformation" among young people. Teachers could fight "sexual ignorance" with
facts, and they could help students clarify their own feelings and values in "free
classroom discussion." The author of the article suggests that one way to avoid
pushing values on students is to organize the curriculum around factual responses to
student-generated questions. One such list of 19 questions generated by high-school
sophomores in Texas is offered as an example, including "How can venereal disease
be prevented? ... Is the sex urge greater in a boy than in a girl? ... How long
should the boy's penis be inserted for fertilization to occur? ... Is it possible for a girl
to get pregnant in a swimming pool?" Only one question on the list pertains to

homosexuality or homosexuals: "How do you go about handling a situation when you become exposed to a homosexual?"[11] This is hardly the kind of question, like the question of whether a girl can become pregnant in a swimming pool, that calls for a factual answer by the teacher. This is a question of how to handle a situation, and so it becomes a subject for "free classroom discussion." There is no indication that the teacher is responsible for helping students unpack a language of "exposure," as if homosexuals were carriers of a disease or a stigma. Without the active intervention of a teacher willing to challenge the implicit homophobia in such a question, this questioning of the "problem" of "exposure" to the homosexual is likely to reproduce rather than challenge dominant homophobic narratives. A 1973 article in *Educational Leadership* also framed sex education in terms of avoiding the "debate ... about what should be taught, [and] when the teaching should take place," focusing on "cognitive information" when needed, and on the clarification of "affective domain" values when needed.[12] In a sex-education workshop for parents offered as an example, participants are asked to make individual decisions about controversial issues. The instructor begins with "fairly easy decisions such as asking for positions on capital punishment." This is, at this point, still a question often raised and debated in social-studies and civics classes. But this "easy" decision is to be followed by taking a position on "legalizing abortions, premarital sex, extramarital sex, homosexuality, masturbation, and sex crimes." This is an odd assortment of crimes and misdemeanors of a sexual nature in the eyes of "normal" society; and if homosexuality may be subcategorized with masturbation as a mis-demeanor, it might also be subcategorized with sex crimes. The very placement of homosexuality in this unnamed category of crimes and misdemeanors is itself a decision, and one with consequences for how the participants frame their own decision making. A second activity designed to make participants more comfortable with homosexuals and homosexuality involves viewing "two fully clothed women embracing, or of one man kissing another on the cheek." Participants are then asked to complete a checklist to reveal how they feel about the pictures, which then provides a basis for small group discussion. The hope is that participants become more aware of "mental and emotional barriers" to "accepting a multiplicity of human sexual behaviors." But the activity need not be framed as an activity about homosexuality at all, so it is hard to see how it necessarily promotes accepting sexual diversity. What it may promote is a bit more comfort in touching someone of the same gender. On the other hand, because it associates homosexuality with touching someone of the same gender, it may have the opposite effect, of discouraging same-gender contact and reinforcing homophobic fears. Value clar-ification ironically often ends up accepting and even reinforcing participants' own values and interpretations, even when they are homophobic.

The 1970s was a decade of "values clarification" in sex education, especially when homosexuality was being discussed. But, by the end of the decade, there were signs that health educators and sex educators were ready to take sides in the public battle over homosexuals and gay rights, to switch sides and now declare that many of the "facts" about homosexuality and homosexuals that the profession had endorsed for decades were really myths that sex educators now needed to dispel. A ground-breaking text in this regard was *Sex Education: Theory and Practice* (1981) by Clint Bruess of the National Center for Health Education and Jerrold Greenberg, a health educator at the University of Maryland. The text incorporates values-clarification activities, but then uses these activities to promote acceptance of homosexuals as "around 10 percent" of the population, and "as individuals with the same rights, responsibilities, and feelings as the other 90 percent." This discourse of homosexual sameness is grounded on the debunking of dominant myths, "that homosexuals look a lot different than other people, ... that homosexual males are effeminate and weak while homosexual females are masculine and physically strong, ... that homosexuals lurk at every street corner waiting to pounce upon innocent children and seduce them into a life of homosexuality, ... [and] that homosexuals obtained their sexual preference because of problems in their early family relationships." The discourse of homosexual sameness includes the facts that physiologically, "homosexuals respond exactly as heterosexuals do ... [and] homosexuals are as amenable to treatment for sexual inadequacy as heterosexuals." The text even states that evidence supports the contention that "among established couples, homosexuals get more pleasure from lovemaking."[13] This is an apparent reference to one of the conclusions of the studies by William Masters and Virginia Johnson, published as *Human Sexual Response* and *Human Sexual Inadequacy* in 1966 and 1970 respectively.

The discourse of homosexual sameness in the text is also interrupted by the suggestion that homosexuals may be gender nonconformists. Discussion questions for the section on the homosexual include: "How do you feel about a man taking over the household chores? How do you feel about a man hairdresser? How do you feel about a woman who becomes a lawyer?"[14] The suggestion here is that students who have a difficult time accepting people in gender-nonconforming roles are also likely to have a difficult time accepting homosexuals, but also that homosexuals are more likely to be found in gender-nonconforming roles. All this points to tensions between a discourse of sameness and a discourse of difference that have continued to run throughout the treatment of the homosexual in sex-education texts and in American popular culture. Homosexuals are just like everyone else, but they are also different. If and when they are different it is because some act like the "opposite" gender. But this nonnormal performance of gender is to be accepted as part of the natural diversity of human sexuality and gender, rather than treated as a psychological disorder, a deficiency, or an abnormality. Even those who fit the stereotypes of the butch lesbian and the effeminate homosexual male are to be respected for being "who they are." What this represents is a recognition that people are the same in fundamental ways, and that they are also different, and that rather than trying to erase, mask, or assimilate that difference, rather than trying to make it "normal," difference itself can be valued. This change in thinking amounted to a seismic shift in the health profession and within sectors of the American public. It did not signal the end of homophobia and gender inequalities; but at least it established the discursive parameters for redefining the "problem of the homosexual" as a problem of homophobia.

The text also does not attempt to resolve another tension, the tension between the claim that sex educators must respect students' "strong moral feelings about homosexual behavior" and the claim that homosexuals need to be respected rather than condemned. Yet it is apparent that this commitment to respecting those who morally condemn homosexuals is presented primarily as a disclaimer, to appease conservative Christian critics and parents. The tone of the book is one of fighting stereotypes and bigotry against homosexuals. The issue of sexual preference is important for teachers, nurses, counselors, and administrators, according to the text, because "you are likely to come in contact with a few who are concerned about the issue, and the way you react could have a significant effect on these students."[15] The text's interest is with the homosexual more than homosexuality, suggesting a movement toward understanding what the text calls "sexual preference" as fairly fixed and stable over a lifetime. Homosexuality is referred to only once, in a separate section from the homosexual, and under the subject of "homosexual experimentation" among the young, particularly those "not sure about their sexual preference." The language of "sexual preference" did, however, suggest more fluidity and flexibility than "sexual orientation," the term that would replace it by the early 1990s.

By 1980, the health and psychiatric "experts" had done a complete turnaround in their treatment of the "facts" and "myths" about homosexuality and homosexuals, and while this served to maintain the credibility of the "experts" in the eyes of many, it also raised questions about how the facts could change so quickly. Perhaps, some began to say, the experts were merely cloaking particular sets of cultural values in a scientific language to make them sound objective and disinterested. Perhaps we should not place our trust in the medical establishment, or the educational establishment, to tell us how to run our lives, no matter what they might tell us. That is the argument advanced by Thomas Szasz in his popular book *Sex by Prescription* (1980). Szasz was a practicing psychiatrist and professor of psychiatry at the State University of New York at Syracuse who had previously published *The Myth of Mental Illness* (1974). Szasz was advancing in the 1970s an idea that would become closely associated with Foucault and cultural studies in the 1980s and 1990s, namely that the psychiatric and medical professions were organized around a project of bringing people and populations under a disciplinary gaze, regulating and controlling their lives, and making them believe they had mental diseases that needed to be treated by medical professionals. Szasz charged that sex educators and therapists had become captives of a "sex as disease" perspective, and that this was unavoidable so long as they accepted the medicalization of sex education and therapy. While once religious clerics were recognized as the authorities when it came to sin, and invested by the church with powers to punish sinners, the modern medical profession is accorded special powers to treat and cure the sick. Szasz remarks that the psychoanalysts who opposed the APA declassification of homosexuality as a disorder acted as if they were being deprived of a valuable possession—their "perverts" to treat. He quotes one psychoanalyst to the effect that homosexual groups in the 1960s revolted against their persecutors, but also began "to turn against their medical (psychiatric) protectors who offered help and hope."[16] The hope, presumably, was of a cure for a disease that never really was a disease in the first place, a futile hope that a psychoanalytic industry had been built up around.

Szasz observed that even some "liberal" psychotherapists, who had abandoned the notion that homosexuality is a disease or disorder, were still offering treatments for homosexuals who wanted to change their sexual orientation. Here he referred specifically to Masters and Johnson, and the basic thesis they advanced in their 1979 volume, *Homosexuality in Perspective*. That book had received press attention for its claim of "homosexual superiority," that homosexuals are more "sexy" and less inhibited sexually than heterosexuals. Masters and Johnson wrote in *Medical World News* that heterosexual partnership is "handicapped by cultural pressures on heterosexuals to regard coitus as the be-all and end-all of sex." Homosexuals "had more fun" because they felt less restricted.[17] This, to Szasz, was only a variation on the popular liberal or "revisionist" cultural narrative, in which the oppressed are treated as superior to "us" in some ways, so that "normal" folk can learn lessons from the oppressed. "To the special virtuousness of the poor, the special spirituality of the Negro, and the special authenticity of the mad," Szasz wrote, "they have now added the special sexual prowess of the woman and the special sexual sensitivity of the homosexual."[18] Szasz's point is not to deny that the oppressed are oppressed, but rather to critique the liberal response of finding something that can be adopted or appropriated from the oppressed. So the conforming, "married with children" heterosexual is now to study the sexual behavior of the homosexual in order to learn new "tricks" and become more satisfied with his or her own sex life. At the same time, the homosexual may go on being oppressed and marginalized—and treated. Szasz chastises Masters and Johnson for making this view of homosexuality compatible with their argument that homosexual "patients" may still receive treatment from psychotherapists if they are unhappy as homosexuals and want to change. In some ways this sounds very much like the rationale currently used to legitimate gender reassignment surgery for transgendered people. Szasz, in fact, does draw parallels between psychotherapeutic reassignment therapy for homosexuals who want to become heterosexual, and reassignment surgery for transgendered people, and opposes both. But gender reassignment surgery is at least about becoming the gendered body you feel you "naturally" or "authentically" are, whereas sexual-orientation reassignment therapy from homosexual to heterosexual would imply attempting to overcome who you naturally or authentically think you are, to fit in to social norms and avoid being stigmatized. Should such therapy be viewed as acceptable practice, on an ethical ground? That is not a question Szasz entirely answers, but he does at least insist that the question be framed as an ethical question, and a question of values, rather than a question of medical, scientific evidence as to whether treatment "works" or not. "Homosexuality is like a minority religion persecuted by the majority," Szasz wrote. In 15th-century Spain, the Jews were such a minority religion persecuted by the Christian majority. Those Jews who sought conversion to the Christian faith to avoid persecution, and those who married into Christian families and learned to hide their Jewishness, were—in Szasz's view— very much like homosexuals who wanted to become heterosexuals so that they would not have to face persecution and stigmatization, and so that they could "fit in." The practice of turning homosexuals into "healthy" heterosexuals presumed the individual had to change rather than the culture, that there was still something wrong with being a homosexual, like there was something wrong with being a Jew in the time of the Spanish Inquisition. At least acknowledge, Szasz argues, that this business of reassignment—of gender, "sexual preference," or religious/ethnic identity—is done for these reasons and not because of medical, scientific evidence about what is natural and well adjusted. To support reassignment theory for homosexuals is, consequently, "a denial of the minority's right to be different."[19] Their difference is viewed as threatening, as something that has to be erased and displaced.

This is, I believe, a sign of a major shift in the language of sexuality and sex education. Although Szasz was somewhat of a lone wolf within his profession, the approach he took toward medicine and psychiatry, as I said earlier, foreshadowed Foucault's work on the disciplines of medicine and psychiatry as regulatory and disciplinary apparatuses of power, not so much engaged in making people happier as in bringing them under tighter surveillance and categorizing and labeling them as normal or abnormal. The acceptance of human difference and diversity is never an option from this perspective, for once difference becomes okay rather than abnormal, immoral, or disordered, then the professions assigned to normalize people—to treat their "disorders" and make them "normal" or healthy—have less power over them. A democratization of sexuality education would mean thinking about sexuality education as the study of sexual difference and diversity rather than "normal" and "abnormal" categories of sexual behavior, and linking it to an ethico-political study of sexuality and social justice. This potential is all still underdeveloped in Szasz analysis, but at least he represented a perspective that would lead toward thinking about adolescent sexuality less in terms of regulation and repression and more in terms of helping young people negotiate their own sexual relations and sexual identities within a framework of equity, respect, and empowerment. The homosexual as a social and personal problem had largely vanished in sex-education texts by the end of the 1970s, to be replaced with the problem of heterosexual prejudice. The homosexual was still referred to primarily as the homosexual rather than as gay or lesbian, but the long era of pathologizing homosexuality and the homosexual was over. Again, analogies between psychiatry and health shifts in thinking and religious shifts in thinking are probably not coincidental. At the same time that the mainstream human sciences and helping professions began to question whether homosexuality was a disorder, mainstream religious orders and liberal Christian groups began to advance the notion that it is not sinful to be gay. It need hardly be said that the historic linkage between sex as sin and sex as sickness had not been fully broken. When the AIDS crisis erupted in the 1980s, the narrative of the homosexual as sick and sinful would take on a whole new meaning.

The "problem" of the homosexual teacher would also continue to remain a problem, although here too there was at least the beginning of an attempt to reframe the problem by the late 1970s. The dismissal of "known" homosexual teachers had been a consistent practice across the U.S. throughout most of the 20th century. In the early 1930s, Willard Waller wrote in his book *The Sociology of Teaching*—a text often used in teacher education—that homosexuals should not be allowed to teach for two primary reasons. First, the homosexual teacher represented a threat to young people because "nothing seems more certain than that homosexuality is contagious." As a disease, homosexuality could be spread through casual contact. Again, the contemporary reader cannot escape being struck by the parallels between the language of homosexuality as a contagious disease in the 1930s, and a 1980s narrative of AIDS as a contagious disease spread by homosexuals. So it becomes possible to see that the framing of the whole public dialogue on AIDS was connected to this history of homosexuality as a contagious disease. The homosexual teacher might spread his or her disease to the innocent victims, his or her students. There is no talk of sexual molestation as the means of transmitting the homosexual virus, although that presumably is in the mind of the 1930s reader. The homosexual teacher presumably only needed to be around young people to spread the virus. The second reason Waller offered for not hiring homosexual teachers, especially at the high-school level, was that they were prone to developing "ridiculous crushes" on students. "The homosexual teacher developed an indelicate soppiness in his relations with his [sic] favorites … and makes major tragedies of minor incidents when the recipient of his attentions shows himself indifferent." Waller went on to argue that because homosexual teachers were always prone to such "crushes," this was inevitably "fatal to school discipline." Since all this supposedly makes homosexuals ineffective as teachers, Waller encouraged administrators and teachers to be on the lookout for "latent homosexuals" when prospective teachers were being interviewed for teaching positions. But how was the "latent homosexual" to be detected? Waller encouraged educators to look for "such personality traits as carriage, mannerisms, voice, speech, etc."[20] In effect, all teachers who violated the normative performance of femininity and masculinity were presumed to be "latent homosexuals," even if they were not aware of it themselves. It need hardly be said that this effort to identity the latent homosexual teachers during the interview process according to their performance of gender led to many more heterosexual than homosexual teachers being denied jobs. Waller's representation of the "latent homosexual" teacher as "contagious" was still the reigning truth in public education through much of the 1970s, and while this truth has more recently been recognized as a myth, gay, lesbian, and transgendered teachers, as well as all teachers perceived as gender nonconforming, are still discriminated against in hiring, and in many districts may be dismissed if they are perceived as being too "out" and "in your face" about their sexual orientation. The U.S. military's "don't ask, don't tell" policy thus reflects what LGBTQ (lesbian, gay, bisexual, transgender, and otherwise queer) teachers have understood for a long time, and it makes sense that the military has done away with its policy before public schools have. After all, LGBTQ people in the military are not viewed as role models for impressionable youth, who may catch their "disease." But with the emergence of the gay-rights movement, at least this dominant narrative of the latent homosexual teacher as contagious began to be challenged, and the teaching closet began to open just a bit.

The first victory in the battle to open the teaching closet was won in California in 1978, when the so-called Briggs initiative was defeated which would have barred gays and lesbians from teaching in the state's public schools. California state senator John Briggs had hoped to capitalize on the momentum of the antigay-rights movement that was becoming a national force after the successful defeat of a gay-rights ordinance in Miami-Dade county, Florida, in 1977—a Christian right campaign in which Anita Bryant, a has-been popular singer known for her television commercials for Florida orange juice, became the visible spokesperson. The day after that victory in Florida, Briggs began mobilizing for a California campaign, this time targeting "out" and "known" gay and lesbian teachers. But lesbian and gay activists were also mobilizing for a fight, and determined to stop the momentum of the anti-gay-rights movements. Harvey Milk became a visible symbol of the anti-Briggs initiative, and even debated Briggs—events described in the film *Milk* (2008) about Harvey Milk's life and times. Leaders of the anti-Briggs initiative made a strategic decision to meet with Governor Reagan to see if he might be won over to their cause. In private meetings, they offered two reasons why they thought Reagan should oppose the initiative. First, if passed, the initiative would have an adverse impact on classroom discipline since students could blackmail teachers, threatening to "out" them as homosexuals (again, even if they were not). Second, the initiative would almost certainly be challenged in the courts, and this would involve the state in a long period of litigation at the taxpayer's expense. These were pragmatic arguments, not designed to appeal to Reagan's sense of what was morally or ethically right, although Reagan also did express his opposition to initiatives that legalized discrimination against particular social groups. Reagan became an odd sort of hero for the gay community after the Briggs initiative defeat, in which his opposition was taken to be decisive. Yet, in his public statements in opposition to the Briggs initiative, Reagan's primary argument was that "innocent lives could be ruined." He imagined a case in which Johnny, who, after receiving bad grades in a math class, might accuse his teacher of being a homosexual. This could all cause "mischief" he believed. And the "innocent lives" ruined were those of heterosexual teachers who might be mistakenly identified as homosexual. They would be the real victims of this initiative. Of course, Reagan was right on one level. But by making it seem as if heterosexual teachers were the "innocent victims," it implied that perhaps homosexual teachers were not so innocent, and perhaps should not be allowed to teach, but that the effort to drive them out of teaching would have too many unanticipated consequences on "innocents." As Craig Rimmerman has observed, "while Governor Reagan had helped to secure victory in the Briggs initiative fight, the ushering in of his conservative presidency in January 1981 provided new political opportunities for the Christian Right."[21] And when the AIDS crisis hit, he would respond through a discourse of moral panic and blame.

Although it was possible by the mid-1970s for gay and lesbian teachers to speak within their profession, they still had to speak from behind the veil and from within the closet. In 1977, *Phi Delta Kappan* published an article by an anonymous homosexual teacher, who begins by posing a question that has been taken as a presumption by many: "Do homosexual teachers, as role models, influence children toward homosexuality?" Rather than turn to scientific evidence from psychology and psychoanalysis to respond, the teacher rejects the normal framing of a response by these "experts," and reframes and redirects the question. He asks readers whether they would consider Plato, Socrates, and Michelangelo good role models. He dismisses the idea that young people may be influenced in their sexual identity, and asserts that "the vast majority [of homosexuals] lead useful, productive lives." Still, because of discrimination against them, and the fear of being fired, they need to have their privacy rights protected. This assertion of a right to the protection of the closet, to a private identity and lifestyle that is not made public, is ironic in an era in which the gay and lesbian rights movement was affirming being "out and proud." It indicates that there was, and continues to be, some level of protection in the closet in a deeply homophobic and heteronormative culture, so lesbian, gay, and transgendered teachers had to work to protect their privacy, to stay in the closet. In concluding, the anonymous teacher shifts to a more personal voice, writing of his hope for a world in which children will be able to play on a playground and not hear the words "faggot" and "queer," an age when young people will not be forced to listen to "bigoted preachers speaking about the sin of sodomy." And he longs for a time when homosexuality will not be viewed as an "illness" to be treated by counselors who promise cures. "All we gays ask," he pleads, "is the right to choose our own life-style, free of persecution and condemnation." These are limited claims: not inclusion in a diverse community as out gay educators, but the claims of privacy, of a space to live a lifestyle that is outside the norm, so long as it does not hurt anyone. He pleads for political leaders to affirm the goal of "justice and equal opportunity" in education, and not to fall victim to "the stereotypes and misconceptions about homosexuality." But this plea is mixed with disappointment. He notes that when liberal Florida governor Reubin Askew was asked whether he would be upset if he knew his children were being taught by "known homosexuals," he replied that "I do not want a known homosexual teaching my children." Just as disappointing was President Carter's statement: "I know that there are homosexuals who teach, and the children don't suffer. But this is a subject I don't particularly want to involve myself in."[22] To side with gay and lesbian teachers under attack was still politically risky, even for liberals.

This "problem" of the homosexual teacher—both the "latent" and the "known" homosexual—was always framed as being a problem of exposure, contagion, and influence. So it always contained a hidden curriculum message to young people in schools: "homosexuals are bad people whom you should stay away from as much as possible. The school is a safe space, designed to protect you against exposure to those bearing this possibly contagious disease." The school was, throughout most of the 20th century, constructed as a safe space for homophobia, purged of all signs of homosexuality or the homosexual, and actively involved in promoting a homophobic ideology. When, several decades later, LGBTQ activists began demanding that public schools be safe spaces for queer youth, they would have to confront this dominant homophobic narrative of the school as a safe space. So long as schools continue to be safe spaces for homophobia rather than those victimized by it, so long as this ethos of the heteronormative school continues to be the norm, efforts to affirm sexual diversity and difference must involve working against the grain, and against dominant narratives.

5

THE PLAGUE

AIDS/HIV Education and Activism in the 1980s

In June 1981, the first cases of what the Center for Disease Control (CDC) initially called "GRID" (gay-related immune deficiency), began to appear in the U.S., and already it was a term that carried as much implicit, hidden, subliminal meaning as it did clinical, medical meaning. Language has a hidden curriculum to it, teaching us both more and less than what it appears to. The clinical marker GRID seemed logical enough since it was designed to capture those aspects of the disease most recognizable, that made it stand out and announce itself as a threat—its emergence within the gay male communities of New York City and San Francisco. Patients were dying of opportunistic infections their bodies should have resisted, and early newspaper reports called it the "gay cancer." The CDC's rush to label the disease as GRID was an attempt to be more accurate, but also to counter some of the antigay prejudice being stirred up in the media around fear of a gay cancer. But "gay-related" was not much of an improvement; and gay-rights leaders pressured the CDC to come up with a better designation for the disease, one that did not associate the disease with being gay. When the CDC finally settled on "acquired immune deficiency syndrome" (AIDS), that seemed to remove any politics from a clinical naming process. As Carol Reeves observes in her history of the language of science, the term "acquired" indicated that the disease was not the result of being gay per se. The disease was acquired through individual behavior. At the same time, the word "acquired" carried an additional meaning, that of behavior causing infection, "that placed blame on the infected for 'acquiring' the disease in the first place." For these reasons, the CDC since the mid-1990s has encouraged a shift toward a language of AIDS/HIV, or just HIV, which is designed to erase all negative connotations.[1] AIDS education has thus slowly evolved into HIV education.

But does "HIV" stand as a purely medical, scientific signifier, without cultural connotations? Might it not encourage some to think of HIV-positive individuals as viruses in the body politic? And what interventions might such an analogy require? My point is not to disparage the search for a better name for a medical disorder and disease of the body. It is instead to say that this search can never entirely succeed. Even deliberately and self-consciously neutral names placed on stigmatized groups by the dominant culture become stigmatizing, and so pressure will exist to find a better, less-stigmatizing name. The term "persons with AIDS" (PWAs) implies an attempt to reclaim control of the naming process by those inflicted and those stigmatized. Through this naming and renaming (gay cancer, GRID/AIDS/HIV/PWA), the AIDS crisis has helped us understand that the "truth" about a disease is as much socially constructed as it is medical. It might have once been possible to see language as just a neutral lens for revealing a "truth" already out there. The AIDS crisis and the national response to it demonstrated the power of language to produce what people see and feel when they look into the face of AIDS. Treating the immunosuppressive disease was one thing. Treating the social disorder—the fear of the new plague and of those groups and individuals perceived to be its carriers—was another. AIDS/HIV education would be constructed as a response to both the medical and the social condition. It would blend health and social-justice language together in a powerful new discourse, with broader implications for reframing sexuality education. And when political leaders and public schools proved not up to the task of doing what had to be done, AIDS educators and activists would create new forms of education through community agencies and drop-in centers, political theater, and political activism.

The Reagan administration pursued a two-sided (some would say two-faced) educational response to the AIDS catastrophe. On one side of the issue within the Reagan administration was William Bennett, who served as chairman of the National Endowment for the Humanities from 1981–1985, when he became Education Secretary, a post he held until 1988. But Bennett was not alone as the voice of social conservatism in the administration. He formed powerful allies with Gary Bauer, then a domestic-affairs advisor to the President (later to lead the conservative Family Research Council and Focus on the Family), and Patrick Buchanan, the President's communication director. Together, they called for sex education grounded in the teaching of traditional family values and moral virtues. Theirs would turn out to be the more powerful and persuasive voice within the administration, particularly since it was consistent with the Republican Party's Christian right constituency that could no longer be ignored. In 1989, after resigning his post as Education Secretary to become drug czar in the new Bush administration, Bennett and Bauer published a booklet *What You Need to Know About AIDS* in which they called for the testing for the HIV status of all Americans, and "contact tracing" of all sexual partners for those identified as having the virus. This they positioned in opposition to what they characterized as progressive sex education, which preached "moral relativism."[2] In a time of crisis, there was no time for moral relativism, they argued. Playing on a term that was being popularized among progressives at the time—"safe sex"—Bennett and Bauer called for safe-sex education for all young people. They reterritorialized the language of safe sex from a usage that implied caring for the self by taking precautions and using condoms, to a usage that implied learning how to "just say no." For those "intravenous drug users and male homosexuals" who threatened the "contamination of our nation's blood supply," the only virtuous response, Bennett and Bauer argued, would be to protect the public by quarantining those with AIDS.[3] Elsewhere Bennett had argued that "in the face of this terrifying AIDS epidemic" the moral teachings of the Catholic Church offered the "only solution possible, chastity."[4] The triumvirate of Bennett, Bauer and Buchanan also tried to position the battle against AIDS as a battle against the moral degeneracy they associated with the "homosexual agenda and lifestyle." Buchanan had written in his newspaper column before he joined the administration that "the poor homosexuals have declared war on nature and now nature is exacting an awful retribution."[5] The language of God's retribution infected policy discourse throughout the Reagan years, even if it had to be officially framed as a secular discourse. God was punishing not only the homosexual, but also the nation as a whole for its permissive attitudes toward the "homosexual agenda."

The alternative, more enlightened voice in the Reagan administration was that of Surgeon General C. Everett Koop. From the beginning Reagan had made it clear that he appointed Koop because of the latter's strong antiabortion stance and his conservative religious values. Women's rights and gay-rights leaders initially were outraged by Koop's appointment. In 1985, when the AIDS crisis could no longer be ignored or go unnamed, Reagan asked Koop to issue a report on AIDS, with the expectation that he would endorse Christian moralistic responses. Instead, the report, released in October 1986, turned out to be quite the opposite of what was expected. The release of the Surgeon General's report is often considered by AIDS educators to be a turning point in the fight against AIDS. Koop began by declaring that those looking for "value judgments" in the report would find that they are "absent." Instead, this was an "objective health and medical report." Without a cure, he called on people to "take the responsibility of protecting" themselves and others, "through preventative measures that are simple, straightforward, and effective." The disease had evoked "highly emotional and often irrational responses," he warned, compounded by the fact that those most immediately affected by the disease—homosexual men and intravenous drug users—evoked strong personal feelings of moral condemnation among many. The best protection against infection, he argued, was education, and "barring abstinence, … use of a condom." As for calls for compulsory blood testing of all Americans, Koop argued that it was "unnecessary, unfeasible, and cost prohibitive." Furthermore, testing could cause "irreparable harm." If someone recently infected had not developed antibodies yet, the test would encourage them to feel safe to engage in unsafe sexual practices; and if they tested positive, they could face job loss and stigmatization. Quarantine also had no role in AIDS prevention, according to Koop, since AIDS was not spread through casual contact.[6] Following release of the report, Koop went on a national tour to promote AIDS education through television, radio, and newspapers. His message was everywhere the same. "We can no longer afford to sidestep frank, open discussion about sexual practices, homosexual and heterosexual." Young people had a right to know "the behaviors to avoid to protect themselves from exposure to the AIDS virus."[7] He recommended a vastly expanded sex-education program in the nation's public schools—with sex education to begin in elementary education and with adolescents to learn about proper use of condoms. Although Koop apparently continued to hold conservative religious values, including a belief in abstinence until marriage, he somehow had managed to rise above, or at least set aside, these values in the face of a medical-health crisis where he felt called to assume responsibility as the nation's first physician. By calling for a massive public education project to help check the spread of the epidemic, Koop also implicitly was critical of his own administration for not doing enough. He began to publicly question why he and other government officials were still occupied writing reports on how to respond to the AIDS crisis (which were then largely ignored by political leaders) when physicians already knew what was needed.[8]

As liberals and progressives rushed to Koop's defense, the President remained silent—and his silence spoke volumes. Progressive columnist Anne Lewis, wrote that "if silence remains the response of national leaders ... then those leaders will no longer have any credibility to discuss moral values."[9] The word "AIDS" was not even spoken publicly by the President until 1987, at the Third International AIDS Conference held in Washington, DC. His administration had done little to speed research on a vaccine or treatment, and had done virtually nothing to promote AIDS education in public schools. His only proposal of substance at the AIDS conference was for widespread, routine testing of people for the virus, although it was not clear why, since there was no effective treatment, and information on someone's HIV status could be stigmatizing and used to deny them employment. According to one observer, Reagan seemed "clearly uncomfortable with a major health problem that targeted those at the margins of American society."[10] And so Reagan would largely ignore AIDS throughout his first term, which would prompt the gay-rights activist and author Randy Schilts to name his book on the AIDS epidemic in the Reagan years *The Band Played On*—in reference to the band that continued to play as the Titanic sank.[11] The U.S. Supreme Court finally had to intervene through the 1987 School Board of Nassau County, Fla. v. Arline case to protect the rights of those with HIV/AIDS from discrimination in federal agencies and in federal contracts. In the summer of that year Reagan did appoint the Presidential Commission on the Human Immunodeficiency Virus Epidemic, both to appease those who were calling for a more coherent federal response and to appease his Christian right base by including in the study group outspoken opponents of AIDS education. The final report called for a massive federal response, including more AIDS education, although by the time it came out it was virtually ignored by the administration. In denouncing federal aid to AIDS education on the Senate floor in October 1987 Senator Jesse Helms held up a comic book he said was published with federal funds (a false claim, it turned out) by the Gay Men's

Health Crisis of New York, that promoted "safe" homosexual sex. For Helms, that was a contradiction in terms, and not the message we should be sending young people. His sentiments, while overtly homophobic, represented a broader sentiment among Republicans and conservative Southern Democrats, who joined with Helms in supporting an amendment to the AIDS appropriation bill to prohibit the use of federal monies for AIDS education materials designed to "promote or encourage, directly or indirectly, homosexual activities." At a time when AIDS education for queer youth in particular was critical, such education was explicitly prohibited by law.[12] By the time of the 1988 elections, candidate Bush embraced the "just say no," moralistic, family-values themes of the previous administration, but went beyond Reagan in calling for mandatory HIV testing to identify those infected. While president, he continued a policy of restricting immigration and tourism to the U.S. by HIV-positive individuals. As it became ever more clear that leadership on AIDS education would not come from either the President or Congress, and that public schools would avoid AIDS education like the plague, the attempt to educate the public would have to occur elsewhere—and in this regard the mass media, particularly the press, would step in to fill the void. If press coverage of the AIDS crisis, at least initially, reproduced many taken-for-granted narratives circulating in the public, it would also begin (ever so slowly) to disassemble the dominant mythology of AIDS and its victims.

In the first years of the plague, the mass media would take for granted, and also perpetuate, a distinction between deserving and innocent AIDS victims. The assumption among many in the press and within the most affected groups (particularly gay men) was that in order to promote sympathy for AIDS victims, the media needed to tell stories of "innocent" victims, the kinds of victim the public could relate to and empathize with, whom the public could imagine as deserving to have their rights protected as human beings. The language of victim rights could then be used to deconstruct the binary opposition that distinguished between innocent and noninnocent victims, to suggest that none are deserving victims, that all should be treated with respect as victims of a disease that did not discriminate. The AIDS narrative that would change everything, that would awaken and reignite a politics of fear, stigmatization, exclusion, and scapegoating on the one hand, and on the other awaken in broad segments of the American public a recommitment to "do the right thing"—to borrow the title of Spike Lee's 1989 film about race in America—was the Ryan White case. Ryan White would serve as the poster boy of the innocent AIDS victim, and his story—narrated over the course of several years in the popular press—would stir the nation and begin to reframe the conversation. Ryan was a 13-year-old boy in the late summer of 1985—a hemophiliac who had contracted the HIV virus in a blood transfusion. The *New York Times* narration of the Ryan White story developed over five years in a number of articles, beginning in August 1985, and it provided a compelling educational text for the nation.

Coverage in the *Times* began with a photo on August 1, 1985, with a caption provided by the Associated Press: "Ryan White, 13 years old, in his room yesterday in Kokomo. The seventh grader contracted AIDS while being treated for hemophilia and was barred from returning to Western Middle School for fear he might pose a health threat to other pupils. 'I'm pretty upset about it,' he said. 'I'll miss my friends mostly.'"[13] At a time when so many young people were skipping classes and dropping out of school, Ryan affirmed a desire and right to go to school because his school friends were a type of family. He thus came to represent wholesome, Midwest family values. As for the fears of local parents and administrators in Kokomo, Indiana, whenever these fears were voiced in an article they would always be accompanied or followed by the viewpoint of the medical community that "the disease can apparently be spread by sexual contact, contaminated needles and blood transfusions, but there is no evidence it is spread by casual contact."[14] Nevertheless, most of the school-system's teachers and parents agreed with the superintendent's decision to require that Ryan receive instruction at home—via a telephone speaker in his room. But the sound quality was poor in the bedroom so he heard little of what the teachers were saying in class. In spite of this, the school principal told the *Times* reporter that "Everything went well with the initial tests for the system."[15] The *Times* articles and headlines consistently positioned "the system," against "the AIDS victim," and so the story was framed as an example of victimizing the victim, or "doubly victimizing." Soon the decision of school officials in Kokomo, Indiana, was being used to justify similar actions around the country. In early September 1985, the *Times* borrowed a phrase from a state health official in Florida to characterize a decision in Miami-Dade County, Florida, not to let three girls with AIDS attend classes. "AIDS is two epidemics," Dr Jeffrey Sacks is quoted as saying, "It's an epidemic of disease and death, and it's also been an epidemic of fear." The Miami-Dade County case involved triplets born with AIDS, whose mother had died of AIDS. Rather than refusing to allow the girls to attend school and thereby incurring the wrath of progressive groups in the community, officials in Miami-Dade County decided to allow the girls to attend a school of their own. A teacher volunteered to teach them in a largely empty school building removed from other students. The school had its own audiovisual equipment, playfield, lunchroom, and even food service. The three young girls and the volunteer teacher were alone in what was beginning to be called at that time "quarantine" conditions. AIDS victims were to be isolated from the "healthy" population in special facilities, like lepers in a leper colony, but with all their needs attended to.

The fear of AIDS in the schools even swept through New York City in the first week of September 1985.[16] On September 3, the *Times* published an editorial critical of the rising tide of AIDS fear in the city's schools, titled "The New Plague, in Perspective," and reiterated that there was no medical reason for preventing students with AIDS from attending school, or legal reason either. On September 4, school officials from Kokomo schools, who had barred Ryan White, traveled to New York City where they had been invited to speak at a news conference in support of two community school boards in Queens who had announced defiantly they would not let students with AIDS attend school, no matter what the central district board or the chancellor said. The next evening, in the middle-class Ozone Park section of Queens, a group of approximately 500 parents gathered in a packed school auditorium and cheered loudly when a member of the local community board asked them to "join us in standing in the schoolhouse door" to prevent children with AIDS from attending school in the community. On the next day, the New York City Board of Education announced its decision to admit "AIDS sufferers" to all schools in the city, declaring that it was the right thing to do, and also the legal thing to do according to school district lawyers. When push came to shove, the board members in Ozone Park decided not to "stand in the schoolhouse door," fearful of the inevitable picture that would appear in the press, and the inevitable comparison with an earlier defiant act of standing in the schoolhouse door in the 1950s in the South. The local board member who made the comment about "standing in the schoolhouse door" had defended it as innocent, but of course even if he did not explicitly mean to draw a comparison with the era of segregation in the South, many presumed that he unconsciously had the comparison in mind. At any rate, his words could not be taken back, and the comparison to the segregation era stuck. At that point, a discourse of basic civil rights and moral principles began to reframe the issue. Those who sought to block children with AIDS from attending school were increasingly represented as those narrow-minded bigots of an earlier era, and perhaps these comparisons were not unfair. In a letter to the editor published in the *Times* on September 23, 1985, a Yale Law School professor concluded that "behind the legal issues is a moral one. ... Fear does not justify doubly victimizing."[17]

Meanwhile, a federal judge in Indianapolis refused to order the admission of Ryan White to school until he had exhausted four levels of state appeal. When a state medical officer ruled that there was no medical reason why he could not return to school, he showed up for classes on February 21 only to find that 43 percent of his classmates had stayed at home. That day, a *Times* reporter followed him around, and the narrative he wrote was subtitled "Like Everybody Else." Ryan was represented as a normal child and student, as someone to whom most young people and their parents could relate. The reader learns that "Ryan arrived wearing the standard student outfit of jeans and high-top tennis shoes," and he is quoted as saying that his fellow students (those who had not fallen victim to their fears) treated him "just like everybody else."[18] But when he returned from school that day, he learned that a local judge had barred his continued attendance, only to find that another judge would soon overturn that decision. It was not until July 1986 that a group of local parents would drop their efforts to prevent his attendance in school, but not because they had a change of heart. Their attorney is quoted as saying: "Nobody feels differently about AIDS in the classroom. The finances just happened to be the biggest stumbling block."[19] Ryan is reduced to "AIDS in the classroom," a disease rather than a human being who is a member of a caring community. His name is, conveniently, erased and replaced with the new scarlet letter, the marker "AIDS," which he is made to represent—even if the parents cannot directly accuse him (as they would other AIDS victims) of sexual crimes and sins. When he did return to school, certain concessions were made to the politics of fear in the community. The *Times* reported (in an Associated Press story) that Ryan had to use a separate bathroom, and he had to eat with disposable plastic utensils and plates in the cafeteria. But the article added that "scientists view such arrangements for AIDS patients as unnecessary." The evidence continued to mount, according to the article, that the disease is transmitted only through "direct exchange of blood or semen."[20]

In September 1987, the *Times* reported that Ryan White, now 15, had attended his first day of classes at Hamilton Heights High School, and used this as a way to introduce a broader discussion of how public schools across the nation were· responding to the AIDS crisis through the development of AIDS curricula. From the examples cited in the article, AIDS curricula were clearly not about countering a politics of fear, linked to a politics of scapegoating, exclusion, and stigmatization. In fact, the article makes clear that the politics of fear was spreading by noting that in Arcadia, Florida, the home of three hemophiliac boys with the AIDS virus had been burned after they were admitted to school. Instead of responding to this climate of fear, the AIDS curricula cited by the *Times* were curricula of disease prevention, designed to teach young people about risky behaviors and how to minimize the risk of contracting the AIDS virus. A New York State Board of Regents AIDS curriculum for kindergarten through high school included frank information about condoms and their proper use, as did a 100-page "Learn to Live" curriculum in Massachusetts. In less liberal states and parts of the nation, the response was more in the way of teaching abstinence and avoidance of risky sexual practices in particular. Very quickly, the AIDS curricula were bringing back a moralistic tone to sexuality education, and the normal–abnormal binary was reasserted with a vengeance. The Arizona superintendent of schools is quoted as saying that such a fear-based AIDS curriculum is legitimate when it is "a matter of life and death." But even talking about risky sexual practices and lifestyles meant speaking their names, bringing them out of the closet so to speak, and to some conservative groups, this was tantamount to endorsing these practices and lifestyles. The *Times* quoted a spokesman for a Rhode Island Catholics of Life group in opposition to a new AIDS curriculum in the state as saying: "They're going to be teaching our children the act of sodomy."[21] The AIDS curricula were not designed to challenge this spreading homophobia and moralistic condemnation of "sodomy" (that broadly inclusive category of perversion), and, consequently, even when they appeared progressive—in calling for education about, and distribution of, condoms in schools—they used fear to teach "healthy" sexual practices. And fear of the disease easily becomes a generalizable fear of plague and of those who are presumed responsible for the plague, who become not only doubly victimized (victims of disease and victims of fear), but also triply victimized (if they are gay) and multiply victimized (if they are poor, black, gay, etc.). Because Ryan White was white middle class, and presumably heterosexual, and because he was an "innocent" AIDS victim, the press was able to package and sell his story around a narrative of double victimization that white, middle-class heterosexuals could understand, in their terms.

The hope among gay and black AIDS activists, and among progressives more generally, was that the Ryan White story could be used to help the public take the next step, to understand victimization more complexly, and to link it to social justice agendas rather than just disease prevention. When the *Times* returned to follow up on the Ryan White case, it was in the context of a review of a made-for-television movie, *The Ryan White Story*, that aired on ABC on January 16, 1989, and this time with a more critical eye to how the story, even at its best, had been narrated in the mass media. "Once more," the review began, "prime-time television entertainment is approaching the subject of AIDS through the case of a hemophiliac youth," even though "the vast majority of AIDS patients are homosexuals and drug addicts." The reviewer observes that television apparently was not yet ready to "explore these groups with any degree of compassion." Instead, it preferred to tell stories about "innocent youngsters trapped by circumstances beyond their control." Such stories provide "easier dramatic hooks for uplift exercises." After saying this up front and at the beginning, the reviewer acknowledges that these stories of innocence are both "heartbreaking" and do serve as vehicles for exposing public ignorance and prejudice about AIDS. The movie presents the story as revolving around a failure of leadership. According to the review: "It is a story not only about ignorance but also about an almost total lack of enlightened community leadership." While residents are represented as being "understandably concerned and frightened, ... panic is allowed to take over." The local media also come in for blame in the movie: "A radio station broadcasts vicious bilge. The print and electronic press push for sensationalism." The movie ends, however, on a note of hope. "Enlightened" leadership finally emerges to do the right thing, and the truth about AIDS wins out over people's misconceptions.[22] This is, as the reviewer concludes, a good lesson, and so it is a story worth telling. Perhaps it is, and there were by 1990 some positive signs that Americans might at last begin to move beyond the panic response of the 1980s, although that panic was allayed largely because of two factors. First, the white, middle-class, heteronormative public was convinced that the disease had been largely contained to the gay and black communities and was not "leaking" out of these stigmatized subpopulations. Secondly, the first AIDS drugs were beginning to appear, which would transform AIDS from an automatic death sentence to a manageable chronic disorder. Without these two factors being present, there is little reason to believe that the politics of fear and panic would not have prevailed over the politics of "enlightened" leadership.

On April 9, 1990, Ryan White died at age 18, and the *Times* story was subtitled: "His Struggle Helped Pierce Myths." One of those myths, according to the story, is that people with AIDS are somehow different from us, or abnormal. Ryan "often said he only wanted to be treated like an ordinary teenager [and he] had a date for the senior prom." Elsewhere the story refers to Ryan's desire "to be a regular kid." But it acknowledges that the myth of Ryan as a "regular kid," one he promoted himself and sought to live, was not quite true, that "he was not quite a typical teenager in Indiana."[23] He lived through notoriety, isolation, and celebrity status all in a few brief years. If he is made to represent an innocent, "regular," "typical," "normal" child, even the most liberal and progressive media outlets such as the *Times* generally failed to question their own taken-for-granted use of the normal–abnormal binary opposition to narrate the story of the AIDS crisis. Ironically, the Ryan White story had nothing and everything to do with sexuality education. It had nothing to do with sexuality education because he contracted the HIV virus through a blood transfusion rather than sexual behavior—and consequently his story was largely ignored within the professional discourse on sex education. But his story had everything to do with sexuality and sexuality education in another sense. As it was covered in the mass media, Ryan's story was about a normal, typical, small-town, Midwest, white, middle-class, heterosexual boy—an "innocent" young man—and the moral of the story is that bad things can happen to even "innocent" victims of disease and of mass hysteria and panic. At best, through the narration of this "innocent" victim's story, we learn to empathize with the social stigmatization all victims of AIDS must face, including those who are gay or black or both. But at worst, we may learn to reinforce our commonsense beliefs about innocence and lack of innocence, about those who are diseased through no fault of their own, and those who are made to bear the burden for their "dirty," "unnatural," "immoral," and "shameful" sexuality in the mark of AIDS. The *Times* review of the movie *The Ryan White Story* laments, for example, that the public is not exposed to stories about AIDS sufferers who are "homosexuals and drug addicts" rather than "innocent" victims. In the conflation of the male homosexual and the drug addict—particularly the poor, black, drug addict—the dominant culture was able to continue to understand the AIDS crisis as about normal versus abnormal, good versus bad, and clean versus dirty sexuality, even if (in the liberal scripting of the story) the abnormal Other was now to be the object of sympathy rather than stigmatization and shaming.

Many Americans came to the conclusion that they had an interest in fighting the kind of fear mongering, public hysteria, scapegoating, and stigmatization that the AIDS epidemic brought out in people—no matter who the victims were. Like the doctor in Albert Camus' *The Plague*, who was fighting the plague of fascism, many ordinary Americans began to affirm that "on this earth there are pestilences and there are victims, and it's up to us, so far as possible, not to join forces with the pestilences." And like Camus' character, they began to ask: How can we, in every predicament "take the victims' side, so as to reduce the damage done?" That would require facing the truth "that we all have plague, ... [and] that one must do what one can to cease being plague stricken."[24] The plague is not just or even primarily AIDS in this case, but rather a sickness of the human spirit that makes people victims of their fears and stereotypes, that brings out the worst in them rather than the best. This fear goes by many names, including homophobia and racism. One might say that in the 1980s through the mid-1990s, the height of the AIDS hysteria in

America, the politics of fear gripped America and led to a search for evil enemies, both without and within. In this context, the Ryan White story, taken as a whole, would do more to reframe the AIDS epidemic in a way that appealed to the best rather than the worst in Americans.

Quite early on, in the first year of the plague, it became clear that the epidemic could have a devastating impact on the gay community both personally, but also in terms of the social stigmatization associated with this linkage between the "homosexual lifestyle" and sickness, death, and contagion. The AIDS crisis would encourage people to replay an old story, to confirm what they thought they knew about the homosexual. In short, the AIDS crisis threatened to undo all that had been done over the course of the past decade by the gay and lesbian rights movement to make gay and lesbian people "respectable," and "normal." AIDS refocused public attention on gay men in particular as "sexual outlaws," who only sought the right to sexual freedom and the right to be promiscuous and spread disease. The AIDS epidemic in the 1980s seemed only to confirm a "truth" that had long been established about homosexuality in the public mind—namely, that it was a disease, and one that could be contagious. The language of homosexual disease and contagion, and the need to protect impressionable young people from this contagious disease, had a long history already by the time the real disease struck. This meant that the real AIDS epidemic became easily assimilated into the reigning cultural narrative of the homosexual and homosexuality. It developed and extended a story that many people already knew quite well, a story that reinforced their fear of the homosexual Other as a sexual "pervert" and carrier of contagious diseases. It also was a story that in a somewhat contradictory fashion comforted many white, "straight," middle-class Americans in its assurance that the plague could be contained within urban gay communities, where it would wreak havoc, but at a safe distance.

In the face of a governmental response that was pathetically underfunded, and also suspect, the gay and lesbian community began to mobilize its own support network, thereby creating the model for a new type of community-based health advocacy education in Gay Men's Health Crisis of New York (GMHC). GMHC was founded in the summer of 1981 in New York City by a group that included the author Larry Kramer, to provide a support network of AIDS-related services to PWAs, using volunteers to help connect people to counseling, medical advice, support groups and other services, in an environment "founded by the gay community for the gay community." GMHC resisted bureaucratization and the professionalization of control by developing an ethos of service around two key ideas and practices: the "buddy system" and "crisis intervention." Volunteers served as care providers (or "care partners") and as crisis counselors. Through direct intervention in the lives of PWAs, volunteers were introduced personally to "the world of compounded human suffering." Volunteers filled many roles, including lobbying for disability rights legislation for PWAs, making sure that a new PWA client who lives alone and needs help with chores is assigned a buddy who can visit him that day, helping develop outreach strategies for people of color in various communities, helping a mother with AIDS find long-term care for her children, and helping an undocumented immigrant with AIDS get needed services.

All these activities were considered to be educative, and all aspects of what Philip Kayal called "bearing witness."[25] Kayal's very personal account of the GMHC and the politics of AIDS was published in 1993, still before protease inhibitors came along and when gay men in New York and elsewhere were still dying in increasing numbers. "Bearing witness," became a theme at GMHC linked directly to gay/ AIDS volunteers as activists, and as being educated through their activism and speaking out—and to speak out was considered an intervention, an activism. To bear witness, Kayal writes, was to speak out and speak up as a response to a lack of response, "to being defined and treated as 'an Other.'" For Kayal, as for Kramer, to bear witness was to put a human face on what was happening, and who it was happening to, to resist dehumanization by telling stories, bearing witness to the suffering of PWAs both physically and psychically as the face of "exclusion and marginalization." This meant resisting the medicalization of AIDS, the statistics, and the facts about transmission, to reframe AIDS. Of community-based agencies serving PWAs or any other marginalized group, Kayal claimed that "there is no other way for empathy to develop and the human face of AIDS to be known." GMHC as an educative initiative organized around this theme of "bearing witness," provided a space for volunteers (most of whom were gay men and/or PWAs) to experience "self-recognition" and "a rebirth of the spirit, of the will to survive." In looking into the face of stigmatization and exclusion, volunteers recognized their own stig- matization and exclusion as gay men, and this led to discussions of how AIDS was a metaphor for gay oppression, and how gay liberation had to begin with "self- acceptance," which to Kayal meant "acknowledging the community that one is identified with as an extension and reinforcement of the personal self." The homosexual was to become one with his gay identity, and identity would provide many white, middle class, otherwise privileged, gay men with a politics and a language of struggle, although that politics often did not involve—at least initially— much of a sense that other struggles might also be important. It was a politics of finding a safe space to protect themselves from the homophobia that was all around, and to develop counterservices and counterstories for support. The theological concept of "bearing witness," according to Kayal, means "taking on the cross or the suffering of others as if it were one's own."[26] Through this active call to justice, he argued, "the gay community becomes the biblical *anawin*—the poor of God of the prophetic community that calls people out of isolation and into commitment to one another in a way that challenges and resists the internalization of homophobia."

The language Kayal used to describe GMHC was a language that circulated throughout the organization by the mid-1980s, and it is significant in several ways. First, the GMHC overtly politicized a viral epidemic, linking its spread and the lack of response to "oppression." The word would be uttered, and that would change everything else, and this at a time when the major gay and lesbian rights groups were trying (somewhat successfully) to "de-gay" AIDS so that it was not perceived in the public mind as a gay disease. GMHC and the new gay voices were out and proud, refusing to feel ashamed because they had AIDS, and fighting against those who would stigmatize them for it. They would turn to the gay community for their support, and the community would turn inward, although this very inwardness had helped spread the virus in the first place. Within the protection of the gay community, new discourses of freedom would circulate, discourses that spoke of humanization and dehumanization, about the process of turning people into an Other, about internalized oppression and self-hate. By naming the problem as oppression, education and outreach efforts became exercises in what Paulo Freire called a "pedagogy of the oppressed," designed to help oppressed peoples break through the ideological chains that keep them oppressed.[27] Freire's work was just beginning to be known in the U.S. by the time of the AIDS crisis, and he brought a language of oppression and social justice with him that provided a useful tool for groups like GMHC to reframe the debate, and to think of education as a praxis or intervention in the world in order to change it rather than just "know" it. Education, from this perspective, was active rather than passive, something that happened to the body as well as the mind, and something that called on people to respond when it was just as easy not to respond.[28] This question of the call to respond, to bear witness to the suffering, injustice, and final humanity of the dead and dying, is—as I have argued elsewhere—basic to teaching for social justice and learning for freedom.[29] If this is a language that has roots in religious heritages, it finds its secular version in the democratic, progressive tradition of the call of the teacher to profess a commitment to the truth, and to bear witness to inconvenient or uncomfortable truths. In this context, it is also a call that is answered in relation to one's community of identity, as one's home and *habitus*, and as one's family. In the mid-1980s, when the New York City Gay Men's Chorus performed an AIDS concert at Carnegie Hall, it brought the house down with its renditions of "We Are Family" and "That's What Friends Are For," two anthems performed again and again that held up the hope that those excluded and stigmatized by their families of origin could find a new family, a new home, in the gay community, a family and set of friends who would be there for you when you needed someone. This, as I have already said, was deeply contradictory, for the community was also a ghetto of sorts, a zone of sex shops and bars for quick pick-ups. This commercialized, bar-based gay culture was part of the problem, and so gay activists would have to re-educate the gay community they represented, calling on gay youth fleeing homophobic homes to embrace the gay community as a safe space to be gay. Some of this tension comes through in the movie *Milk*, about the life and times of Harvey Milk in San Francisco as Milk confronts the depoliticized bar and street scene in the gay community there in the 1970s.

This turning inward to the gay community, if it was to be transformative, had to engage the community in critiquing its own complicity in the plague, and the power of commercialized bar culture in taking over the community. Community re-education was thus just as important as educating those outside the community that gay people were "normal" and no threat to them. This is where Queer Nation and AIDS Coalition to Unleash Power (ACT UP) would play an important role—in repoliticizing sexual politics, and in engaging young people in acts of embodied and discursive resistance; that is, resistance through and with the body, and also through the naming of what it is that oppresses the body. So "silence = death" became a signifier employed by Queer Nation to remind people how, at an earlier time in Germany, many had remained silent when some groups (including homosexuals) were targeted and scapegoated. In a similar way, the pink triangle of ACT UP referred back to the triangle worn by gay men in German concentration camps, and thus connected the past and the present in ways that made people think differently about the "problem" of AIDS and who had the problem. Queer Nation was organized out of AIDS activism in New York City, when, in 1990, people were looking for some way to respond to a series of beatings of lesbians and gay men in East Village by gangs of young toughs doing what they had done for decades in the East Village without any police action. A younger generation of AIDS and HIV activists decided to mobilize what they called a "cultural happening," a form of cultural terrorism that involved action in public spaces aimed at disrupting heteronormative culture. Queer Nation sought, in the words of Sally Munt, "to make the nation a space safe for queers, not just in the sense of being tolerated," but safe for in-your-face queers who embodied their sexuality.[30] As Lauren Berlant and Elizabeth Freeman argued, "being queer is not about the right to privacy: it is about the freedom to be public."[31] ACT UP was primarily a gay male organization engaged in symbolic protests and designed to make heterosexuals aware of their tacit support of homophobia although they aligned themselves with such groups as Women's Health Action and Mobilization (WHAM!) and Lesbian Avenger. On December 10, 1989, ACT UP and WHAM! organized a protest inside and outside St Patrick's Cathedral in protest of Cardinal O'Connor's opposition to AIDS education in schools, along with his commitment to overturning the Roe v. Wade decision that legalized abortion. While thousands protested outside, a "plant" inside publicly refused the Eucharist when presented it by the Cardinal—an action considered to represent desecration by Roman Catholics. While the media event did attract much attention, it also polarized people in ways that mainstream gay and lesbian rights leaders felt were counterproductive. It may be best to view groups like ACT UP and WHAM! as engaged in political guerilla theater, while the more established rights groups were involved in a campaign of normalizing gays and lesbians. Both played a role in moving the public to become more accepting of difference.

Warren Johansson and William Percy, in their 1994 queer history of being "out," noted that the idea of a queer nation implied something different from the idea of a gay community. "Our ranks," they wrote, "are too diverse as well as too widespread to form a community in the traditional sense." The lesbian and gay communities in urban areas across the U.S. were traditional in the sense that they served to situate the homosexual within an urban, ghettoized space, albeit a space of partial freedom and mobilization to fight stigmatization. That is, they contained the Other within an urban space of both confinement and freedom. These spaces also were privileged in the sense of being carved out for the most part by white, middle- and upper-middle-class gays and lesbians, and they were spaces where—because of their privilege—people did not seem anymore to have much of a political agenda, other than the freedom to enjoy themselves sexually and consume large quantities of alcohol and drugs—often at the same time. The more political Queer Nation young people took this for internalized oppression, and sought to reconnect queer youth, wherever they might be and from whatever their backgrounds, to a deprogrammed mind, one free (as much as possible) of the need to conform and seek approval from those who have despised and "othered" them, out and proud in public, and even willing to flaunt their deviant desires by holding hands, kissing, and in other ways exhibiting themselves in public. To do so was a radical act of public pedagogy from the perspective of Queer Nation, for it once more served to make straight people aware of how they took heterosexual public intimacy for granted, yet reacted through shame and disgust to homosexual intimacy or displays of affection in public. All this was to help the broader culture unpack homophobia, by naming it and by unpacking fear. "Queer Nation" also implied a mobilization and movement that went far beyond life in the urban gay ghettoes, that sought to be inclusive of people of color and of people of all classes and locations on the national and global grid. Lauren Berlant and Elizabeth Freeman wrote of Queer Nation in the early 1990s that "we have no community ethos ... but common dangers and enemies are fostering a political will to resist."[32] The gay revolution had not, it turned out, eliminated homophobia, and the Christian right had grown in response to the cultural movement to normalize homosexuality and treat homosexuals as "normal" people—as the same but different. As Christian conservatism spread an antigay message through the new, alternative evangelical mass media (television, music, and movies), and as more young people were "out," in some ways it was less safe to be a homosexual in America in the 1980s than it was to be one in the 1950s. The "out" lesbian and gay man, particularly when they dared to "flaunt" their sexuality in public places, were subject to possibly brutal, even lethal, reaction by those (typically men) "disgusted" by seeing such public behavior, by even seeing "out" gay men and lesbians in public. What Queer Nation understood was that this "disgust" had to be elicited, produced through the performance of queer, embodied sexuality and sexual identity in public spaces outside the gay community. "We're here, we're queer, get used to it" served as a rallying cry for the movement, and it sent a powerful message out to straight Americans that, in spite of systematic efforts to silence, closet, and then assimilate gayness as the same, many lesbians and gay men were demanding that their differences also be acknowledged and that straight America get over its uneasiness with their sexuality.

Within the gay community, Queer Nation engaged in what the Brazilian political activist Augusto Boal called the "theatre of the oppressed," a dramatized performance, in part improvisational, in which the oppressed perform themselves as the oppressed, and also play the role of their oppressors.[33] Through this role playing and role switching, and in dialogue, the performers learn to critique their own victim mentality and internalized oppression, and to "name" that which oppresses them. Frederick Corey provides an example of ACT UP's version of a theater of the oppressed in his autobiographical essay about his involvement in ACT UP in the 1980s. "I used to be a gay man," Corey began, "Now I am queer."[34] To be gay was a "private matter," an identity reserved for personal relationships within a small circle of friends and coworkers. To be queer, on the other hand, is a "public matter," something that comes with a politics; and here Foucault gets invoked. The domination of homosexual people, Corey argued, has been about the regulation of homosexual desire and the production of the homosexual body as a subjugated body. Homosexuals were ashamed of their bodies and desires, and learned to perform this shame as part of who they were. Gay men and lesbians sought to replace shame with a desire to be "normal"—just like everyone else, only different. What would it mean to perform a queer identity? We get some inkling of what it might mean in Corey's description of his own life in the late 1980s. At that time, his gay partner was dying of AIDS, and he remembers how he looked: "wearing a purple mock turtleneck from the Gap, a pair of faded inverse silhouette Levi blue jeans, London Fog black loafers, a black belt, white socks." To be an urban gay male, according to Corey, was to become a brand-identified image of the fashion-conscious "queen." Gay men understood the performance of identity, but risked becoming nothing but a stylized performance of the dominant image of a gay man. Then there was the image of the gay man as ethereal, a mind without a body, represented by Corey, who, as an assistant professor in a liberal arts college, delighted in reading obscure, romantic poetry to an undergraduate audience, never daring to speak of his own life in his poetry, "because after all, we [gay men] cannot really talk about who we are or what our bodies know."[35] These performances of gay male identity are largely taken for granted and unquestioned before Corey attended a performance of *Sex/Love/Stories* in Santa Monica, California, in 1991. The author of the play, and the sole performer, was Tim Miller, a member of ACT UP and a prophet of queer consciousness. The audience consisted mainly of white, gay men, mostly in their twenties and thirties—like Corey himself—and he immediately feels solidarity with everyone in the theater. Whereas the bar is a gay space, characterized by darkness and hiding—the very physical manifestation of the closet mentality—this is a public theater and a public event that brought together a more political group of people to create a queer space. Of course, the theater has historically been defined as a gay-friendly space. It is also a white, middle-class space; none of which Corey questions. But the performance he witnesses is at least expressive of a new sensibility, which began to be named "queer." Miller's performance was a stylized re-enactment of a protest conducted by ACT UP at Los Angeles General Hospital. The author/performer begins by reading the inscription on the hospital's facade to the effect that no citizen will be denied protection of health and life. Yet inside the hospital PWAs look at "blood-stained walls" and are forced to sit on a hard wooden bench, all in a row, as they receive their chemo, and then often throw up in front of others. The narrator taunts the audience that many of them would rather "go shopping" than care about what was going on in the hospital. Miller then begins to disrobe, and slowly transforms his body into a stylized version of St Sebastian, tied up and pierced with arrows. In this way, the performance affirms homosexual and homoerotic desire and eroticism in the very throes of death.[36] This form of performance of the body as an oppressed body, a body in chains, turns out then to be a performance of the body as unashamed of its desires. As I have said, the contradiction of such a performance is that it takes place in a very privileged space, and speaks to an otherwise privileged audience. Still, in some important ways, AIDS and homophobia made otherwise privileged white males know what it feels like to be oppressed. At the same time, this did not necessarily lead to the kinds of alliances across class, race, gender, and linguistic differences that would be needed to seriously address AIDS as an epidemic and as a social phenomenon involved in stigmatization and exclusion.

If more women became AIDS victims than men, their responses were more likely to focus on the support group as a central educative and re-educative space; and through support groups in urban spaces, women with AIDS struggled to work through their differences and fears and to come together in solidarity. In their study of a multiracial and multiclass support group in Columbus, Ohio, for women with AIDS in the early 1990s, Patricia Lather and Chris Smithies wrote that "AIDS is a rainbow disease, affecting women from all walks of life. Some are poor and some live in the suburbs. Others use drugs, and still others have professional jobs, and some have rarely, if ever, entertained a positive thought about self." The HIV support group served as a "catalyst for women from very different backgrounds to come together," the authors concluded. At the same time, differences among the women were a cause for continuing "anger, alienation, exhaustion, [and] distrust."[37] The support group provided women with an opportunity to make meaning of AIDS in the context of their lives, and to move toward activism and community. Still, the authors resist the easy temptation of a "feel-good" conclusion, refusing to provide the reader with familiar stories that presume to know the unknowable. The "truth" about AIDS is linked to the truth about "sex, blood, drugs and death," which push its meaning beyond the limits of medicine to address social differences and inequalities. The authors turn finally to the stage for an image that conveys something of what AIDS can mean. They wrote that Tony Kushner's play *Angels in America*, which premiered in San Francisco in 1991, "captures the movement of a weary world toward forms of community that respect differences." After wrestling with an angel, the character Prior follows her to heaven, where he refuses her request to let him die so as not to suffer further. He chooses life in the face of suffering, and thus affirms life. They quote Prior's words to the angel: "This disease will be the end of many of us, but not nearly all, and the dead will be commemorated and will struggle on with the living, and we are not going away."[38]

Simon Watney, in his history of how the AIDS crisis was represented in popular culture, observes that AIDS was almost always represented through references to gay males, African Americans, and the African continent. Through these representational practices, "Africa becomes a 'deviant' continent, just as gay men are effectively Africanized." In a similar way, it becomes possible to see how this language of a contagious disease fits with a controlling image of the pregnant, inner-city, African American or Latina teenager as infected. Now, the infection was real, and many children were born in America's urban neighborhoods in the 1980s to poor black and Latina women already infected with the disease. The child of the welfare teenage mother long had been treated as an unfortunate mistake, the fetus an unwanted cancer in the womb. Now the fetus and the child carried their diseased nature in their blood. So too, black and brown men in the U.S. historically had been represented as sexually "dirty" and promiscuous, and the AIDS crisis not only confirmed what the dominant culture thought it already knew about them, it also legitimated blaming black men as spreaders of disease. The burden of AIDS, it turned out, would fall heavily upon the African American community, especially after 1990. When the first cases of AIDS were diagnosed in the early 1980s, most of the victims were gay white men or hemophiliacs. But by the mid-1990s, the proportion of known cases among whites in the U.S. was steadily declining, while the rate of infection among African Americans exceeded for the first time the rate among whites. By 2005 the rate of infection for what was by then known as HIV/AIDS was ten times higher for black than for white Americans. Even more disturbing, the rate of HIV infection among African American women was 23 times higher than among white women, and among African American men it was eight times higher than among white men.[39] Whereas African American teenagers represented 16 percent of the total population in the early 21st century, they accounted for 69 percent of all reported HIV/AIDS cases in the U.S.[40] This is a crisis of major proportions that has been growing and getting worse, and yet it has gone largely under the radar in the mass media, and even among many within the black community, who would rather hide this problem. In combating a growing public perception that what once had been a gay disease was now a black disease, leadership in the black community, including health educators, have emphasized that the virus strikes those who engaged in certain risky behaviors, not members of a racial or sexual orientation group, and that poverty is itself a risk factor. In a recent study by three black health educators that reviews the history of AIDS in the black community, the authors note that "there are no known genetic factors that place African American people at a greater risk for HIV/AIDS than other racial/ethnic groups." The virus is most commonly spread through unprotected anal and vaginal intercourse, or the use of infected needles so that "AIDS has highly effective and uncomplicated methods of prevention." Poverty enters the picture in its connection to intravenous drug use, but also because "HIV/AIDS is most often spread by people who are unaware of their status with the virus"—which includes most people living in poverty.[41]

Along with sexual contact with intravenous drug users, or those who have had contact with them, there was the problem of transmission of the virus through male-to-male contact in the black community. Because homosexuality was morally condemned within the black community, even more so than in the white community, many young homosexual or bisexual black men learned that they could not be gay and black at the same time. Partially, as a result, the phenomenon of black men being on the "down low"—having sexual relations with other men, usually without protection, never thinking of themselves as gay and of spreading the virus to their wives and other men—began to come out of the closet, although it would prove difficult to talk about. As the authors observe, "many in the African American community are less accepting of homosexuality than are members of other racial and ethnic groups." Young homosexual African Americans face "fears of social isolation, discrimination, and verbal/physical abuse." This not only hurts homosexual youth, it also means that African American men who engage in homosexual behavior are encouraged to mask their behavior, to "nondisclose" to their sexual partners that they have engaged in risky sexual behavior with others or that they are HIV-positive. "Disclosing" behavior, they write, "could be viewed as creating a high risk for embarrassment or potential loss of a relationship."[42] The authors call for an acceptance of homosexuality and gay and lesbian youth in the black community as one way of getting beyond these problems. They also call for the more widespread distribution of condoms and birth-control information. As in the gay community, the condom would be the first and best line of defense against AIDS in the black community, and making sure that condoms were readily available and that people got used to using them was much of what the educational campaign was about. People could not, in the end, presume or expect that their sexual partners would disclose their HIV status and sexual history—they had to learn to protect themselves. But with little governmental support for either condom distribution or clean needles for intravenous drug users, HIV/AIDS would not be controlled in the black community, only contained there. When it became clear that most white, heterosexual, middle-class Americans were not in imminent danger, health educators and politicians would have a hard time selling HIV/AIDS education to the public, or getting beyond a blame-the-victim mentality to seriously address the epidemic as a public-health crisis and as a civil-rights issue.

The AIDS crisis might have brought people of color and the gay male community closer together in bonds of common victimization, stigmatization and shaming; and in some cases it did. But the disease served to divide its "noninnocent" victims as much or more than it brought them together in solidarity. In 1989, Inge Corless and Mary Pittman-Lindeman, in their book on AIDS in the black community, wrote of the "plague" and its politics in terms of privileged AIDS victims and socially disadvantaged AIDS victims—and they left little doubt that gay white males were privileged, and that their privilege was countered by the neglect of AIDS in black and brown communities. First, there was the fact that "gay men of color constitute a significant portion of the total gay population," yet as nonwhite gay men, "they did not share in the wealth of information that has influenced change in the white gay community." Gay men of color in the inner city were victims of "ignorance, denial, and drug abuse," and also rejected for being gay by black leaders. "This homophobic reaction of black and brown leaders further alienates and isolates those persons of color at risk as well as those already infected with the virus." At the same time, people of color with AIDS, when they sought support and services at gay male community-based agencies such as GMHC, often were treated as if they were invisible or their concerns not taken seriously. "This of all times tends to be the moment when racism rears its ugly head," they wrote, "preventing normally eligible citizens from reaping the benefit of much-needed access to support systems that are already established for and often by the gay white male." But it is also a time when homophobia in the black community raises its ugly head, for, as they observe, groups such as the National Association for the Advancement of Colored People (NAACP), the Urban League, and the National Black Social Workers Association were "reluctant at best to comment and take action of the issue of AIDS." If the role of these groups was "vital to the education and prevention effort within the nonwhite communities," as they claimed it was, it would remain lacking—for the most part.[43] The black caucus in Congress assumed some leadership in the 1990s in pushing for more federal money for AIDS education and prevention in black communities by framing the epidemic as a "public-health emergency." The black caucus, along with the National Black Leadership Commission on AIDS, formally requested that the Department of Health and Human Services make such a declaration, which would require immediate and substantial federal and state responses. Representative Maxine Waters of California went so far as to declare what others feared, that "the AIDS epidemic could literally wipe out the black community if it continues to go unchallenged."[44] This language of genocide, without invoking the word, situates the scourge of AIDS in a long history of racial domination and colonialism.

If it was still possible to keep homosexuality out of the discussion in family-life sexuality education, it was not possible in AIDS education. Furthermore, within the AIDS education movement there were a good number of "out" gay and lesbian voices by the end of the Eighties. New voices also were entering the field of sexuality education and AIDS education who drew upon feminist theory. The practitioner-oriented journal *Feminist Teacher*, begun in 1986, is a good case in point. In a special issue in 1989 devoted to feminist perspectives on AIDS education, the emphasis in the articles is on using a language of "homophobia, racism, and classism" to analyze societal responses to the epidemic, particularly as a women's health issue. In the leading article, homophobia is defined as a form of oppression manifested in "an irrational fear and hatred of those who love and sexually desire those of the same sex," and also "the fear of being perceived as gay, lesbian, or bisexual." The language of oppression suddenly enters the discourse in a radically unsettling way, and gets linked with subversive categories such as "homophobia" and "heterosexism." Suddenly, the heterosexual is no longer the invisible, unquestioned norm which various Others aspire to be treated like. The center, the normal, the typical, is now also the heterosexist, the oppressor, and the taken-for-granted, commonsense language of the oppressor is being called into question. At the cultural level, "gay men, lesbians, and bisexuals—if visible—are presented as oversexed, deviant, and sick," while heterosexuality is held up not only as a norm, but as the "ideal."[45] Rather than call for changes in the AIDS education curriculum, the authors shift the attention to teachers' own commonsense beliefs and values, and how they may "reinforce, even indirectly or unintentionally, the misguided values and beliefs of our audiences [students and parents]". Teachers are called upon to question—to begin by questioning, and to continue questioning their actions when educating about AIDS. "Do I talk about 'high risk groups' or 'high risk behaviors'? Do I make heterosexist assumptions? … Do I ignore homophobic remarks? … Do I ever give credit to the gay community for its effective reaction to AIDS? … Do I use educational materials which assume all my students are heterosexual? Do my students see me as a safe person to talk to when it comes to their concerns about sexual orientation?"[46] The central questioning is to be of language. Do we refer to anal intercourse as "homosexual intercourse," when heterosexuals clearly practice it? Do we call penile–vaginal intercourse "normal" or "regular" intercourse? A step is being made here to move beyond heteronormative language in a way that would not have been thinkable a decade or so earlier. For to even raise these questions, to understand them as questions, teachers must be at a new level of awareness; and it seems reasonable to assume that the readers of *Feminist Teacher* were raised to this level of awareness at least partially through reading the journal. Feminist perspectives in the journal also served to politicize the AIDS crisis. One article on AIDS education begins: "The feminist axiom 'the personal is political' is the analytical Rosetta Stone needed to decipher the socio-cultural AIDS text."[47] AIDS has become a text to be read, a cultural-studies curriculum, and in this shift we see the movement toward a new discourse in sexuality education that is social constructionist and understands gender oppression as folded into forces of homophobia, racism, and classism.

Still, studying AIDS as a cultural text does not, for this author, mean engaging popular culture. It means "values clarification," in which young people discuss the degree to which they agree or disagree with statements such as: "AIDS is God's curse on homosexuals," "HIV infection is 'not a significant risk' for heterosexual students," and "AIDS is as much a moral issue as a medical issue." Studying AIDS as a cultural text also means, to this author, role-playing members of affected groups, such as drug users, HIV-positive women, and gay men and lesbians. In this regard, not much has changed from a decade earlier. "Affective" education is still understood to be the primary way of unpacking young people's commonsense beliefs and attitudes about sexuality rather than, or in addition to, a rigorous, critical reading of movies, television, video games, and so on. The only reference the author makes to the media is in a values-clarification exercise, in which students are asked to agree or disagree, strongly or weakly, with the statement: "Because of AIDS, negotiating safer sex should be part of the media's presentation of sexuality." The implicit message is that the media is partially to blame for the AIDS epidemic by valorizing adolescent sexuality and encouraging young people to engage in "unsafe sex." But one might as well blame the media, then, for the sexual revolution, for the increasing visibility of the sexualized body in popular culture and youth culture is not just about exploiting and objectifying bodies—although that is largely what it has become in the age of global marketing of commodified sexual images. It is also a reflection of a new openness in youth culture, a new freedom of sexual expression, that is important—at least if you believe that Herbert Marcuse was basically right, that the next democratic revolution would be a revolution of long repressed desires. In a culture that is still hyperrepressive and in which people are still alienated from a more natural, liberatory expression of sexuality, some noncommercialized elements of popular culture and youth culture have been transgressive and radical. AIDS educators, even some feminist AIDS educators, still were assuming that the media should replace representations of "risky" or "dangerous" adolescent sexuality with representations of "less risky" or "safe" sexuality. Whether intentional or not, these concerns (even among some feminist educators) that the media should "clean up its act", so to speak, that "negative" images should be replaced with "positive" images, may reproduce the "innocent"–"not innocent," "healthy"–"unhealthy," "normal"–"abnormal", and "moral"–"immoral" binaries that have governed the discourse on sexuality education from the start.

Something else is going on in this series of articles in *Feminist Teacher* in 1989 that signals a shift in the terrain of speaking and acting about AIDS. While the authors offer their perspectives to educators and community-health professionals generally, the exemplary programs they cite are from higher education. By the late 1980s, women's studies programs, and even gay and lesbian studies programs were being offered on many liberal arts campuses around the nation. The emergence of black studies, women's studies, and (now) queer studies was beginning to remake higher-education communities, and the newest cultural-studies perspectives were beginning to be brought to bear on the teaching of undergraduates about diversity, inequity, and social injustice. Furthermore, the liberal arts college and university had emerged from the 1960s as a relatively open, critical space for teaching, even as public high schools moved, and have continued to move, in the opposite direction. It was possible to use a language of heterosexism, institutional racism, oppression, and social justice in the nation's college campuses, even as this language became still largely "unthinkable," and thus surely also unspeakable, in the nations high schools. Another one of the facilitating factors in linking AIDS education with a democratic project in higher education was the emergence of diversity offices and initiatives. In an article in *Feminist Teacher* that describes an AIDS-education initiative on a Midwest college campus, the reader learns that the AIDS task force worked closely with the campus Gay and Lesbian Student Association in creating a workshop on AIDS that was conducted with various groups on campus. During the presentation part of the workshop, the intention is to "thwart the tendency to blame the victim," and also to counter "negative stereotypes of individuals in high incidence groups."[48] AIDS education, from this perspective, was about teaching people to respect the "dignity of infected individuals," and it was to be grounded in the development of feminist values of compassion and unconditional caring for the victims of the disease.

In the 1980s, when the spread of HIV was still largely unchecked, when the public knew little about how the virus was transmitted, and before protease inhibitors made AIDS a chronic, manageable disease, education became the front line of defense. The government, at both federal and state levels, proved unable to provide the needed leadership in mounting an educational response to the crisis, and this was largely because AIDS and its victims had become inextricable from culture wars being waged by those on the Christian evangelical right against the "sins" of homosexuality and the sexual revolution. AIDS was transformed into a new plague by those on the Christian right, like one of those plagues God inflicted on his people in the Bible when they had gone astray and displeased him. AIDS education, for Christian conservatives, should call for a return to moral condemnation of homosexuality and all sexuality outside the "sacred" institution of marriage, tied to the traditional family with clearly distinguished gender roles. AIDS was the curse of God upon individuals and a nation that permitted "perversity." Much AIDS education occurred within evangelical churches, through sermons and special classes and events that reached out to young people. A whole genre of Christian rock music developed that brought this conservative Christian approach to AIDS education—with its message of abstinence, virginity, and antihomosexuality—directly to adolescents, and in a language they could understand and appreciate. Christian conservatives proved to be not conservative at all when it came to adapting their message to the latest trends in youth culture and music, although there is irony in the fact that Christian conservatives turned to the "devil's music" to reach young people with a very traditional message about sexuality.

Public-school, sex-education textbooks, meanwhile, continued to include little if anything about AIDS or HIV throughout the 1980s. Even when students were taught facts about the transmission of the disease in health classes, they almost always received a strong explicit or implicit warning that all sexual contacts are "dangerous" and "risky" before marriage.[49] The AIDS crisis was used to reinforce a message that had been around for a long time in the sex-education curriculum: namely, that adolescent sexuality is dangerous and unsafe. This was a message that many adolescents rejected, as well they should have if that is all that sex education had to teach them. When AIDS or HIV was acknowledged in the curriculum, it was treated only as a health and medical concern, rather than as a disease that carried social meaning, that came with a politics, and that mobilized a politics of fear around discourses and practices of stigmatization, exclusion, and moral blame. Nietzsche spoke of moral blame as a particular type of *ressentiment*—anger and blame projected upon a person or group presumed to be responsible for one's sorry predicament, or the nation's sorry predicament, or the race's sorry predicament. This is the common refrain of rightist politics in the U.S., and the politics of *ressentiment* found a new target and thus new life in the 1980s—the individuals and groups marked with the sign of AIDS, the new "Scarlet Letter."

The response to this rightist politics of *ressentiment* would be led by the gay and lesbian movements. Perhaps it is fitting that a group of people who were no strangers to stigmatization and scapegoating, who had endured already a long history of it, would now be called on to lead the fight against the stigmatization of all people who suffered with AIDS, no matter how they had contracted HIV. The "liberal" press and mass media also played an important role in AIDS education, as the *New York Times*' coverage of the Ryan White story indicates. Slowly, by dispelling fears about how HIV is spread and by telling victim's stories, the press began to address head on the language of stigmatization, exclusion, and blame. There is also evidence that some educators, like those writing in the special issue of *Feminist Teacher* I mentioned earlier, began to broaden the scope of AIDS/HIV education to include a discussion of human rights, civil rights, and social justice, and of the need to avoid victimizing the victim. Throughout the professions of social work, nursing, health, and teaching there was a growing concern by the end of the 1980s with professional training that included the development of "positive attitudes" about caring for PWAs.[50] The politics of resentment and fear did not in the end win out, although it never disappeared either. HIV/AIDS education was being addressed in a number of educational sites by the mid to late 1990s, including: school-based health services, sex-education classes, and family-life or life-skills education, along with civics, social studies, and "moral education." HIV/AIDS education had, in effect, became a wedge to open a space for a frank and open discussion of sexuality in many schools, and for teaching the importance of recognizing and respecting diversity, and respecting and valuing all people as full individuals.[51]

6

THE ABSTINENCE-ONLY ERA AND THE WELFARE REFORM ACT OF 1996

Once, when progressive sex educators were most influential in shaping state policy, the religious right had battled to keep sex education out of the schools. Janice Irvine, in her history of the religious right engagement with sex education, notes that the religious right opposed "talk about sex" initially, so that the battle was framed as between supporters and opponents of talk about sex in the school.[1] To speak of something is to acknowledge it, to give it a name and face, to see it and make it visible to others, and so Christian conservatism in the U.S. sought to keep sex education out of the schools entirely under the false presumption that "ignorance is bliss." But keeping young people "ignorant" and thus supposedly unaware of sexuality has always been a losing battle, and it became even more so in a media-saturated age in which youth could no longer be "protected" from sex talk. Consequently, by the 1980s social conservatives were beginning to follow a different tactic, one of supporting their own brand of sex education and working to ensure that it was translated into the law of the land. By the mid-1990s, Christian and social conservative groups had mobilized enough power to do just that—through an amendment to the Welfare Reform Act of 1996 funding abstinence-only sex-education programs in public schools, in cooperation with religious-based organizations and movements. The religious right's construction of the "problem" of adolescent sexuality, with abstinence until marriage as the solution, would prevail in public policy and in public-school practice, beginning in 1996 with the passage of the Welfare Reform Act. Once more, sex-education initiatives would be tied to the "problem" of unwed welfare mothers, although the solution was not more access to family-planning services and contraceptives, or more opportunities for education and job training. The problem of young welfare mothers bearing children out of wedlock was located in the bad "family values" of single-mother families, and the solution was the re-establishment of a household headed by a breadwinner husband and father—with abstinence practiced before marriage. This was a definition and response to the problem very similar to that advanced in the Moynihan Report on the "Negro family" in 1965, although this time it faced less opposition from established civil-rights groups. In fact, this message of "abstinence in preparation for marriage," linked to the notion that the problem of the young welfare mother could be solved only through the re-establishment of a "traditional" two-parent, heterosexual household, was appealing to a broad spectrum of the black and Latino/a middle class by the 1980s. And it certainly reinforced the commonsense beliefs of many white Americans of diverse class backgrounds. This is what made the Christian right's framing of the problem of adolescent sexuality so hegemonic, so dominating that it drove out almost all other framings of the problem. The commonsense wisdom of the Christian right's framing of the problem and the solution to the problem was hard to resist. Young people should "wait" until the right person, their "true love," came along (presumably of the opposite gender), and then they should get married and live happily ever after. If this has been a commonsense wisdom that appeals to many if not most adults—particularly parents—it is out of touch with the reality of adolescent sexuality, and it sets unrealistic expectations and standards for adolescents. In effect, it continues to treat them as if they are asexual children until they marry, when they are suddenly to become adults with sexual feelings and needs for intimacy. It fails to recognize that they might have rights to a sexual life, since they are not asexual children, but, rather, young adults.

The power of the religious right had first been felt under the Reagan administration, when the discourse of abstinence-only sex education first began to circulate in policy circles and take legislative shape. In 1981, Congress passed the Adolescent Family Life Act (AFLA) with a provision in it to fund abstinence-only and abstinence-only-until-marriage family planning—an act that was quickly dubbed the "Chastity Act" by liberal critics. Demonstration projects had to counsel pregnant teens to choose adoption over abortion and to teach premarital abstinence."[2] They also were required to "involve religious and charitable organizations, voluntary associations, and other groups in the private sector." Religious groups were even allowed to deliver a complete abstinence-based curriculum program for a school, complete with speakers, movies, and other curricular materials. The U.S. Supreme Court eventually upheld the statute, rejecting an argument that it would lead to an excessive government entanglement with religion.[3] Congressional critics of the bill were at least able to ensure that the abstinence-only demonstration projects were funded at a low level (11 million dollars the first year). In 1993, an out-of-court settlement also stipulated that educational materials produced by religious groups for AFLA-funded programs could not include religious references and had to be medically accurate. As well, religious-based programs had to respect the "principle of self-determination" by referring teenagers to contraceptive services when they wanted that information, and they were prohibited from using church sanctuaries for their programs. This regulated and regularized the new relationship between the religious right and the state; but it did not counter the growing erosion of borders, that once seemed so solid, between religious institutions and movements and the "state," meaning here all governmental institutions and structures, including public education. These borders had been breached as early as 1981, and the Christian right was on its way to being a power player within the nation state. The Christian right had established a beachhead in federal educational policy, from which it was able to slowly extend its territorial claims. Which it did throughout the 1980s. The Christian evangelical vote was split in the 1992 presidential election, but the Democratic candidate, Bill Clinton, was able to win by capturing a large share of the evangelical, white voting bloc—largely because he came from a working class, Southern Baptist family and continued to profess his faith in public. Once in office, however, Clinton proved more liberal than evangelical Christians hoped he would be on social issues, and his support for comprehensive sexuality education found its way into a major piece of legislation in his first term, the Welfare Reform Act. In 1994, conservative Republicans gained control of Congress in part because of a backlash among Christian evangelical, white voters against a president whom they felt had let them down. With a new Congress elected in good measure because of its support, the Christian right insured that the section of the Welfare Reform Act funding comprehensive sexuality education was removed and replaced with a section mandating abstinence-only sexuality education.

The Clinton administration bill had included a Teen Pregnancy Prevention Grant Program in which 1,000 schools and community-based groups would have received grants in comprehensive sexuality education. The six-page summary of the grant program emphasized the importance of three interrelated ideas: "premature," "delay," and "developmental readiness." In invoking a development approach to adolescent sexuality, the administration bill encouraged grant applications from programs that taught that sexual intercourse is "premature" for early teens, and should be "delayed" until at least the age of 16 or 17, at which point some are "ready" while others may not be. Much depended on the young person's maturity level at any given age. The bill also mandated that equal attention be paid to the "delay of sexual activity" and the "prevention of pregnancy before marriage" (through contraception). It concluded that "programs that combine these elements have shown the most promise."[4] This was, in fact, a position on comprehensive sexuality education that mirrored that of SIECUS—which had been instrumental in helping shape the Clinton administration bill. In 1995, timed to gain support for Clinton's Welfare Reform Act, SIECUS released its report of the National Commission on Adolescent Sexual Health, titled *Facing Facts*. On the commission were leaders from mainstream religious organizations as well as education leaders, health professionals, medical doctors, and scholars. Whereas it might be best (according to the report) for adolescents to abstain from sexual activity, the "fact" was that they were adolescents and sometimes let their impulses override what was best for them. And whereas it might be tempting to treat all adolescents as if they were not ready for sexual relations, the "fact" was that they differed developmentally, so that what was good for one teenager was not necessarily good for another. The message and information conveyed in sexuality education had to be adjusted and modified, bearing these two "facts" in mind. To use the language of popular culture, we might say that SIECUS and the Clinton administration wanted a reality-based approach to sexuality education that did not expect adolescents to always live up to the ideal of abstinence. To "get real" also meant, from this perspective, being open to the possibility, and even probability, that some older, more developmentally mature adolescents will be engaging in relatively active sexual lives while still in high school.

Once in power, Republicans were able to ensure that the SIECUS-inspired Teen Pregnancy Prevention Grant Program in the Welfare Reform Act of 1996 was redrafted to mandate abstinence-only sex education. The new draft had been written with the help of the Christian Coalition and the Family Research Council, along with the Heritage Foundation, a conservative think tank.[5] As Christian conservatives had sought to move their social agenda into public policy and legislation, they looked to think tanks like the Heritage Foundation to help them translate a religious-based discourse on sex education into one that was secular, nonreligious, and legalistic. The Heritage Foundation could argue for the importance of public support for religious approaches to sex education, if the argument could be framed in terms of public interests and responding more effectively to public problems like teen pregnancy and welfare dependency. In a sense, religious conservatives hid behind a secular and, ostensibly, rational and scientific language, letting think tanks like the Heritage Foundation do much of the policy work needed to rebuild America around a return to traditional family values and religious faith. The religious right also found common ground with social critics on the right who were concerned about how—in spite of everything that had been written on welfare reform since the Moynihan Report in 1965—the welfare system kept getting larger and the Aid to Families with Dependent Children Program continued to grow. One obvious explanation—but one that did not appeal to those on the right—was that post-industrial America was a place in which millions of people could not find jobs to support themselves, in which young women of color with children were particularly vulnerable to being trapped in poverty, and that the only alternative was to let these millions slowly die on the mean streets of American cities. One set of solutions to welfare dependency was jobs with a living wage tied to job training and education, along with state-supported child care, and an end to discrimination against young mothers of color in the workforce. But these would all require expanding the role of the state, and taking on class, race, and gender inequities. The conservative solution was much simpler: bring back the "traditional" family to replace welfare dependency.

The way had been paved for passage of the amended Welfare Reform Act by a special Congress Assessment Project Study released by the Heritage Foundation in March, 1995, provocatively titled *Combating Family Disintegration, Crime, and Dependence; Welfare Reform and Beyond*. In 1995, as the report noted, nearly one out of seven children in the U.S. was enrolled in Aid to Families with Dependent Children (AFDC), "with Uncle Sam's welfare check serving as a surrogate father." The welfare state had assumed the role of the absent father in a large part of the new American underclass, and had even played a role in breaking up families. This is all something that has to be acknowledged by liberals and progressives, but welfare is also essential to provide a basic quality of life to those who are members of the growing underclass of women in America, unable to support themselves in the new economy. The fact that two out of three black children in the U.S. were born out of wedlock, up 25 percent since the 1960s, and that increases in illegitimacy were also occurring among low-income whites, is also hard to dispute.[6] But these numbers have to be understood in terms of the history of the break-up of black families in the U.S., and the fact that a high proportion of African Americans continued to be economically oppressed and marginalized in the new economy, which had a crippling effect on family stability. The Heritage Foundation report, however, put a whole different spin on these facts. The problem, according to the report, could be solved only by dismantling welfare, discouraging abortions, and teaching (or preaching) abstinence before marriage. All this was framed in the language of scientific evidence that abstinence-only programs work in reducing teen pregnancies— evidence that was hotly contested by supporters of comprehensive sex education. Scientific "evidence" was also marshaled to support the contention that abstinence-only sex education was particularly important for young men from the "underclasses." Here the authors of the report drew upon recent, very controversial and contested research by Charles Murray.[7] Through an examination of available data on standardized test scores, Murray had argued that there was a new "cognitive underclass" in America, with welfare mothers at the bottom of the hierarchy of intelligence. A few years later, Murray, along with Richard J. Hernstein, published a book that was widely distributed, *The Bell Curve*, and that developed this argument through an elaborate analysis of test-score data.[8] The brunt of the argument was that, in a meritocracy (as supposedly existed in the U.S.), the social elite is also a "cognitive elite" and the underclass a "cognitive underclass." Over time in a meritocracy, and due to people's propensity to choose sexual partners from within their own class, the cognitive elite and underclass became ever more unequal in terms of intellectual endowment. The result, according to this argument, was that the cognitive underclass was becoming less capable of caring for itself, and more dependent on the cognitive elite to take care of it. According to the report, "the very low cognitive abilities of the average welfare mother" underscored "the futility of reform schemes aimed narrowly at making unwed mothers employable and self-sufficient." It was better for all concerned if they stuck to mothering, at least until their children were grown. But they need not be welfare mothers, encouraged to raise more children out of wedlock so they could get more support from the state. The solution proposed was simple: defer child rearing until the woman can have the financial and supposedly cognitive support of a husband. "It is very difficult," the report concluded, "to raise a child while also working to support the family."

Through marriage, the young woman could continue to be a primary caregiver for her children, with a husband as the primary income provider. If this commonsense solution to the problem may make some sense, it is also nonsense to the extent that (first of all) the days of the single-wage household are over. In the new economy, the "stable," working-class marriage, with the wife at home as child-care provider and the father off at work at the factory or office, is no longer realistic. Secondly, it is a solution that seeks to restore the patriarchal, heteronormative family. Finally, it is a solution that does not address underlying structural economic and cultural realities. All that is needed, from this perspective, is a strong dose of morality and family values to overcome welfare dependency and the "epidemic" of illegitimacy. The report ends with the claim that "the battle against expanding underclass culture" was of utmost importance, and that religious institutions along with public institutions had to work together in holding young people to the same high moral standards.[9] "For the well-being of American children and the safety of society, a moral sense of responsible parenthood must be restored," and that was possible only when the parents were married and "committed to a life together," and when they could "sustain a family without large amounts of ongoing financial support from the larger community."[10]

In a follow-up background report on welfare reform published by the Heritage Foundation in August 1995, the specter of an illegitimate nation is raised. "Soaring rates of illegitimacy," the report began, "are threatening America's social fabric." The use of the word "illegitimate" to refer to children usually referred to as having been "born out of wedlock," is a crucial discursive shift—reframing the "problem" of teen pregnancy within an ancient language with patriarchal religious origins, but also one that worked its way into secular legal discourse in both ancient Greece and Rome. The early Christian church adopted canonical laws of illegitimacy that denied illegitimate children rights of succession, inheritance, and support by their fathers. In religious law, the illegitimate child was denied these rights because he or she was presumed to be "morally tainted" by the immoral acts that led to their birth.[11] The victim was blamed for his or her own bastardization and denied the basic human rights reserved for "legitimate" members of the faith community. In the American South under slavery—and here the parallels are very direct—the children of slave women and white men were denied the legitimate rights of white citizens and relegated to the status of a disenfranchised, disempowered, and oppressed minority. Consequently, to speak of the children of welfare mothers as illegitimate, either overtly or tacitly, invokes this history. The language of "illegitimacy" brings to law the force of a moral condemnation, a moral imperative to punish the sins of the flesh, and the product of these sins. In the modern discourse of the Heritage Foundation, illegitimacy results in the social curse of entrapment in a culture of poverty, which effectively prevents young people from exercising their full rights as equal citizens. Boys born into welfare families without fathers, according to the report, "are raised by peers on the streets, without social norms, achievable goals, or hope." It is ultimately the lack of a stable father figure, the report suggests, that dooms these children of welfare mothers to illegitimacy. Thus, the "illegitimacy crisis" can be solved only when all children are born "legitimate"— that is, born into a traditional, heterosexual, married family. That means abolishing the welfare system as we know it, so as not to encourage welfare dependency and single-mother families living on welfare. It also means an aggressive sexuality-education campaign, with a "new emphasis on responsibility, virtue, and sexual abstinence in a broad cultural setting." Abstinence until marriage was to be the one standard for all young people, and it needed (according to the Heritage Foundation) to be enshrined in law. Homosexuality and homosexual youth need not be named; but their very absence speaks volumes. They face only two real options—a lifetime of sexual abstinence and self-renunciation, or marrying and having children and living a life of self-renunciation and hidden sexual encounters and affairs. This was a direct attempt to roll back everything that had happened over the past three decades to recognize gay men and lesbians, and also to recognize gay and lesbian families—all by saying nothing about them.

The Welfare Reform Act of 1996, as passed by Congress and signed by President Clinton, did not use the archaic and stigmatizing language of illegitimacy and sexual immorality. But the spirit of this language was woven throughout the text, which spoke of "abstinence outside marriage as the expected standard for all school-age children." Adolescents entered the law as children rather than young adults, and they were to be treated more like children and less like adults. Just as younger children are not ready for sexual relations (so the logic went), neither are older children. They are all, after all, children, and their innocence needs to be protected. Sex-education programs funded under the Welfare Reform Act had to teach that abstinence is the only certain way to avoid "out-of-wedlock" pregnancy and STDs. Indeed, the law mandates teaching that "all sexual activity outside the context of marriage is likely to have harmful psychological and physical effects."[12] Behind these medicalized claims lies a puritanical worldview that emphasizes sex as sin (outside "legitimate" procreative purposes in marriage), that stigmatizes and marginalizes sexual difference, and that makes illegitimate a whole class of young people raised by poor black, Latina and white, welfare mothers. God rewards those who can take care of themselves and punishes and stigmatizes those who cannot. Finally, the new Puritanism was like the old Puritanism in its insistence that the U.S. is a Christian nation, and that Christian values should determine public policy and community standards. But that only begged the question of who speaks for Christians, for, by the 1990s, mainstream American Christian churches were deeply divided over issues of sexuality and homosexuality and over abortion and women's rights. The Christian community was as divided as the broader culture. Yet, those who came to speak most forcefully of Christian family values were those on the political right, and they knew how to mobilize power to insure that their version of Christian and family values was incorporated into the law of the land. Under President George W. Bush, federal funding for abstinence-only sex education was expanded so that, by 2007, over $1 billion had been allocated, and states contributed at least as much in mandatory matching funds.[13] This was, in fact, the largest investment ever made by the federal government in sex education.

Much of this money ended up in the pockets of the religious right and spawned a veritable cottage industry of abstinence-only educational materials and resources. Since public schools had to teach abstinence-only sexuality education, mainstream and progressive sexuality-education movements like SIECUS were effectively locked out of schools. Instead, school districts often contracted with religious-based, abstinence-only organizations and movements to deliver all or part of a sexuality-education curriculum. The most powerful of these movements, and one that has helped coordinate all abstinence-only programs and curriculum materials in the U.S., is the Abstinence Clearinghouse, founded in 1997. It provides resources for accessing information, speakers, and curriculum materials for abstinence programs.[14] It also sponsors national and regional conferences and publishes the *Abstinence Network*, a quarterly newsletter. Its advisory council includes representatives from Focus on the Family and the Heritage Foundation, along with members of various pregnancy centers that council unwed pregnant young women against abortions and for adoptions. In its educational campaigns, it has added one more supposed problem with adolescent sexual activity—the claim that it can lead to depression and possible suicide. According to a report issued by the Abstinence Clearinghouse, medical studies had proved that there was a causal link between "clinical depression in adolescent boys and girls ... related to sexual activity and drinking." It seems that, according to the report, "with every act of sexual activity the persons involved release oxytocin ... which creates permanent bonds in the brain, linking the two people together." Thus, breaking this "bonding effect," especially in adolescence, "can lead to depression and suicide."[15] The "bonding effect" thus seems to require that sex only occur in marriage, when the individuals involved are guaranteed a steady supply of the "drug" they need to stay upbeat and happy. If the person has sex with someone only once, or even a number of times with different people, the initial "bonding effect" is broken and the individual sinks into despair and thoughts of suicide. Is there any truth to this claim? And if so, what kind of truth? One might reflect on the tragic fate of Romeo and Juliet as an adolescent tragedy, told over and over in movies and books about teenage lost love. The irony is, of course, that most of these tales of lost love are among young people who are abstinent. Their love is consumed through romantic obsession rather than sexual intimacy, and one might even say that their abstinence feeds the flames of their romantic obsessions and their suicidal thoughts. In the hands of the Abstinence Clearinghouse, this Romeo and Juliet narrative becomes a scientific "fact." Even one sexual encounter can supposedly lead to a lifetime of clinical depression or, alternately, an early suicide. Young people and their parents are expected to worry not only about STDs and unwanted pregnancies, but also the person's mental health, which is supposedly put at risk through sexual activity outside heterosexual marriage. The objective of sexuality education is to be the inculcation of fear.

This pedagogy of fear is quite explicit in curriculum materials from Sex Respect, an abstinence-only sexuality-education organization founded by a former teacher, Colleen Mast. The mission statement of Sex Respect emphasizes that "teaching kids about sexuality is more than passing on facts. It's passing on attitudes and values"— the kind of family values that are presumably both healthy and good. At the same time, a distinction is made between telling young people to be abstinent "just because I say so," and encouraging young people to say no themselves by appealing to "the intellect and the heart, treating these kids as the intelligent human beings they are." In fact, the Sex Respect curriculum appeals much more to fear than reason. According to the organization's webpage, "Kids are not animals. They can control their sex lives. You can teach them to say 'no.'" But how is this to be done? Are young people to be reasoned with, since they are not animals? Not at all. They are to be treated as animals, kept celibate out of fear. Sex Respect claims that "statistics indicate teens refrain from sex for two reasons—FEAR of Pregnancy and FEAR of Disappointing their Parents."[16] Aside from the fact that homosexual teens are left out of the picture in such an assertion (intentionally or unintentionally made invisible, not recognized as teens), there is the fact that education is to be about fear more than about the rewards of abstinence—presumably because it is hard to sell abstinence to adolescents as something that they will enjoy or get rewards for. Furthermore, this is not just a cultural politics of "fear," but of "FEAR"—of the great power that lies in fear to induce people to "behave." There is, of course, also great irony in a Christian-based movement emphasizing fear more than love; but it is consistent with traditional religious beliefs about the need to instill fear in children through corporal punishment. Mother Teresa is invoked as a spokesperson of fear. She is quoted on the Sex Respect website to the effect that love between a girl and a boy (presumably adolescents) is beautiful, "but don't spoil it, don't destroy it. Keep it pure." If love is not "pure" and thus chaste, it is spoiled and ultimately destroyed, bringing down everyone and everything, from the young couple to civilization and "the future of family life."

The bulk of the Sex Respect curriculum consists of a set of short videos—fictional teenage romance stories designed to inspire, and also tales of teenage depravity designed to instill fear. Textbooks, student workbooks, a parental guidebook, and a teacher's manual accompany the videos.[17] In effect, a school district purchases a whole-curriculum Sex Respect package, and one that is "teacher proof," as they say; that is, so scripted in advance that teachers are turned into script readers and given prompts on how to respond to student questions. Each video in the Sex Respect series is short—between 15 minutes and half an hour in length—and each is designed to drive home one narrative theme in a way that taps into youthful fears and other emotions. *Done That ... Changed my Ways* is, according to publicity for the video, a "heart-warming true story" with two messages: "First, save sex for marriage; secondly, if you have made the mistake of engaging in premarital sex, you can change your ways." The story concerns a young man committed to remaining a virgin until he marries, who gets drunk at a party and "lost his gift of virginity to a girl he didn't even know." The good news is that he hated what he did and embraced "secondary virginity, the practice where teens stop engaging in premarital sex and wait until marriage." Virginity thus becomes an attitude more than a bodily fact. You can always become a virgin again if you lose your way once, or twice, or more times presumably. The contradiction in this message is that it suggests to young people that they can engage in sexual activity and still become virgins again the next day. *Done That* is followed by a video titled *Not Doing It*, which is a "celebration of the rewards of saving sex until marriage." Here the drama revolves around a young woman committed to maintaining her virginity in the face of a boyfriend's assertion that "If you love me, you'll prove it." In promotional materials for the video, a "teen" is quoted to the effect that "It's like watching MTV, only it has good values and morals." A third video in the Sex Respect series, titled *Dating: Predator or Partner?*, suggests that there are really only two types of young man when it comes to dating. *But You Can't Hide* tells the "tragic but true" story of a young woman who "fools" herself into believing that "common sense and contraception will protect you." According to the producers, this video "will shock and sober its teen audience."

Sex Respect videos and instructional materials became popular in school districts throughout the country, and their slick, youth-oriented production qualities made them particularly appealing. Progressive groups responded by attacking the videos for "lying" to young people, and for using scare tactics to sell an abstinence-only message. *Sex, Lies, and Politics*, a 1997 report on abstinence-only curricula in California public schools by the Applied Research Center, a progressive public policy institute based in Oakland, argues that Sex Respect curriculum materials and videos preached against premarital sex, but did not provide young people with the facts and information they needed to avoid unwanted pregnancies and STDs.[18] In one instructional video mentioned in the report, a student asks the teacher, "What if I want to have sex before I get married?" The teacher replies, "Well, I guess you'll just have to be prepared to die." The reality, the report notes, is that 80% of men and 75% of women in California report having sex before the age of 20; and 84 % of California parents want their children to be taught about contraception. The videos and curriculum materials also were open to the criticism, according to the Applied Research Center report, that they promoted and legitimated homophobia in not recognizing homosexual behavior as acceptable in any circumstances, and in linking homosexuality exclusively and inaccurately to HIV/AIDS. In one workbook, AIDS is described as "the STD most common among homosexuals and bisexuals." Elsewhere, students learn that AIDS is nature's way of "making some kind of a comment on sexual behavior." Along with a rather overt homophobia, the Sex Respect curriculum materials reinforce racial and ethnic stereotypes and biases. According to the report, stereotypes used in Sex Respect videos included: "that African Americans are promiscuous; that African-American men are uncaring, unfaithful and irresponsible; and that African-American women have grown up in troubled homes, aren't physically attractive, and need male attention for self-esteem."

The youth-culture appeal of Sex Respect curriculum materials—their MTV quality, but with a very different message—has also been an important selling point for True Love Waits, the first national abstinence education program, founded in 1993 by LifeWay, through a Southern Baptist Church in Nashville, Tennessee. Young people in the program participate in a commitment ceremony before friends, clergy, and family, at which they pledge: "Believing that true love waits, I make a commitment to God, myself, my family, my friends, my future mate, and my future children to a lifetime of purity including sexual abstinence from this day until the day I enter a biblical marriage relationship." Along with the commitment ceremony, pledgers have the opportunity to purchase jewelry, teddy bears, stationary, books, music, clothing, buttons, and bumper stickers that declare their chastity.[19] In many communities in small-town America, True Love Waits, or another movement like it, essentially assumed responsibility for writing the local sexuality curriculum, and even delivering it. In the widely circulated Christian book *Why True Love Waits*, which touts itself as a definitive guide for parents, clergy, and youth on how to help kids resist sexual pressure, author Josh McDowell mixes discourses of fear, moral panic, and social costs in presenting the case for abstinence before marriage. McDowell asks the reader to imagine a typical American shopping mall. It's a Saturday afternoon and the place is "crawling" with teenagers. Now imagine, he says, that roughly half of them are sexually active. "They're either having sexual intercourse, practicing mutual masturbation and 'outercourse,' or performing oral sex." As these sexually active teens talk about the "sexual exploits" with their peers who are not yet sexually active, they encourage them to have sex. Now imagine, McDowell says, that of about 40 young people in the mall, 20 are sexually active, and of this group approximately five or six are "infected"—carriers of STDs. "Some will have to deal with an incurable infection for the rest of their lives. One of them may even die as a result of his or her disease." Then the reader is asked to think about how, of the "uninfected kids hanging out with the infected kids," every time one of them "sneaks off to have sex," they may become infected.[20] We learn of a young woman who had a blocked fallopian tube because of an infection due to chlamydia or gonorrhea, and that the fallopian tube had to be removed. "A dream she had cherished for years," of having children, was crushed—"a heavy price to pay for her sexual experiences with multiple partners."[21] This is followed by the story of Tina and Wade. "As they began making out, Wade whispered, 'Just once, Tina. After all we're almost married.'" This attempt to weaken Tina's resolve works, and soon, to her dismay, she learns she is pregnant, Wade wants an abortion but she doesn't because she is a Christian, Wade leaves her, and the child grows up one more victim of welfare dependency. All this is designed to reinforce the message that young women must resist the seductive language of "just once" by rehearsing their response over and over again.

Aside from producing curriculum materials that have appeal to young people—designed to frame traditional morality tales in terms of a contemporary youth culture and the perennial fears and insecurities of adolescents—the Christian right also has proven to be quite savvy when it comes to producing a scripted narrative for news coverage of "purity balls" and other such rituals of abstinence, and the press has been mostly sympathetic. After all, most of the press, national and local, represents mainstream conservative or, perhaps, liberal values and beliefs, and the discourse of abstinence makes a lot of sense to many Americans, perhaps particularly parents of adolescents. In the climate of the day, abstinence is represented as an ideal, perhaps not always realizable, but nevertheless worth promoting. *Time* magazine, in a 2009 article "The Pursuit of Teen Girl Purity," about purity balls and pledges, concluded that while there is no evidence that providing adolescents information on contraceptives encourages promiscuity, purity pledges do communicate that "sex is serious," and it should not be entered into "recklessly." Research indicates, according to the article, that teenagers "may be more capable of high standards than parents are." Abstinence is the "high standard" that unfortunately, adults do not always live by. For parents, according to *Time*, the message is clear. It is not enough to say "do as I say, not as I do. … Children can spot hypocrisy very quickly."[22] There is to be one "high standard," and adults are to role model this standard for their children.

Adolescents committed to abstinence in preparation for marriage also are expected to serve as role models among their peers. Alaska governor Sarah Palin—who had been an outspoken supporter of abstinence before marriage—found herself in an uncomfortable spot in 2009 when it was revealed that her daughter Bristol was pregnant and did not intend to marry the father. Bristol had publicly spoken out in support of abstinence before marriage, and was something of a poster child for the abstinence movement. Thus, her "outing" as pregnant out of wedlock became a media event. It was interpreted by liberal and progressive commentators as a sign that abstinence pledges did not "work" to prevent teen pregnancies. But Christian conservatives sought to use Palin as a symbol of what not to do, and to convey the message that while she loved her child, being a teenage mother was a lot of work, that you had to change a lot of diapers, and that being a mother had changed her life in ways that were not so good. With the support of the Candie's Foundation, a fashion-industry group dedicated to educating American youth about "the devastating consequences of teenage pregnancy," Bristol was sent on a national tour of local talk shows, and she appeared on both *Good Morning America* and the *Today Show* on March 6, 2009, as part of a campaign for abstinence. When Matt Lauer of the *Today Show* asked her if she would do the same thing again—she replied that she would not, but that she loved her son and viewed him as a "blessing." The contradiction in this message was not hard to see. Lauer subsequently asked, "doesn't that put you in the position of saying, 'do as I say, not as I do'?" She agreed, but reiterated like a broken record what she had been told to say, and also no doubt felt: that while her son was a blessing, he was also a lot of work. It may well be that Bristol's tour of talk shows had the opposite effect of what was intended. Instead of reinforcing the message that abstinence before marriage can work, that it is realistic, and that it is the only safe way to prevent unwanted pregnancies, Bristol conveyed a more nuanced message that perhaps represented the views of many teenage, unwed mothers. She was both blessed, and regretful that this "blessing" was bestowed on her, at least at this early age. But the hypocrisy of the message she had been scripted to convey—which boiled down to "do as I say, not as I do"— revealed the underlying contradiction of Christian conservative approaches to sexuality education. Christian conservatives often preached one thing in public but did something else in their "private" lives; and even that seemed to be okay, so long as you did not get caught. If you were caught, like Bristol Palin, you were obliged to say that you had made a mistake and would not do it again—in more religious terms, that you had sinned but recognized your sin and vowed not to sin again.

The Bristol Palin story, as it was covered in the national news media, was often quite openly critical of abstinence pledges and the hypocrisy of those on the Christian right who supported them. For the most part, however, press coverage of the abstinence movement has been more positive and supportive than critical or questioning. In particular, local press coverage of purity pledge campaigns most often narrated and framed coverage in a positive manner. That is the conclusion of a recent study by three highly respected scholars in health education—Felicia Mebane, Eileen Yam, and Barbara Rimer—that analyzes press coverage of purity campaigns between 1987 and 2001 in 329 U.S. newspapers and newswire services.[23] Published in the *Journal of Health Communication*, the study was grounded in the idea, basic to media literacy, that language and images portrayed in the media frame the world, revealing some things and making other things invisible, outside the frame. A frame is also an "interpretive package" used to assign meaning to events according to predictable scripts and narratives. In this case, at issue is how local newspaper coverage of purity or pledge campaigns gets framed. The study suggests that, at the local level, Christian conservatives have been far more effective than progressives in influencing how the news media frames sexuality education, and this is probably due to a combination of factors. For one thing, local press coverage typically takes for granted rather than challenges conventional, commonsense, "family-friendly," beliefs about the importance of a religious upbringing, imparting "good" values, and so on. Thus, local news coverage seems a particularly friendly media for the "family values" promoted by Christian conservatives. Secondly, the abstinence movement has been able to control much of its own representation in the local press, and it has made sure that events like chastity balls and ceremonies get local press coverage. Local press reporters often rely on prepackaged press releases and background materials provided by groups such as True Love Waits, and news stories often devote considerable space to quoting from spokespersons and event organizers. As a result, Christian conservative groups have been effective in getting their message out through local reporting.

The study found that the most common narrative framing of purity campaigns in local press reporting was that abstinence is the new "in" thing among young people. The presumption is that it was once not "in," particularly back in the days of the "old" sexual revolution, but that the tide has turned, or is turning, toward a more responsible and mature attitude about sex. Phrases such as "new sexual revolution" and "new era of chastity" were used frequently to describe the True Love Waits program. According to a teenager quoted in one newspaper: "there are kids who, a year ago would have been ashamed to admit they're virgins. ... It's cool now." The "coolness" of virginity pledges also is linked to high-profile athletes and entertainers—like Phoenix Suns' basketball player A.C. Green, and the singer Juliana Hatfield—who are "out" and public about their decision to wait, and who often show up at local events.[24] Closely related to this trope of the growing "coolness" of abstinence among the young is that of a reverse youth rebellion, reversing the sexual revolution of the 1960s, which presumably encouraged impulsiveness and instant gratification. According to one newspaper report: "A quarter century after Woodstock, a new youth rebellion is afoot. The anthem of this new generation: True loves waits." This reversal of values, this reaffirmation of what was supposedly devalued, in which that which was "old-fashioned" becomes "new" and "in," plays on a desire to think of abstinence as fashionable, as something young people are even drawn to in order to differentiate themselves from their parents' generation. Abstinence is, like Pepsi, represented as the brand of a younger generation. A third, somewhat less influential trope or theme in local press coverage of purity campaigns has to do with the importance of trusting that young people are mature enough to keep abstinence pledges. One young man quoted in a press story remarks, "a lot of adults think we're sexually active and we're a bunch of animals who can't control ourselves." The contrast established, either explicitly or implicitly, is between progressives who want to teach teenagers about contraceptives because they do not trust that they can rise above their "animal" impulses, and social and religious conservatives who do trust teens. So the former comes across as setting low moral expectations for youth, the latter as setting higher moral standards. Consequently, comprehensive approaches to sexuality education were often criticized in local press reports for encouraging young people to have sex. The only critical framing of purity campaigns in local press reports raised questions about the effectiveness of pledge campaigns in affecting the sexual behavior of teenagers. Newspaper reports that employed this frame deliberately sought to balance quotations in support of abstinence-only sex education with scientific evidence and arguments. A state public health official is quoted in one article that "vows of abstinence break more often than condoms do."[25] Yet overall, this final, more critical framing of the issues was identifiable in only a quarter of the articles surveyed. One of the reasons is that both sides had their own evidence, and the interpretation of the evidence was contested. Another reason is that local reporters focused on telling personal narratives and covering events. Scientific evidence, even when it is compelling, does not shape local perceptions and attitudes on the "problem" of adolescent sexuality as much as values, community and family norms, and commonsense beliefs.

At the policy level, however, it is only permissible to speak in a scientific language of "what works." Throughout the abstinence-only era, in which religious agendas were advanced through state policy, that policy has to be officially based on scientific evidence about what works to reduce teen pregnancy rates (primarily) and

STD rates (secondarily). No one working within the great halls of justice and law, the seats of governance, could be allowed to utter or even acknowledge what everyone knew: that abstinence-only legislation and policy did not emerge out of a reasoned presentation and analysis of the "hard facts" about "what works." Policy at least had to claim to be the result of a reasoned analysis of scientific facts and evidence about what works best in reducing teen pregnancy and STDs—since that is defined as the public interest in sex education, and the only interest the public (through the state) is allowed to have. A moral crusade for abstinence and sexual "purity" had to be translated into a secular campaign of reducing teen pregnancy rates. And the way to do this has been through sponsored research studies, and the selective interpretation and reporting of research data.

The Heritage Foundation, perhaps not unexpectedly, has played a major role in this regard. It published report after report presenting and analyzing scientific data on the effectiveness of abstinence-only sexuality education, even as the supporters of comprehensive sexuality education (such as SIECUS and the Guttmacher Institute) marshaled their own evidence to prove just the opposite. One reason for these contradictory findings, which just so happened to reflect the biases of the researchers, was that none of the data was very conclusive. In effect, both sides have made much of relatively minor differences in the outcomes for students enrolled in abstinence-only programs and those who are not. Both sides cited studies, and sometimes the same studies, to support their claims. A good example of this battle over the "facts" about whether abstinence-only sex education "works" was played out in the national press in 2005 around claims made by the authors of an article published in the *Journal of Adolescent Health*. That study by two highly respected sociologists— Peter Bearman and Hannah Bruckner—focused on the effectiveness of sexuality programs that involved virginity pledges, such as True Love Waits, in reducing STDs among adolescents.[26] Bruckner and Bearman analyzed data from the National Longitudinal Study of Adolescent Health, a national representative study of students enrolled in grades 7–12 in 1995. In a follow-up survey conducted in 2001–2002, respondents were asked to provide urine samples, which were then tested for various STDs. The authors could find no difference between pledgers and nonpledgers when it came to STDs, and they concluded that "pledging does not appear effective in stemming STD acquisition among young adults."[27] This was significant because it indicated that while abstinence-only programs might change some attitudes in the short run, they did not result in adolescents being less sexually active. Furthermore, when they were sexually active, the evidence suggested that those who had comprehensive sexuality education were more likely to use condoms and practice safe-sex techniques than those who were in abstinence-only programs. While pledgers delayed sexual relations by up to 18 months compared to nonpledgers, once they did become sexually active they took more risks.

The authors ended with a question: "Because most adolescents eventually become sexually active during their teenage years, is it really wise to ban discussion of contraception and STD protection from sex education?" They feared that the "all or nothing" approach of abstinence-only sex education may create barriers to knowledge about safe sex and protection.[28] SIECUS put out a press release on the article on March 18, 2005, titled: "Virginity Pledgers More Likely to Engage in Risky Sexual Behavior Including Oral and Anal Sex."[29] Part of what this was all about had to do with the definition of "having sex." Many pledgers adopted the belief that oral and anal sex were not "having sex" and therefore not a violation of their pledge of abstinence. The press quickly picked up the story and within several weeks it had become accepted as the truth. The Associated Press reported, "teens who pledged abstinence are just as likely to have STDs as their peers."[30] The *San Francisco Chronicle* reported, "Virginity pledgers are just as likely to contract sexually transmitted diseases as other teens."[31] And a CBS *Sixty Minutes* news show segment reported that "kids who take virginity pledges are just as likely to have sexually transmitted diseases as kids who don't." To counter this growing commonsense wisdom in the press that virginity pledges did not work as an effective response to the "problem" of adolescent sexuality, and that they might even encourage young people to engage in "risky" behavior, the Heritage Foundation quickly released its own assessment of Bruckner and Bearman's article.[32] By using the same database that Bruckner and Bearman had used, but by shifting around some variables and redefining categories, and by using a different type of regression analysis, the Heritage Foundation report concluded that virginity pledging did reduce STDs, although the difference "falls short of statistical significance by a razor thin margin." Furthermore, the Heritage Foundation report argued that virginity pledging has a positive impact on other important outcomes of sexuality-education programs. Such programs seek to "improve the mental health of youth; help youth develop true respect for others; prepare young people for healthy marriages as adults; reduce the risk of teen pregnancy and out-of-wedlock childbearing; and reduce the threat of sexually transmitted diseases."[33] So it was unfair to determine the effectiveness of virginity pledge programs by looking at STDs in isolation.

One may well question whether any of this debate (one might even say battle) over statistics in the attempt to prove "what works" ever has mattered much in public policy or educational practice. The abstinence-only era in sexuality education was not ushered in by an objective analysis of the data or a reasoned assessment of the "facts." Rather, it was the result of a political movement among social and religious conservatives to use the state and public schools to teach their version of "family values." They then saw in the data on the effectiveness of abstinence-only education programs what they wanted to see. As did the progressives at SIECUS. Progressives were more willing to view some adolescent sexual activity as "natural" and even "normal," which meant that withholding of information on contraceptives or condom usage, for example, is unethical and a violation of young people's right to know. If social and religious conservatives and progressives were both driven by firmly held values and ethical imperatives, much of the policy and public debate over sexuality education was bogged down in a seemingly endless battle over statistics and what they proved or did not prove. In fact, everyone conveniently overlooked one "fact" that emerged out of all these studies: it really did not matter much what kind of sexuality education young people had in school, or even whether they had sex-education classes. If sex education was about preventing or delaying sexual activity among adolescents, there was no indication that it was making a difference. This was a "truth" and a "fact" that neither side in the battle preferred to face. For they had invested much in the battle over sex education that had been waged almost nonstop since the 1950s when it first began to appear in U.S. public schools. That battle mattered because, presumably, what was taught in sex-education classes mattered. But did it? Even at the height of the virginity pledge movement in the Nineties, an estimated 12% of adolescents in the U.S. had taken a pledge of abstinence before marriage.[34] The religious right did not win the battle over sexuality education, but then neither did the progressives. Most young people had tuned out and had tuned into the popular culture sexuality curriculum.

While the battle raged over abstinence-only education, with both sides presenting evidence that it either "worked" or did not "work" to reduce rates of teen pregnancy and STDS, the law of the land required that teachers tell young people that abstinence is the only sure way to protect themselves. Consequently, progressives, along with social conservatives, staked out their positions and battle lines on a language terrain in which abstinence was taken for granted as the ideal, and in which scientific quantitative analysis was taken for granted as providing the answer to the question of "what works" to reduce a presumed "epidemic" of teen pregnancies and STDs. If public schools and universities wanted federal or state grants, they had to adhere to these linguistic rules of the game, rules that regulated what can be talked about and what cannot, what would count for truth, and what would not. This establishment of a commonsense discourse about abstinence and what works represented a major victory for social conservatives and the religious right. They were successful in establishing the linguistic rules and commonsense beliefs that sexuality educators and policy makers have played by since the early 1990s, and the battles have been played on their turf. One might even go so far as to say that social conservatives and the religious right established the discursive terrain for talking about the problem of adolescent sexuality. In Janice Irvine's history of the religious right and sex education, *Talk About Sex* (2004), the author observes that, at the turn of the 21st century, most public schools in the nation offered sex-education programs of some type. But very few offered anything like the comprehensive approach to sexuality education advocated by SIECUS. Even those schools that claimed to be doing comprehensive sexuality education used "comprehensive" to mean programs that stressed abstinence, but also taught about contraception.[35] Homosexuality was rarely in the curriculum, since homosexual youths were not presumably open to the risk of unwanted pregnancies—although in fact they are.[36] Irvine writes that "the turn of the century marked a widespread erosion of what could be said about sexuality to young people in many classrooms."[37] The right was able to control the language of policy and practice in sexuality education, and thus how the issues were framed and what got talked about. Most of the policy debate, consequently, has been between advocates of conservative and religious positions and those advocating a more "modern" position, with contraceptives as the backup, for when abstinence didn't work.[38] The power of religious rights movements lay in their capacity to articulate some good commonsense—about learning to respect yourself and resisting pressure to do something you do not want to do, and that might not be in your interests. "Sex Respect" is a great slogan, and one that progressives might have come up with if the Christian conservatives had not stolen the language of "respect" from them.

Some progressives have sought to reappropriate a language of respect, and even a language of abstinence, in sexuality education—when it is tied to a project of young women reclaiming control over their futures and their bodies. In an article in *Teachers College Record* in 2000, Lois Weis presented a case study of an abstinence-based program in Buffalo, New York, that, she argued, offered opportunities for "working against the grain—challenging representations and controlling images of women as victims, and exploring these images within their own racial/ethnic and class cultures of origin."[39] The article reports on a multiracial, poor, working-class support group, established on a voluntary basis for girls who had decided to stay abstinent. This group was facilitated by a Latina counselor supplied through WomanFocus, a nonprofit agency focused on women's rights issues and the abuse of women. Under the careful guidance of a Latina group leader, Weis observed, "mainstream sexuality programming" was being used for very progressive ends, "ends that encourage young women across race/ethnicity to explore their own gendered subjectivities and, most of all, resist ... violence and control."[40] One of the ways they affirmed their commitment to control over their bodies and not getting involved in abusive relationships was by distinguishing between themselves and what they called "lost" girls, who put up with abusive boyfriends and lived a life of victimization and internalized oppression.

By constructing their own identities in opposition to "lost" girls, the girls in the support group were able to construct self-affirming gender identities in solidarity with each other. This case study speaks to the importance of working in what limited space exists within public schools for progressive purposes, and of trying to open up more progressive spaces from within the abstinence-only movement. But it also is a case study of a program in a progressive state, in an urban magnet school for the performing arts, where progressive approaches to abstinence are more likely to prevail, and where teachers subvert the narrow intent of abstinence-only legislation to promote "abstinence-based" education—which, as Weis observes, is something quite different. Abstinence-based programs, like the one used in the support group, offer information about "safer-sex" techniques and contraception, for when adolescents decide not to choose abstinence. To the extent that "comprehensive sexuality education" existed in public schools in the age of the abstinence-only curriculum mandate, it did so in the guise of "abstinence-based" education or "abstinence-plus" education. So it is clear that the law was subverted, and that in some districts and individual schools around the country something like the SIECUS version of comprehensive sexuality education was being implemented.

Nevertheless, and as Weis admits, there are real and significant limits to working within abstinence discourses of sexuality education, even in their most progressive forms. Homosexuality was never discussed in the support group she observed, and the presumption was that everyone was heterosexual and that this was "normal." She writes that the support group's aim was "helping young women to gain strength and control within the boundaries of heterosexual relationships."[41] For these reasons, sexual orientation was never brought into the conversation. Of course, it is already part of the conversation, as that absent presence which is not talked about. Weis has, nevertheless, a valid argument, that it is okay and sometimes even useful for young women to form a support group that focuses on their victimization by heterosexual males—without, hopefully, encouraging the young women to think of all men as potential victimizers and abusers, or other young women who make different choices as "lost." This binary that separates the "saved" from the "lost," or even "damned," may well come as part of the baggage of abstinence approaches to education, I'm afraid, even those that attempt to use abstinence as a technology of the self that is empowering.

The long battle between Christian and social conservatives in support of abstinence-only sex education and progressive health professionals in support of "comprehensive" sexuality education goes on, and the battle over the "evidence" and what counts for evidence thus also goes on. However, the terrain of battle has narrowed over time, with each side endorsing a version of abstinence education. "Comprehensive" sexuality education is also commonly called "abstinence-plus" education, because it begins with a curriculum that stresses that abstinence is the best way to avoid unwanted pregnancies and STDs, then offers information about contraception and condoms for when adolescents do not "wait." Under President Obama and with a Democratic Congress, this "comprehensive" approach to abstinence education has received more policy-level support. In March, 2009, Congress passed the Responsible Education About Life (REAL) act, authorizing funds to public-school programs that provided "medically accurate, age appropriate" information about contraceptives to young people, with the stipulation that the programs had to teach that abstinence is the best and only certain way to avoid the risks of pregnancy and STDs. "REAL" connoted "getting real" about adolescent sexuality—a major progressive theme in the battle over sexuality education. "Getting real" meant acknowledging that, as the secondary-school reformer Theodore Sizer once commented, "high school is hormones." The word "responsible," meanwhile, implied that young people had to learn how to make "responsible decisions" about sexuality, including "how to avoid unwanted verbal, physical and sexual advances and how to avoid making verbal, physical, and sexual advances that are not wanted by the other party."[42] These two themes—"getting real" about adolescent sexuality and promoting "responsible decision making" about sexual behavior—have been mainstream progressive themes throughout the abstinence era in sexuality education, endorsed by almost all public health and health education professionals. These themes, finally legislated into educational policy in the REAL act, represent a significant shift in the discourse of abstinence education toward something called "comprehensive" sexuality education. At the same time, the aim remains the same. This means that nowhere in the act is there anything about serving the needs of LGBTQ youth. The exclusive focus is on delaying or discouraging heterosexual relations that may lead to unwanted teen pregnancies before marriage. It is almost as if the act, by focusing so narrowly on the problem of teen pregnancies, makes homosexuality irrelevant and nearly invisible. Ironically, to discourage religious-based organizations from applying for funding under the act, language was added to prohibit discrimination in hiring on the basis of sexual orientation and gender identity. Gay or lesbian teachers, even transgendered teachers, could not be prohibited from teaching in REAL-funded programs, although they were to remain largely invisible in the curriculum for decades after the Stonewall riots. The act also assumed, inaccurately, that LGBTQ youth were not at risk of getting pregnant, or getting someone else pregnant. The act relegates discussions of sexual orientation to a sidebar. Funded programs are to provide factual information on "abortion, masturbation, and sexual orientation." This is an interesting trio of the same old topics that presumably need to be "frankly" and "honestly" discussed somewhere in the sexuality curriculum, but which are not really the heart of the matter.

The act did speak of the need to increase education about HIV/AIDS among those groups most impacted, but refers only to African American and Hispanic youth, not gay youth. According to the act, while African American youth represents 17% of the adolescent population in the U.S., it accounted for 69% of new AIDS cases among adolescents in 2006. Young Latinos/as represented 18 percent of the youth population that year, but accounted for 23% of new AIDS cases. This includes AIDS diagnoses among both male and female youth. It is unclear what proportion of these new infections and AIDS cases are the result of homosexual contact, particularly anal intercourse among male adolescents, but infection rates are presumed to be quite high, with around half of all new infections among adolescents the result of homosexual relations. White, middle-class, gay males are also more likely to get early screening and treatment for HIV infection so that they are less likely than poor black and Latino/a adolescents to actually be diagnosed with AIDS. To acknowledge these high rates of infection among African American and Latino/a youth thus makes good sense since it focuses attention on the disproportionate impact of HIV/ AIDS on youth of color and the need to reach these youth with a comprehensive sexuality curriculum. At the same time, it makes little sense to ignore the dis-proportionate impact of HIV/AIDS on LGBTQ youth, and the particular needs of LGBTQ youth in African American and Latino/a communities. However these statistics on HIV/AIDS among adolescents are to be interpreted, to even acknowledge the continuation of high rates of infection and diagnosis, as the act does, is an unintended, but nevertheless forceful, indictment of sex education as an element of a field that seems to have had minimal impact on the sexual behavior of American youth, neither to encourage adolescents to abstain from "having sex" altogether, nor to protect themselves when they do.

The central "problems" that organized, modern, sex education as a field of research, a policy discourse, and an educational practice—the problem of teenage pregnancy, the problem of STDs, and the problem of homosexuality and the homosexual—still organized the field at the end of the first decade of the 21st century. It might be argued that substantial shifts have occurred in how the "problem of homosexuality" was represented and understood in sex-education discourse. Sex education no longer blames the homosexual for being a problem, but instead frames the problem as one of intolerance, a lack of understanding, and even homophobia. But homosexuality and LGBTQ youth are still marginalized as "topics" within a sexuality curriculum that continues for the most part to be organized around heteronormative "family values"—mandated by state and federal policies. Fearful of stirring up those on the religious evangelical right, policy makers and school administrators have sought to reduce conflict potential by making the curriculum noncontroversial. But even this is not enough for parents who elect to keep their children out of all sex-education classes—something they cannot do for other classes. Another way of managing conflict is to reduce the "space" within the curriculum and the school day for sexuality education of any sort. This indeed is the trend. Concerns with health, both individual and public, are unable to compete for space in a curriculum increasingly about economically functional literacy, math, and science skills pegged to standardized tests. These trends have not entirely gone unnoticed by progressives or conservatives. For conservatives, the shrinking space within public schools for sexuality education is a victory of sorts, even though they have controlled much of what is presented. Social and religious conservatives would, for the most, prefer that public schools get out of sex education entirely and leave it to religious groups working with families. Progressives too have begun to wonder whether sex education as we have known it is worth fighting hard for and whether there might be another way of framing sexuality education outside its narrow borders, even outside the field of health education. Over the past two decades or so, an alternative progressive discourse on sexuality education has emerged, linked to a shift toward cultural-studies perspectives and theories of sexuality and identity. I now want to turn to that movement and to the newer perspectives on sexuality that began to emerge out of the liberal arts academy by the 1990s.

7

FOUCAULT, DISCIPLINARY POWER, AND CARE OF THE SELF

Beginning in the 1980s, the tide had turned against progressive approaches to sexuality education in state and federal policy and in school practice. In response to the discourse of abstinence education, progressives advanced "comprehensive" sexuality education, which also went under the name of "abstinence-plus" sex education. Progressives thus played on a linguistic playing field in which abstinence had to be promoted as the ideal so that a discussion of condom use, for example, had to be presented as something young people needed to know in case they "slipped up" and had sex. Progressive sex educators, consequently, were working in an abstinence discourse that limited what it was possible to say or think about sexuality and the "problem" of adolescent sexuality. This meant that progressive models of sexuality education and progressive formulations of the "problem" of adolescent sexuality ended up looking more similar than not. In the end, both conservatives and "liberal" progressives were interested in finding better ways of managing the "problem" of adolescent sexuality. Arguments were thus waged over what the scientific evidence revealed about the "effectiveness" of both approaches. In public policy it was impossible to raise other questions or understand sexuality education in a different way, through a different lens. Meanwhile, the space for sexuality education in the curriculum kept shrinking for a number of reasons, including the continuing decline of health and physical education, where sexuality education has continued to be located in most school districts.

Ironically, as the battle over "sex education" reached this state of affairs, something that we might now know as "sexuality education" was being invented outside the battle, in the liberal arts academy, under the banner of cultural studies. It is true that the term "sexuality" had been around in health-education discourse for some time. In family-life education a distinction was often made between an education that was only or primarily about the "facts" of sex (sexual organs, mechanics of the sex act, birth control, homosexuality, and so on), and an education that addressed "sex" as part of the "whole child" and the child's development. "Sexuality" implied a concern with the sphere of human relations within which "sex" happened, including, for example, concerns with "healthy" boy–girl relationships and "healthy" families. But in the new cultural-studies scholarship, sexuality implied something else and something more. Certainly cultural-studies scholars would agree that sex is about much more than just "having sex," and it has much to do with human relations. But it also has to do with cultural politics: the way power is mobilized and distributed according to categories of class, race, gender, sexual, and other identities, and according to practices of equity and freedom or authoritarianism and domination. This is to say that sex education has a cultural politics. Cultural-studies scholars, working outside the field of sex education, were able to critically address its cultural politics, challenge the commonsense or conventional wisdom within the field, and ask whose interests were being served in sex education. At the time of this writing, cultural-studies perspectives on sexuality education have only a relatively minor impact on the practice of sex education. But that influence seems to be growing. Furthermore, cultural studies implies a much broader concern with the "problem" of adolescent sexuality that cannot be contained within the health field alone.

A general framework for a cultural-studies perspective on sex education and the problem of the adolescent was provided by the great social theorist and historian Michel Foucault in his three volume *The History of Sexuality* released between 1976 and 1984 in French, and one and two years later as English translations. He died of AIDS the year the last volume in the series was released in French. Foucault was a homosexual, and supported the struggle for gay and lesbian rights. But he was also the father of "queer theory," in that he questioned the binary oppositions within which sexual identity was regulated and understood in the modern age. These binaries, he felt, were all about establishing and privileging "normal" sexuality, as defined by dominant groups, and at the same time setting it up against "abnormal" sexuality—and the treatment, surveillance, and regulation of abnormal sexuality. This obviously has suggested a rethinking of the "problem" of homosexuality and the homosexual as the problem of establishing a rigid "norm" associated with an idealized version of a white, middle-class, heterosexual, familial sexuality to which everyone is expected to conform. Any performance of sexuality outside this "norm" threatens the stability of the norm, especially when sexual abnormality is not represented and is portrayed as a psychological disorder or as immoral. So too, the sexuality of poor black and Latina unwed mothers must be represented, if it is to be represented at all, as deviant and irresponsible. Foucault's history of sexuality explores the notion of "normalization" in a broad cultural context, and he associates it with the rise of what he called "disciplinary power"—the power of the scientific and medical disciplines over the body and its "health," and a power that disciplines sexuality along with the body to make it more utilitarian and docile.

In *The History of Sexuality*, Volume 1, Foucault takes on the dominant historical narrative of progress, which he identifies with the "repressive hypothesis," the idea that people in the Victorian era were more repressed, prudish, and silent about sexuality than we are today. Part of the appeal of the repressive hypothesis, no doubt, is that it fits neatly within the framework established by dominant narratives of progress. As people have become more "enlightened" about sexuality (less "old-fashioned" in popular vernacular), they are presumably less prudish and more willing to engage in a frank and open treatment of sexuality. According to this narrative, the scientific disciplines—medicine, psychology, and psychoanalysis— have led the way toward the more enlightened view of sexuality that characterizes contemporary society. History is a story of a long movement from sexual repression, silencing, stigmatization, and moral condemnation toward sexual "liberation." Thus, people in the modern era are understood as generally more enlightened about sexuality, and less prudish and judgmental than their parents and grandparents were. This is a story that gets told again and again in histories and in popular culture. If it is not altogether wrong, its truths are a little too convenient and conventional to be taken at face value, and Foucault means to disrupt its commonsense logic and thereby call into question the modernist narrative of progress that things are getting better, even if we still have a long way to go. For one thing, the modernist narrative of progress sets up a neat binary opposition between sexual darkness and sexual enlightenment or liberation, with sexual "liberation" understood as the polar opposite of sexual repression and discipline. Foucault questions whether a demo-cratic alternative to the dominant discourse on sexuality can be articulated within the binary by merely choosing an unrepressed sexuality. He argues that radical Freudians (like Wilhelm Reich, Herbert Marcuse, and Eric Fromm) are guilty of viewing unrepressed desire as somehow revolutionary in itself, as if capitalism is associated with repressed desire, and socialism with unrepressed desire. Although he finds the radical Freudian argument compelling in some ways, he feels that it too easily slips into a discourse that poses sexual repression and oppression against "something that smacks of revolt, of promised freedom, ... [of] revolution and happiness."[1]

Foucault focuses on the rise of disciplinary power and a normalizing discourse in Europe from the 17th century through to the 19th century, with some rather direct implications for sexuality education. Again, he wishes to refute, or at least modify, the "repressive hypothesis" that positions this past as a "dark ages" of sexual repression and the silencing of sexual language in all spheres of public and private life. What he finds instead is an "incitement to discourse," an almost obsessive interest in sexuality, but a sexuality that is now under the gaze of scientific and medical eyes. As for prohibitions against the use of sexual language in public, the very prohibition against using such language is spoken and written about. It becomes the subject of media attention when words are spoken that are forbidden, by law or public decency, from being used in public or among children. That is, the silences, the prohibitions, the censoring of language is part of an apparatus of power that is rather obsessively interested in sexuality. Even the prohibition not to speak about sexuality in public incites resistances that are in turn the subject of discourse by professional "experts." To Foucault, discourse establishes what can be talked about but also what cannot be talked about. It also incites resistance through the speaking of a "profane" language in public—something teachers and administrators in schools know all too well. But beyond this, he wonders whether prohibition and censorship of sexual language is truly repressive, or rather it might just as well be the opposite, since it focuses attention on the forbidden and encourages the transgressive speaking of the forbidden. But Foucault does not linger long on the silencing and prohibition of sexual language, for it is to him a minor effect of the disciplining of sexuality. The overarching phenomenon he means to study he calls "biopower": "population as wealth, population as manpower or labor capacity, population balanced between its own growth and the resources it commanded."[2] The health of the community, the society, and the nation was tied "not only to the number and uprightness of its citizens, to their marriage rules and family organization, but to the manner in which each individual made use of his [sic] sex."[3] The sexuality of the individual, and of subgroups within the population, was a public and, thus, state concern. Here Foucault is quite clear about some of the early history of biopower in the West, and its association with racist eugenics or a racial-hygiene movement. He observes that biopower takes up the cause of "hygienic necessity," using the fear of venereal diseases and combining this with a concern for "public health" that "promised to eliminate defective individuals, degenerates and bastardized populations." This medicalization of the "problem" of sexuality legitimated racist policies under National Socialism in Germany on the grounds that they were based on scientific "truth."[4] In the U.S., racial hygiene and population health were related to keeping or making the nation "strong" and "virile," and identifying and slowly eliminating "weak" and "degenerate" populations through eugenics marriages and selective sterilization.[5] This eugenics past also serves as a caution against looking to scientific discourse as neutral and objective, rather than itself part of biopower and thus politically interested. Foucault would warn us against investing too much legitimacy in a scientific, "objective" discourse on sexuality when there can be no objective, disinterested truth, and when sexuality is always already about ethics and power.

Not only are the scientific disciplines and professional "experts" not neutral; they have been servants of power for the most part, framing their research and policy discourse according to dominant narratives of "progress" in the long battle against various "social problems"—like the single welfare mother. The human and social-science "disciplines" actually emerge out of and are part of a biopower project of normalizing and disciplining sexuality that is coextensive with the rise of industrial capitalism, and also the modern state and state institutions such as public schools, prisons, and mental hospitals organized to efficiently manage and discipline "inmate" populations. In French secondary schools in the 18th century, Foucault notes, everything is architecturally designed to discipline what is understood to be the natural, trouble-making sexuality of the boys and young men. Far from viewing youth as innocent, the educators viewed them as uncivilized savages who needed to be tamed. "The space for classes, the shape of the tables, the planning of the recreation lessons, the distribution of the dormitories (with or without partitions, with or without curtains), the rules for monitoring bedtime and sleep periods," all these referred back to the public problem of youthful sexuality. Aside from the architectural disciplining of sexuality, Foucault observes that formal sex education emerges as "a whole literature" of clinical cases and medical advice, along with pedagogical techniques and experimental programs. Of one such experimental program, he writes that "a certain reasonable, limited, canonical, and truthful discourse on sex" was initiated in the classroom, and at the end of the term students were given a public examination in which they had to answer questions about the mysteries of sex relations, procreation, and perversions. It was expressly forbidden for any of the young men, or those men and women in the audience, to show shame or embarrassment, and "no unseemly laughter intervened to disturb them."[6] What we have here is not really a muting of language that refers to sexuality, but rather a new language about sexuality, and new "experts" who speak about sexuality and require that students speak of it, but in a way that disciplines it, regulates it, and medicalizes it.

Of all the technologies or mechanisms of biopower, Foucault focuses on one in particular: the ritual of the confession. In picking the confession as a ritual of biopower, Foucault already subverts the "normal" way Western history gets written, as a narrative of development out of a "dark ages" in which religious dogma and moral condemnation of sexuality was the norm, into a more "enlightened" culture that is secular, rational, and nonreligious. The story Foucault has to tell is one of continuities as well as discontinuities between religious and secular discourses on sexuality in the West. The confession provides an example. Confession manuals in the Middle Ages, according to Foucault, called on the confessor of sexual sins to provide a: "description of the respective positions of the partners, the postures assumed, gestures, places touched, caresses, the precise moment of pleasure," which is to say a narration of the sexual act "in its very unfolding."[7] As sexual discretion began to dictate a more circumspect language, one with less detail, more reliant upon coded words, the confession changed. But its scope and power, as Foucault notes, continuously increased. Even sexual thoughts, desires, and dreams had to be told, and entered into the process of confession and penance. By the 19th century this religious tradition of sexual confession had become reconstituted in scientific and medical terms and provided the basis for clinical psychoanalytic practice. The modern psychiatrist with a client on his couch is, Foucault suggests, a direct descendent of the priest listening to a confession in the Middle Ages. But the new confessional is different in significant ways as well. The psychiatrist or psychologist who hears a confession is not empowered to forgive and assign penances, but rather to interpret and decide the "truth" about causation and treatment. The truth does not reside in the confession itself, but in its "decipherment" by the new "master of truth," the psychoanalytic doctor.[8] Gradually, this new approach to the ritual of confession also, Foucault suggests, emigrates toward education, where it is associated with a pedagogy of young people talking about their lives in a therapeutic classroom. This is one form that sexuality education has taken in the U.S., particularly that developed out of family-life education. Of course, the confession is also a well-developed ritual within evangelical Christian "purity" movements, with teenagers expected to talk openly with parents and religious leaders about their sexual impulses and "lapses." In all these forms, the confessional confers power on those who hear and interpret "confessions." Here I use the term "confession" broadly to refer to all peda-gogical rituals in which the teacher expects students to produce personal narratives about their fears, desires, and relations with others, and in which the teacher is positioned as "master of truth" in interpreting and finding meaning in these narratives.

For a long time, according to Foucault, the working classes in Europe were able to escape the gaze of this disciplinary and normalizing sexuality education. The middle class disciplined itself first, so to speak, by deploying a discourse of legitimate mar-riages and illegitimate children, by prescribing strict "technologies of the flesh" in boarding schools, and so on. But, by the early 19th century, Foucault notices that these disciplinary technologies and concerns with biopower were being attached to the working class, with the aim of adjusting them to bourgeois standards of sexual conduct and morality. He identifies three successive stages in the development of a sexuality education for the working class. The first stage involved an incitement to discourse on the problem of birth control among the urban poor, in other words, on the problem of high birthrates among the poor and how this problem might be managed. Next came a concern with replicating the "conventional" or "normal," middle-class family as an instrument of "political control and economic regulation for the subjugation of the urban proletariat." In other words, if only the urban poor could learn to adopt "normal" family patterns like middle-class people, then they would no longer be such a problem. They could be assimilated and adjusted as no longer a threat to the dominant order. The last stage Foucault associates with the development of legal and medical classification and control of perversions, "for the sake of the general protection of society and the race."[9] Interestingly, these remained the central motifs in U.S. sex education in the period beginning in 1950, although the age of the pervert began to come to a close in the 1970s with the declassification of homosexuality as a psychological disorder. Foucault acknowledges that this may seem like progress, that people are becoming more enlightened and tolerant. Prenuptial or extramarital relations are tolerated, "perverts" are no longer condemned in law and in the school curriculum, and the protection of childhood innocence no longer calls for such a strict desexualization of youth. Nevertheless, the incitement to speak about sexuality at all levels, the continuing concern with the problem of adolescent sexuality, and the almost obsessive concern with regulating and commodifying the bodies of young people, suggest to Foucault that what we are now witnessing is not "liberation" from disciplinary and normalizing power, but changes in its tactics and methods, a rupture at best in an age characterized by a heightening of concern with the problem of sexuality.

Volume 1 of Foucault's history of sexuality provided a critical lens through which it became possible to see how sexuality education in its dominant forms, and even in its radical Freudian and bohemian forms, was part of a broader discourse on sexuality that regulated sexuality by talking about it. Through an incitement to discourse, a problem of adolescent sexuality has been constructed and developed over an historical period of at least two centuries. This socially constructed "problem," in turn, justifies various interventions by the state, along with professional experts of various sorts, to "normalize" sexuality in ways that support the interests and worldviews of dominant groups. This is a powerful new narrative on sexuality education that has profound implications for reframing sexuality education. Of course, Foucault appears to be critical of almost everything that sexuality education has come to stand for in the modern era, so his story—at least up through Volume 1—begs the question: What does Foucault have to say beyond criticism in the way of fleshing out an alternative, a more democratic discourse on sexuality? As I have already noted, he did go out of his way to avoid the trap of a narrow critical theory of negation, in which "liberation" of the body and its desires is posed against an oppressive disciplinary power. Disciplinary power is not "bad" or "good" in itself. It all depends on who is using it, and for what purposes. The modern, disciplinary power that organizes sexuality in the West has been a power exercized over people, both as individuals and as populations and subpopulations, in the interests of control and docility. But there have been and are other discourses and practices that discipline sexuality and the body. In Volume 1, Foucault notes that alternative discourses of disciplining sexuality currently exist or historically have existed in China, Japan, India, Rome, and the Arab world. He lumps these together as examples of what the ancient Greeks called *ars erotica*, in which "pleasure is not considered in relation to an absolute law of the permitted and the forbidden, nor by reference to a criterion of utility, but first and foremost in relation to itself."[10] This is a disciplining of sexuality that, in Volumes 2 and 3 of his history of sexuality Foucault will associate with an ethic and practice of "care of the self."

Volume 2 of Foucault's history of sexuality, *The Use of Pleasure*, was published in English in 1985, a year after its French publication and the death of its author. Foucault begins with a brief introduction explaining that he meant to write a history of sexuality in which sexuality is produced as an effect of producing the human subject as a worker, family member, and citizen.[11] Sexuality emerges as a cultural mechanism for organizing and shaping desire, or *eros*, with the aim of constructing or producing certain kinds of "subjects" situated within particular sets of power relations. Sexuality is produced along with a sense of what it means to be masculine and feminine, and also within the context of racial and class-based power relations (between black slaves and white masters, for example, in the antebellum South). Sexuality is also bound up with the social construction of sexual identity, as either "gay," "straight," or "queer." This expands the scope of sexuality education, as I have already said. But it also makes it more difficult for Foucault to put neat brackets around his history, to declare that it is a history of the disciplining of sexuality in the modern age, as he does in Volume 1. Furthermore, he recognizes that to appreciate the modern view of sexuality and the "games of truth" organized around it, the reader would need to imagine how things might be different. And to do that Foucault says that he would need to go back to Western antiquity, where sexuality was organized around significantly different modes and forms of self-production—although he means to reject the commonsense view of "pagan" sexuality as liberated and nonmoralistic, in contrast to a more repressed and moralistic Christian sexuality. To take on a history or genealogy of sexuality in ancient Greek and Roman cultures, he admits, "would carry me far from my original project." He expresses concern that this new history came with risks, including the "likelihood of delaying and upsetting the publication schedule." Without mentioning his own health, Foucault is obviously interested in getting this history completed. He writes that for some of his friends who had waited patiently for an outcome, working in the midst of such uncertainty and apprehension "is tantamount to failure." But he adds, "all I can say is that clearly we are not from the same planet."[12] Foucault called on people to live with uncertainty and ambiguity, and with a personal and cultural history that could not be wrapped up into a neat package of truths. He would charge ahead with an ambitious new project, spanning two volumes, one on ancient Greece, and the other on Rome in the first two centuries AD, completed just before he died.

As in the first volume, Foucault sets up his history of ancient Greek and Roman cultures in a way that counters the common way in which this "pagan" past is represented; that is, as a time of unbridled sexuality and Dionysian sensuality, an immoral and decadent time that leads to decline and fall. Foucault is willing to grant the proposition that Greeks and Romans of that era "accepted certain sexual behaviors much more readily than the Christians of the Middle Ages or the Europeans of the modern period."[13] He also concedes that sexual "misconduct" was less scandalous then than it is today in the West. There was, after all, no power (either medical or religious) that claimed the right to say what was "abnormal" or immoral with regard to sexuality. Once all this has been acknowledged, Foucault argues, it is inaccurate to say that the Greeks and Romans were unconcerned with disciplining sexuality, or with understanding it in terms of moral and ethical considerations. In fact, it is inaccurate to set the pagan off against the Christian, with the pagan era representing either sexual decadence or sexual liberation (depending on your political views), and the Christian era representing either sexual virtue or sexual discipline and punishment. In *The Use of Pleasure*, Foucault finds that many of the concerns about sexuality raised in the Christian era and in the modern era were already part of the discourse on sexuality in 4th-century Athens. These concerns and worries ran throughout philosophical texts, and they found expression in medical texts and popular self-help guides that offered wisdom in the arts and ethics of "self-mastery."

Among free Greek men of high social status, sexuality was organized around an ethics of leadership, authority, and domination of both women and weaker males. "Self-mastery" in this context prescribed a highly disciplined sexuality, with sexual desire understood as weakening men by sapping their strength and distracting them from their duties as family, military, and political leaders. Foucault observes that this was a male ethic "in which women figured only as objects or, at most, as partners that one had best reign, educate, and watch over." It did not establish a set of sexual dos and don'ts, of rigid norms of normal and abnormal, moral or immoral, sexuality. For to do so would be to limit the freedom of these men to exercise power and practice liberty. Men called upon themselves to assume the role of head of a household, but no code of conduct prevented them from having extramarital relations, including relationships with adolescent young men, which were "accepted, commonly maintained, and even prized."[14] Adolescent males were typically referred to as "boys," to emphasize their subordinate status in male society. Interestingly, this suggests that whether we think of adolescents as children or as young adults matters. The Greeks deliberately emphasized the child-like status of adolescent males in order to accentuate power inequalities in the relationship. When "boys" became "men," somewhere in their late teens, they were no longer to be treated as the "passive" partner in sexual relations. As equals to other free men of status and power, they were expected to enter only into relationships in which they assumed the "active" role. Were the Greeks bisexual? For Foucault, that phrasing of the question would not make sense to the ancient Greeks who did not think in terms of homosexual, bisexual, and heterosexual identities. "Men could be distinguished by the pleasure they were most fond of," but most were fond of the love of "boys" (adolescent males) and women. There is, in effect, no particular structure to desire in the ancient Greek world, in sharp contrast to our own. Relationships with adolescent males and females were subject to the same condition, that the "appetite was nobler that inclined toward what was more beautiful and more honorable," rather than toward lust and selfishness.[15]

What was unacceptable, and consequently defined as "abnormal" within patriarchal Greek culture, was the effeminate or feminized male. Many might think, Foucault observes, that the image or stereotype of the effeminate homosexual was a creation of the Victorian era. But he finds it alive and well developed already in ancient Greece. There are countless examples of the effeminate male in Greek texts, characterized in terms of mannerisms, facial expressions, stylish and flamboyant dress, and a feminized body. Socrates complains in *Phaedrus* "of the love that is given to soft boys, too delicate to be exposed to the sun as they are growing up, and all made up with rouge and decked up in ornaments." Gender nonconformity among males is represented in terms of feminizing the body, since there were really only two possible gender and sexual options available: perform the masculine, "active," dominating role, or perform the feminine, "passive," submissive role. Bullying and stigmatization of gender nonconforming males, and perhaps females, was a pervasive practice in Greek culture, and it was directly implicated in the maintenance of patriarchy. Foucault observes that in ancient Greek culture it is possible to see "the very early expression of intense negative reactions and a form of stigmatization that will extend well into the future."[16] This suggests that in a culture in which gender is tied to fixed, oppositional performances of femininity and masculinity, those who do not identify with their assigned gender roles are in the position of having to choose the only other option, to act like their gender opposite. This was an effect of binary oppositional thinking about sexuality and gender.

If we are still haunted by the ghost of this ancient past, which has bequeathed us such a troubled view of sexuality, Foucault seeks to recover what he can that might be useful in constructing an alternative, more democratic approach to sexuality. He finds value in the idea that sexuality is not governed by religious dogma or legal codes of prohibition and regulation, but rather by an ethical code of conduct and practices of bodily and spiritual health. Ethical concerns had to do with not abusing one's power over others, but rather looking out for their interests and seeing that their desires are also met. This is, of course, the heart of paternalism, but it at least establishes the basis for distinguishing between abusive and nonabusive relations, and between consensual and nonconsensual ones. As for holistic bodily and spiritual health, the Greeks practiced a whole array of regimes of bodily cleansing and nutrition, of exercise and rest, of meditation and self-reflection that were designed to bring one's sexuality into balance. Such practices might also include temporary abstinence. Plato remarks in the *Laws* that a certain heroic young athlete in training for the Olympics "never touched a woman—or a boy, for that matter—during the entire time of his intensive training."[17] As Foucault observes, "such extreme virtue was the visible mark of the mastery they [athlete heroes] brought to bear on themselves and hence of the power they were worthy of exercising over others."[18] For most people, Greek sexual ethics offered neither long-term abstinence nor obsessive indulgence as "healthy," but rather offered tools of self-discipline and self-regulation that could be used to navigate a course between excess and abstinence through an ethic of moderation. The use of pleasure was tied to a belief in "satisfying yourself" as a means of appeasing sexual "appetite." Masturbation might be the most direct means of satisfying the sexual appetite, or visiting a prostitute. How sexual appetite was satisfied was less important than that it was satisfied, so that it did not become an obsession. The ethic of moderation thus did not take the form, Foucault argues, "of an obedience to a system of laws or a codification of behaviors; it was an art, a practice of pleasures that was capable of self-limitation."[19] It was an ethic that involved the negotiation of sexual behavior between involved parties, with the best and highest interests of each considered, and in which personal and public interests both had to be considered. People were expected to fall short of this ethical claim at times, and certainly the highly inequitable power relations (subordinating women, children, and slaves) meant that concerns for reciprocity and symmetry were very contradictory.

In *Care of the Self*, the third volume of his history of sexuality, Foucault continues to explore an ethical grounding for sexuality in Greek culture, but extends his history to the first two centuries of the era in Rome. Even more than for the Greeks, Roman sexual ethics emphasized the health of the individual, the family, and the nation or empire. Philosophical discourse becomes less lofty, less concerned with virtue, and correspondingly more concerned with how to care for the self in ways that maintain the strength and vitality of the individual, the family, and the state—which were all linked. This too becomes the concern of doctors, who wrote texts and developed methods to teach health and vitality—what the Romans called *vita activa*.[20] There was, for the most part, a masculinist and patriarchal interest behind this discourse, since only men were expected to assume the "active" role in sexual and other relations. But the health and vitality of women is also of concern, given that they must be healthy to be good wives and mothers and to endure pregnancy and childbirth. While the Greeks were inclined to link this bodily healthiness to the healthiness of the spirit and to noble ideals that transcended the body, the Romans were more inclined to speak of the health of the body. Foucault quotes one Roman doctor's famous saying: "Subdue the soul and make it obey the body."[21] This appears to be a reversal of the Greek ideal, but in sexual matters it meant letting the body have its way, not trying to bring the soul or psyche into it (in terms of moralizing or rationalizing sexual desire). "There is the care of the body to consider, health regimens, physical exercises, ... the carefully measured satisfaction of needs."[22] There are also reflective practices, journal keeping, meditation, and talking with friends and confidantes. These practices do not represent a break from the past, but rather a development of Greek interests in health along a certain path, and within a class that could afford to be concerned with maintaining health. We can see parallels today in a health industry that caters to the middle and upper classes with all kinds of self-help programs and meditation techniques. But Foucault at least sees in practices of "care of the self" a framework for thinking beyond the disciplinary and normalizing discourse on sexuality education he identified in the first volume of his history.

The question that had been so central in Greek philosophy, of the love between "boys" and men, was of such a concern because the honor and virtue of the "boy" had to be respected at all times, and because the love had to be placed within its proper idealistic context of pedagogy and mentoring. Yet this love was, because of power inequalities, subject to abuse. How then could Greek men and young men of a certain age negotiate a relationship so associated with high ideals and fraught with the real possibility for abuse? This was the question that Greeks pondered. Foucault suggests that, for Romans, this had ceased to be a problem, at least a problem of much importance. Sexual relationships between adult males and teenage "boys" and "girls" continued to be common and widely accepted, but they were more often now relationships between Roman free men and young male and female "barbarian" slaves. There was no need to worry about protecting the virtue and honor of slaves. Elite males could care for their own needs and not worry about the needs of others. Along with a discourse of care of the self that empowered middle- and upper-class men, Foucault finds in the 1st and 2nd centuries of our era a growing concern with the dangers of sexuality in general, and a valorization of marriage as the proper place for its fulfillment. The problem with sexuality in general—its tendency, as Plato saw it, to work against the spirit and the higher virtues it represented—began to reinsert itself in Roman culture. According to a Stoic ethic, people were to engage in sexual acts not out of a desire for desire, that is, for a heightening of passions and sensuality, but rather out of a desire to pursue desire through orgasm, "an act of natural elimination," as one might eliminate urine or excrement from the body. Masturbation was supported by the Romans as a quick and effective technique for purging desire when it began to intrude, and it therefore was part of a Stoic philosophy and ethic that veered toward austerity and abstinence. The beginning of the Christian era consequently does not represent a major rupture, a complete reversal, in cultural development. But it did begin to codify this austere Stoic movement in Graeco-Roman culture through law and religious dogma, which meant the end of an ethic of care of the self that is decentered and valorizes moderation rather than a set of moralistic dos and don'ts. The "flesh" will replace the "body" as a site of temptation to sin, and all sexuality that is not productive in the procreative sense is now to be sinful; and even the latter will be governed by the law of "original sin."

With all the limitations of the ancient Greek and Roman ethical discourses of care of the self, Foucault finds in them ideas that are potentially quite democratic, and that might provide a way of thinking beyond the current framing of sexuality education as both a religious and a secular disciplinary and normalizing power. In a democratized form, care of the self would remove sex education from the realm of either morality (in terms of prescribed codes of moral conduct, associated with dos and don'ts) or normalization (in terms of establishing and privileging a norm, with those who do not fit the norm labeled abnormal, deviant, and dangerous). By reframing sexuality education as care of the self, it becomes possible to engage young people in a dialogue on what is caring for themselves, and what is not. How do they take care of themselves so that they do not enter into abusive relationships? How do they care for themselves by knowing how to protect themselves when they engage in sexual relations? How do queer youth practice caring for themselves in an often hostile school and family ethos? How does care of the self translate into caring for others? How does care of the self involve resisting objectification and subjugation of the gendered body? These all become thinkable questions and problems when sexuality education is reframed as the study of sexuality as it is produced within a culture—how it gets talked about, in what terms, according to what fears and problems; how it is related to class, race, gender, sexual orientation, and ability differences; and thus how it is implicated in a cultural politics. There will be no easy answers to the new questions and problems made thinkable and imaginable through such cultural studies of sexuality. But they do suggest responses that are consistent with a pedagogy of equity and social justice. Sexuality education in this sense is still a form of health education. It is just that health education as care of the self takes on a significantly different meaning, linked to a different pedagogy.

Foucault provided the basis for a quite radical critique of dominant discourses of sex education, as biopower discourses concerned with managing and regulating populations and subpopulations, and constituting populations and individuals as subjugated subjectivities—that is, as dominated, docile, and manageable subjects of power. He also proposed, as a possible alternative, discourses and practices of freedom, tied to an ethic of care of the self that he had traced back to the pre-Christian era. Because his history was so critical of dominant discourses of sexuality education, and because he saw something useful in a pagan past typically depicted as a time of decadence and immorality, it should hardly be surprising that his history was not embraced by the health-education establishment, or even noticed for that matter. But Foucault's influence grew dramatically in the liberal arts academy in the 1980s and 1990s, as cultural-studies perspectives became more influential. The field of curriculum studies was the first in education to take up these new cultural-studies perspectives. Since the 1970s at least, curriculum studies had been a space of critique tied to a democratic progressive cultural politics, along with the "foundations" of education (history, sociology, anthropology, and the philosophy of education), where Foucault's work has been most influential.

Foucault was "antifoundational" in that he critiqued the dominant narrative of history as the building of a national or cultural identity upon a solid foundation, an original grounding for all truth and knowing. For Foucault, there is no solid cultural foundation upon which to assemble a discourse and practice of sexuality education, only different culturally specific discourses, which are themselves contradictory, incomplete, and partial. This not only challenges the authority of scientific approaches to sexuality, it challenges the foundational beliefs about sexuality and morality held by Christian conservatives as well. Reason is not a neutral tool to reveal a truth already out there waiting to be discovered. Nor is truth handed down by God as a set of timeless moral virtues and sins. The truth about sexuality is produced by discourse, the "truth games" about which Foucault writes. Different discourses construct different sets of problems, and raise different sets of questions about how to resolve or respond to these problems. If this is a postmodern understanding of truth and reason, it is also poststructural in that it rejects all models of society, or of social institutions, that attempt to explain them in terms of neat, fixed, stable structures. Instead of structure, poststructuralists seek the circulation of discourses in various institutions and spaces that are organizing and distributing power through various microtechnologies and rituals. Discourse is always situated within a cultural, historical, material, and pragmatic context, so it is not an abstract, disinterested language. Rather, it is language in use. And it is language that frames the way we interpret and "see" events in the world. By implication, if we want to think the world anew, we need a new language, a new discourse, a new truth game—which Foucault hoped to assemble around the ancient Greek and Roman ethic of care of the self. It was neither an austere, puritanical, moralistic discourse, nor a discourse of liberation and the surrender to desire. Poststructuralists like Foucault offer no answers or solutions to our problems. If there is hope it lies in our capacity to think and act outside the current binary logic that has organized so many truth games in the West. This also implies that democratic cultural traditions are strengthened and made more open and resilient as they become more multicultural and multilingual, and as the voices of gender, class, race, and sexual Others are heard.

It was not long, as I have said, before Foucault's histories began to disrupt established scholarly traditions and disciplines. He had, after all, challenged scholars in various disciplines (the social and behavioral sciences particularly) and applied fields (medicine, social work, psychiatry, and education) to re-examine their histories and the social "problems" that called them into existence, to explore the extent to which they have been involved in normalizing and regulatory projects. When James Sears' edited volume *Sexuality and the Curriculum* was published in 1992, which contained critical essays written from a number of different theoretical standpoints and positions, Foucault's work was acknowledged by only a few of the contributors, and then without developing any of his key insights.[23] At the same time, the poststructural shift in thinking was visible from the outset in the book. Debra Haffner, then executive director of SIECUS, wrote in her forward that the authors in the volume "raise disturbing questions about sexuality education programs." These questions had to do with "gender issues, cultural issues, ideological conflict, sexual orientation, and pleasure and desire." They also summoned educators and health-care professionals, Haffner wrote, "to look beyond the formal curriculum to the hidden curriculum of sexuality from preschool through college."[24] The concern in curriculum studies with the so-called "hidden curriculum"—the messages communicated through the processes and rituals of schooling rather than the official curriculum—fits in well with Foucault's analysis of rituals (such as the confessional) as a technology of power. Peter McLaren, from Miami University's Center for Education and Cultural Studies, also wrote a foreword that did not mention Foucault, although he did rely heavily upon Marxist and feminist theorists who focused on the body as a site of domination and resistance. He noted that the concept of the body "as a site of social and cultural inscription" was growing in prominence, along with an analysis of desire—spurred on by feminist scholars interested in uncoupling the gendered body from the "machine of corporate capitalism." Educators, he argued, had divorced knowledge from the body, and he quoted Terry Eagleton to the effect that much rebellion against schooling by working-class youth was an expression of "the body's long, inarticulate rebellion against the tyranny of the intellectual."[25] McLaren called for pedagogies of sexuality education that enable young people to "construct knowledge that is lived in the body, felt in the bones, and situated within a larger commitment to social justice and emancipation." The notion of emancipation implied something much more idealistic and transformative than Foucault would have suggested, but Foucault clearly was not about just reforming the currently dominant discourse on sexuality either. He was about rethinking, and that is a transformative project. For his part, Sears did cite Foucault in his introductory chapter to argue that "an informed understanding of sexuality as socially constructed and historically changing" leads one to conclude that there is not a good deal of difference between the two competing discourses of sexuality education, represented by the abstinence-only and the comprehensive sexuality-education discourses. "Their near exclusive focus on teenage pregnancy and sexually transmitted diseases," Sears wrote, was tied to an ideology that denied adolescents the right to sexual expression on the premise of "protecting" them, like children, from the dangers of sexuality.[26]

The next chapter in *Sexuality and the Curriculum* was by me, and in it I presented some of the evidence from my history of early decades of the sex education movement in the U.S.—roughly the first half of the 20th century, that period just before this history begins. I attempted to make sense of the historical conflict over sexuality, particularly the sexuality of youth, through a discussion of three competing "ideologies" of sexuality. I used "ideology" to mean an interested worldview. And, since all worldviews are interested (even, as Foucault argued, the worldview of the scientific disciplines), we are left to choose between competing ideologies. Drawing on a Marxist notion of ideology, I acknowledged that dominant ideologies were linked to the interests and worldview of capitalism, and to the emergence of the modern state to reproduce the conditions needed for the maintenance of capitalism in terms of a sorted, docile workforce with individuals focused on a private world of consumption and pleasure. As I noted, this was close to what Foucault had in mind in his analysis of disciplinary discourse and power. The bulk of that chapter was a discussion of four ideologies and discourses of sexuality education: a *traditional* ideology of sexual sin and sickness; a *progressive* ideology of sexual adjustment and management of sexual "problems"; a *radical Freudian* ideology associated with Reich, Fromm, and Marcuse; and a *libertarian* ideology of individual sexual rights and freedoms (which I associated with Kinsey). While I invoked Foucault's first volume of *The History of Sexuality* in discussing these ideologies and discourses of sexuality, I used Foucault only incidentally, recognizing the importance of his recently published history of sexuality (Volume 1), but not quite sure yet what to make of it. Now I can question what "traditional" means when it is applied to both a religious discourse of sin and a modern, scientific, medical discourse of sickness. In fact, the word "traditional" needs to be questioned since it sets up such a simplistic opposition between "traditional" and "modern"—which was one of Foucault's central arguments. The word "progressive" is less problematic, for what was called progressive in much of the 20th century, and still is today, is a very normalizing discourse and practice, tied to the rise of the modern welfare state and its normalizing institutions (health, education, and welfare). At the same time, the word "progressive" has been appropriated by some quite radical democratic and socially reconstructive movements in the U.S. during this period, and I am concerned in this study with the possibility of a new progressivism that is no longer so normalizing and regulatory, so narrowly focused on the problem of managing subpopulations of "deviants" and lowering the social and economic costs of unwanted pregnancies and STDs. Foucault provides one approach to such a democratic progressivism, although he would insist (as I do) that this word "progress" be interrogated and deconstructed if we are to use it still, given that democratic progress is not guaranteed and that cultural development is not leading to some utopian end of history in which everyone is liberated and *eros* no longer disciplined and bound. This approach to a revolutionary, "liberated" sexuality I associated with the "radical Freudian" discourse, and I follow Foucault's critique of this notion of a "liberated" sexuality as utopian and still working within the reigning leftist binary of oppressive–liberated. But poststructuralists working in the Freudian tradition, particularly Lacan, have overcome some of these limitations that are so evident in the work of Marcuse, for example. So this tradition remains important in the articulation of a new democratic progressive voice on sexuality education. A fourth discourse or ideology I labeled "libertarian," and this still seems to me to add something useful to the mix, even if it is based on a notion of the individual as an autonomous, rational decision maker that needs to be rejected. It does provide some basis for articulating a discourse of sexual rights, including the right of citizens to sexual privacy in the face of governmental intrusion on their privacy (the basis for Supreme Court decisions striking down sodomy laws and antiabortion laws).

The other chapter in *Sexuality and the Curriculum* informed by a reading of Foucault's work was by Lynn Phillips and Michelle Fine. The latter of these two was well known in the field of curriculum studies as the author of a much cited *Harvard Education Review* article in 1988 in which she used the poststructural notion of discourse, and also Foucault's idea that discourse included "silences"—what could not be said, or even thought—and that these silences were every bit as much a part of discourse as that which could be said. Foucault understood censorship as a technology of disciplinary power, associated, for example, with a cataloging of words students were forbidden to say in school. Fine's point was that this "missing discourse," what could not be said, included a discourse of female sexual desire in any positive or self-affirming sense. Instead, there was a discourse (for girls) of "sexuality as victimization."[27] Sexuality education had become little more, Fine maintained, than a technology to construct "normal" gendered bodies within highly unequal and even oppressive gender relations. In their chapter in *Sexuality and the Curriculum* Phillips and Fine wondered whether, in the age of abstinence-only education and an institutional climate of conservatism, educators were becoming "complicit in their own silencing" by constricting their language and the topics they allow themselves to address within the classroom. The sexuality curriculum severed a discussion of the "facts" of sex from any discussion of "gender politics, violence, heterosexism, and the economics of reproduction." It was a curriculum that maintained certain "sexual arrangements and practices as legitimate" (Foucault would say "normal"), and defined others in terms of categories of "Deviance, Disgust, and Disease" (the abnormal).[28] The newer perspectives on sexuality education associated with Foucault and his history of sexuality were just beginning to circulate in the early 1990s in texts such as *Sexuality and the Curriculum*. Throughout that decade, Foucault's work would become increasingly influential in curriculum studies, the cultural foundations of education, and an emerging interdisciplinary movement that crossed the borders of these two fields: the cultural studies of education. If is safe to say that Foucault's work had, by the beginning of the 21st century, reframed the teaching and study of sexuality, adolescence, and sexuality education in much of the academy—with one caveat. The first volume of his history of sexuality has been far more influential at this point than his second and third volumes, on care of the self. As I have already said, this is understandable, given that the first volume dealt with the modern era and is more directly applicable to the study of sexuality education in its dominant forms today. The implications of an emphasis on care of the self in sexuality education are also more subversive and unsettling than a reform of sexuality education in its existing form (such as through adoption of comprehensive sexuality education). Since the early 1990s, progressive reformers have fought for comprehensive sexuality education, while in the academy the groundwork was being laid for a radical rethinking of sexuality education, from the roots up, so to speak. Foucault's work would play a very important role in this rethinking. But his work would quickly begin to be interwoven with and taken up by a new generation of feminist, antiracist, and queer scholars and activists influenced by cultural studies and the poststructural turn in theorizing—a subject to which I now turn.

8

CULTURAL STUDIES AND THE SOCIAL CONSTRUCTION OF THE ADOLESCENT BODY

Aside from Foucault's *The History of Sexuality*, the single most influential book to unsettle thinking about sexuality in the liberal arts academy in the U.S. was Judith Butler's *Gender Trouble*, published in 1990. Butler was an American social theorist who drew heavily on Foucault, but also on a diverse group of other theorists to articulate a performance theory of gender. Over the past two decades this single book has produced a steady stream of scholarship, and a distinctive approach to pedagogy, that has profound implications in sexuality education. Foucault had argued that the "normal"–"abnormal" binary created or constructed the homosexual as the abnormal Other, identifiable and knowable in terms of disorders, diseases, developmental immaturity, and so on. The category "homosexual" thus serves to affirm the normality and dominance of the exclusive heterosexual. Butler, consistent with a long line of feminists from Beauvoir on, argued that much the same thing has applied to the category "woman." Gender categories, both masculine and feminine, have been produced by a patriarchal power that constructs the feminine as lacking in agency, as nurturing, as submissive, and as a sexual object under a masculine gaze. Gender had also been constructed or produced in a way that tied it back to sexuality, and more specifically to exclusive heterosexuality. A woman was a woman because she assumed a certain role in sexual relations with a man, and vice versa. The homosexual was the abnormal Other within this gendered truth game and only intelligible as either a feminized male or a masculinized female. The whole system worked and seemed "natural" so long as everyone agreed to play these expected roles. But homosexuals and women began to question the roles they were expected to play in the patriarchal truth game, and gender began to be decoupled from "sex." When gender was no longer defined in terms of a normative role in sexual relations (with masculinity and femininity expressed in their pure authentic forms in heterosexual intercourse, in "active" and "passive" roles), then the stability of the category "gender" was called into question. Butler does, in fact, suggest that gender is little if anything more than a regulative category, designed to establish relations of domination and submission; which implies that the emancipation of women (and homosexuals) will require "troubling" gender. In this regard, she saw transgendered and intersexual people as the new sexual revolutionaries, even more than the homosexual. How a culture responds to transgender and intersexual bodies and ambiguous and changing gender identities speaks volumes about both how it understands gender, and how much force it exerts to police gender norms and oppositions. Transgender identities and "gender bending" are thus not just of peripheral interest in sexuality education, Butler would say, but close to its very core. Butler, along with Foucault, would become known as "queer theorists," in that they queered or questioned all stable gender and sexual identities, particularly when these identities set up binary oppositions in which some were defined as normal and others defined as abnormal. But it is not necessary to do away with gender completely in order to see that Butler's analysis offers a new way of thinking of gender, as a performance, a stylization of the body, a presentation of self—which opens the possibility of gender being reperformed in ways that are more equitable and less exclusionary. Butler presented the possibility of a new pedagogy of reading the gendered body that was quickly taken up by cultural-studies scholars and educators.

In the 1990 preface to *Gender Trouble*, Butler explains that many feminists viewed debates over the meaning of gender as troublesome in that they "might eventually culminate in the failure of feminism." What would feminism be without some stable sense of what it is to be a woman? But Butler wonders whether the word "trouble" might take on a positive meaning. When she was a child she quickly learned, she wrote, that "to make trouble was ... something one should never do precisely because that would get one in trouble." If you made trouble, you would get in trouble. That is, one might conclude, the golden rule of schooling and sexuality education. For Butler, this "critical insight" led her to conclude that "trouble is inevitable and the task, how best to make it, what best way to be in it." Butler got into trouble with both liberal feminists and with male critical theorists. For the latter group, "trouble" occurred with the sudden "intrusion, the unanticipated agency, of a female 'object' who inexplicably returns the glance, reverses the gaze, and contests the place and authority of the masculine position."[1] But gender trouble, as Butler means it, is also "serious play," the kind represented in the John Waters movie *Female Trouble* (1974). In that movie, according to Butler, the character Divine (who appears in drag) "implicitly suggests that gender is a kind of persistent impersonation that passes as the real." The popularity of drag suggests a parodying of gender that brings into relief "the performative construction of an original and true sex."[2] In sketching out this nuanced meaning of "gender trouble" in a few paragraphs, Butler offers the framework for a complex performance theory of gender. Of course, what Butler had to say was "in the wind" already. The postmodern is a time in which popular culture has redefined reality, so that the image, the performance, is the new reality that real human bodies seek to imitate. Butler saw this as potentially quite insightful, and even useful from a democratic perspective. We are who we perform, she argued, so we had best be aware of whom we are performing, and how we might perform self differently. She wrote that "gender is the repeated stylization of the body, a set of repeated acts," but acts reiterated within a "regulatory frame." Over time, these reiterated performances of the gendered body "produce the appearance of substance."[3] But this substance has no reality apart from the performance, so that gender becomes something you *do* rather than something you *are*. It is a verb more than a noun, a "doing" instead of a "being," even if this doing is sometimes regulated by highly restrictive gender norms and sanctions.[4]

By the mid-1990s, a good deal of research was being published that explored how girls and young women learn to perform a "normal" feminine body. Much of this scholarship, like Butler's, spoke of the construction of the feminine body in a general or universalizable sense; that is, without acknowledging differences of racial and ethnic background, sexual orientation, or even class. In fact, these were studies by white, middle-class women, and, like many feminists in the 1980s and 1990s, what they had to say applied particularly to white, middle-class femininity. Its usefulness, I think, is not that it provides us with a general analysis of the construction of femininity in contemporary American culture, but that it suggests that even relatively privileged white girls and young women are victims of gender oppression in their own ways. Karen Martin, in her 1996 study of puberty, sexuality, and the body, observed that "differential experiences of puberty, along with first sexual experiences ... lead girls to feel more negatively about themselves than it does boys."[5] According to Martin, girls learn through schooling what lies ahead for them as women. They learn to feel "fat, dirty, ugly, objectified or ashamed of their bodies." Martin found that adolescent young women's first sexual experiences with adolescent young men tended to leave them "confused, unagentic, unpleasured, and unsure of themselves, their decisions, and their bodies."[6] Teenagers need to learn more from sex education than "just say no," or "beware of boys," she wrote. As examples of what this means in terms of curriculum, Martin offered only a few hints, but they were clearly in the direction of engaging popular culture and youth culture. Adolescents might be taught to "critique beauty standards portrayed in fashion magazines," she suggested, so that they become more aware of the "socially constructed nature of beauty" as well as consequences of gender oppression on young girls' and women's lives.[7] Joan Brumberg's book *The Body Project* (1997), the most popular of the Nineties books about the adolescent female body, was based on her years of experience teaching and advising young women in an Ivy League college.[9] She argued that the increase in anorexia nervosa and bulimia among her students in recent years was only an extreme example of something more widespread in American culture: the obsessive reworking of the feminine body to meet a norm of beauty established by a patriarchal culture industry. The body has become so central to definitions of feminine desirability that, as Blumberg observed, "psychologists sometimes use numerical scores of 'body esteem' and 'body satisfaction' to evaluate a girl's mental health."[9] One self-esteem test used in the 1990s, according to Blumberg, even asked adolescent young women to indicate how satisfied or dissatisfied they were with their own thighs and buttocks. Young women, she concluded, had become the object of an expert psychological gaze and medical technologies of body restructuring and reshaping, reinforcing the message of the fashion and media industries that the thinner you are the more desirable you are and the more you are "worth" as a person.

Women of color were also entering the conversation to racialize gendered sexualities. Particularly influential was Patricia Hill Collins. In *Black Feminist Thought* (1990), Collins showed how race has intersected with gender in constructing black femininity in the U.S. But she argued as well that class shaped the performance of a black femininity since, historically, black women have occupied one primary role within the economic and social order in the U.S.—subordinated child-care and service workers. According to Collins, this economic and social subordination has been maintained by circulating in popular culture certain highly coded "controlling images" of black femininity. By "controlling images" she meant popular-culture images of marginalized and subordinated groups designed to keep them in their place at the margins, and keep them controlled. These controlling images are thus always negative, although they may—as Collins suggested—be reappropriated by black women. To the extent that black women learn to construct and perform "controlling images" of themselves, they participate in their own control. So Collins proposed an education for young black women that is a history of controlling images, as well as counterimages of resistance and struggle. Collins' analysis emphasized the powerful role of sexuality, and, more particularly, "deviant" sexuality, in establishing controlling images of black femininity in the U.S., with roots that reached back to slavery. In the antebellum South, the mammy was the black woman as a fecund breeding stock of future property—and as a big-breasted and big-hipped mother figure, with babies at her breast and on her knees. This controlling image is both reinforced and subverted in some ways in popular cultural texts such as the movie *Big Momma's House*, in which the comedian Martin Lawrence dresses up as a "big momma" as an undercover FBI agent. Collins even saw aspects of the big momma in Oprah Winfrey, as a powerful black woman— although ironically, Oprah's battles to lose weight may be read as both an attempt to not become the stereotype white culture expects, and also an attempt to construct her body according to a white cultural norm. Even when black women perform the big momma as an image of self-assertion rather than control, Collins feared that they might not be able to completely disassociate this image and performance from its past. The mammy, Collins wrote, has been "shaped by the dominant group's efforts to harness black women's sexuality and fertility to a system of capitalist exploitation."[10] The image of the welfare mother in popular culture is for Collins only a variation on this image of the mammy as subordinated child-care worker and mother of future workers. She is kept dependent and in her place, under the stewardship of the state. This all points to the importance of a sexuality education that connects the past to what Foucault called a "history of the present."[11]

Collins also examined two other controlling images of black femininity that were even more overly sexualized than the images of the mammy and "welfare queen". These are the images of the Jezebel and "hoochie mamma". "Yesterday's Jezebel becomes today's 'hoochie,'" Collins wrote, "pornographic objects" and "sexualized animals" associated with a cluster of "deviant female sexualities."[12] In her next book, *Black Sexual Politics* (2005), she explored these images further by linking them to hip hop and rap. Early on, she argued, hip hop had provided a way of turning the gaze of power back on whiteness and racism, and affirming black power. But by the mid-1990s, she wrote, commercial hip hop and gangsta rap turned the gaze "back upon itself in fascinating and troubling ways, ... [a] sexist reverse gaze, a posture of cursing, crotch grabbing, 'in your face' spectacle that rejects middle-class discourses on Black respectability."[13] Of course, the rejection of middle-class norms of "respectability" could be quite radical if linked to a progressive gender and sexual politics. But Collins' point is well taken, that disconnected from a progressive politics, commercialized hip hop often serves to reproduce controlling images of black femininity. bell hooks, in her 1994 essay, "Misogyny, Sexism, and Gangsta Rap—Who Takes the Rap?" published in *Z Magazine*, took up a similar argument, this time in reference to a Snoop Dogg CD that was popular at the time.[14] It featured on its cover an image of a doghouse and a sign that said "beware of the dog." A naked black female was represented in the doghouse door, her butt sticking out. *Time* magazine, in a November 29, 1993, favorable review of the album, had even reproduced the cover image with no critical comment. This led bell hooks, in her critical essay, to wonder "if a naked white female body had been inside the doghouse" whether *Time* would have printed the cover. But the image does not make her think only, or even primarily, of the misogyny of young black males. Instead, she thinks about "the sexist and misogynist politics of the powerful white adult men and women (and folks of color) who helped produce and market this album." Rap in this commercialized, corporate form was not an "authentic" product of the lived experience of urban black males. In fact, gangsta rap's largest audience, she pointed out, was young white men, and artists like Snoop Dogg did not express their masculinity through their music so much as their "subjugation and humiliation by more powerful, less visible forces of patriarchal gangsterism."

Studies of young Latina women's body image and performance of gender have emphasized their struggles to affirm empowering identities in the face of controlling images in traditional Mexican culture, and controlling images of Anglo beauty in the U.S. A version of the mammy image, of an overweight, mother heavy with child, has kept Latina women in their place as well, although this image works to the advantage of Latina women as they get older. As Oliva Espin wrote in 1997, "middle-aged and elderly Hispanic women retain important roles in their families even after their sons and daughters are married"—as healers of mind and body. At the same time, Latina women "receive constant cultural messages that they should be submissive and subservient to males in order to be seen as 'good' women." The image of the Virgin Mary emphasizes self-renunciation. "To enjoy sexual pleasure," Espin wrote, "even in marriage, may indicate a lack of virtue."[15] This "good" mother and wife image is in tension with the controlling image in machismo culture of the Latina woman as a curvaceous sex object. This, in turn, is in conflict with controlling images in Anglo or white popular culture that emphasize a thin body image. Because the Latina body is constructed at the borders between traditional Mexican culture and postmodern American culture, Gloria Anzaldua has argued that the "guiding metaphor" of the new Chicana feminist is that of the body as *bocacalles*, constructed at the intersection of streets, always being reconstructed and assembled at the borderlands between cultural norms and traditions.[16] This borderline space thus becomes a third space, a *mestiza* space of relative openness in which young women might be able to perform gender in new and more liberatory ways. Chicana feminists have thus served as models for a new postmodern performance of gender that is able to play with controlling images without letting those images control them.

One of the problems with feminist studies of the gendered body as a sexual text is that women were doing all the talking; although that slowly began to change as well. By the early 1990s a new subfield of masculinity studies was coalescing around cultural-studies perspectives, and this time men would take responsibility for turning a critical gaze on themselves. As with some of the earlier feminist work on the performance of gender, the early work on masculinity studies in the late 1980s and early 1990s often overgeneralized about masculinity, without adequately accounting for cultural, ethnic, and racial differences. What masculinity studies did offer was a very useful way of differentiating between "hegemonic" and "counterhegemonic" performances of masculinity. R.W. Connell, working in Australia, is usually given credit with coining the term "hegemonic masculinities," which soon became a central, perhaps *the* central, conceptual category in the new field of masculinity studies.[17] Connell defined hegemonic masculinities as particular ways of embodying and performing masculine identity that secure and maintain the domination of elite males, not only over women, but also over other men. Implicit here is the idea that dominating forms of masculinity are hegemonic because they are largely taken for granted as "the way things are," or "natural." Heterosexual women may internalize a desire for a dominating, even abusive male, for example, or for a man who has power and wealth. And men may accept the notion that wealth and status go with dominating women (and other men) and having men and women serve, and service, them. Support for hegemonic masculinities consequently works to bring men together across their differences of sexual orientation or class background, and this is part of its power. Men are brought together, as Connell observed, around a project of "domination in the world gender order as a whole."[18]

Within this common project, hegemonic masculinities take on different styles and forms for different groups of men. One obvious class-based division is between men who are primarily mental workers (professionals, managers, administrators, and specialized experts) and those who are primarily manual workers (service and industrial workers and those engaged in physical labor). For the former group, masculine sexuality is not invested in the power of the body as such, but rather the body as dressed and performed around financial power or wealth, along with an aggressiveness associated with fighting to rise to the top of the organization. The sexual appeal of such a hegemonic masculinity, as Connell argued, is centered around the power of wealth, but also managing one's body and emotions along with money and women, and detaching oneself from traditional loyalties to firm, family, or nation. In the 1980s television series, *Family Ties*, the teenage son, Alex, sought to emulate this hegemonic masculinity, and in the cultural and political climate of the Reagan era, Alex is represented as having sexual capital with young women, even if he is not a "jock." In the movie *Wall Street* (1987), this type of hegemonic masculinity is both glorified and critiqued—which expresses the public's love–hate affair with this masculinity of greed and wealth, of "being on top" and sleeping your way to the top.

The star athlete represents an image of hegemonic masculinity that more young men can realistically aspire to, and do through participation in high school and college sports—with football stars at the top of the masculinity hierarchy. At the same time, becoming a star professional athlete is totally beyond what most young men can or should hope for, and thus this hegemonic image may, in a contradictory way, set up many inner-city youth for disempowerment. The male athlete is invested with the "physical capital" of sexual power, expressed through the size and shape of the body, speech, gait, and general deportment.[19] He is the image of a performance of masculinity that is both dominating and aggressive, and at the same time and simultaneously conforming or normalizing. In popular culture about high-school life, for example, the star athlete is most often paired up with the most popular girl (traditionally a cheer leader) who represents hegemonic femininity—the kind of teenager every good, respectable, middle-class and working-class family wants and hopes for, and the kind of young people school administrators can control for their purposes. Sexually, the male athlete represents an image of "good," "clean," "wholesome" sexuality, even if the reality may be something quite different. Even when the star athlete does not live up to the image of wholesome, family-oriented sexuality, his stature may rise among other men because he is a "lady's man." The recent media representation of Tiger Woods is a good case in point. The dominant media narrative of Tiger Woods was framed by the hegemonic image of the good, clean-cut, "family man" that he represented, and which had become his brand or trade mark for commercial exploitation. When the "real" Tiger Woods was revealed to be a "lady's man," he lost some of his marketing appeal because he could no longer represent the image he had. At the same time, his stature as a "lady's man" and a "bad boy" gained him a good deal of sympathy from men in particular for representing another form of hegemonic masculinity, one threatened by women's values and beliefs in monogamy. Of course, athleticism and the development of athletic talents, including participation in team sports, is not at issue here. Rather, it is a particular form of hegemonic masculinity that performs a sublimated, disciplined, family-oriented sexuality in public life and a "bad boy" masculinity in "private" life, thereby re-inscribing a public–private binary on the face of masculinity. The star athlete is the sexual athlete that other men hope to copy. If high school in particular offers some young men a space to act out this jock fantasy, it does little to prepare them for life beyond being a star quarterback on the football team. Yet, young men and boys, perhaps especially poor young men of color, cling to the belief that they have a future as professional players and never take their education seriously.

Hegemonic masculinities and sexualities also began to be framed in terms of intersectionality by the end of the Nineties; that is, in terms of the interplay between race, class, and sexual orientation in the performance of masculinity. In his history *The Gender of Racial Politics in America* (2001), William Pinar used the notion of hegemonic masculinities to interpret the construction of black and white masculinity in relation to a history of slavery and its legacy.[20] On the one hand, Pinar charted a long history of homoerotic desire between black and white men—expressed, for example, in the gaze of white men on black male bodies "from the auction blocks to basketball courts, from slave to professional athlete."[21] On the other hand, white hegemonic masculinity is organized around fear of the black body as a violent body, as a potential rapist—of white women to be sure, but also, Pinar makes clear, of themselves as white men. Here he explores a whole history of prison rape, particularly rape by black men of young white inmates—as an expression of rage and anger, and as a way of turning the tables on the white man. It is a way of reasserting black manhood in the face of the historic emasculation (literally and figuratively) of black males by hegemonic white masculinity. The hyperaggressive sexuality of black masculinity is thus constructed in relation to racial domination, so it is too simple (and part of the problem) to blame black men for their rage and their assertions of manhood, even if these assertions are often displaced.

In discussing prison rape, Pinar raised questions about the adequacy and stability of the straight–gay and heterosexual–homosexual binaries, arguing that this binary is in historic crisis as its contradictions and effects become clearer. Yet, what replaces this reigning binary, if it is in crisis, is not so clear. Pinar finds something like the ancient Roman form of hegemonic masculinity operating in some cultural and social spaces in the U.S., where manliness is associated with assuming a dominant sexual and social role—in either heterosexual or homosexual relations. Rape becomes an extension, then, of a hegemonic masculinity of domination in which the phallus is used like a sword to prove one's manhood.[22] This configuration of masculinity and sexuality is patriarchal and oppressive to women as well as to men defined as "passive." So simply disrupting the hetero–homo binary is not in itself antipatriarchal. At least it becomes possible, once we recognize the instability of this binary opposition in masculinity construction, to imagine other ways of performing masculinity that do not require domination of an objectified and passive Other. In the language of psychoanalytic theory, Pinar called for a reclaiming by men of those parts of themselves defined as "weak" that they have projected upon the female Other, but also the "effeminate" or gender-nonconforming male Other (whether heterosexual, homosexual, or bisexual). His hope was that "through such a self-restructuring a public political program supporting the democratization of society might follow."[23]

In calling into question the stability and adequacy of the hetero–homo binary, Pinar invoked "queer theory," a movement in cultural studies whose founding theorists are often identified as Foucault and Butler, although neither used the term "queer" in their work. The term "queer theory" was first used in a conference in gay and lesbian studies organized by Teresa de Lauretis at the University of California, Santa Cruz, in 1991, and de Lauretis acknowledged using the term as a tool to upset the perceived wisdom in the field of gay and lesbian studies—that each individual was, by nature, either gay or straight, a homosexual or a heterosexual.[24] She used the word "queer" in reference to a pregay-rights era when homosexuals were "queers," and sought to reappropriate some of the subversive meaning attached to that earlier usage, to proudly proclaim "we're here and we're queer," which also meant being a threat to heteronormative culture. Gays and lesbians were, by the 1990s, no longer threats, she argued, since they just wanted to be treated as "normal," with all the rights and respect "normal" people deserve. To be queer was to be subversive, and that meant calling into question the hetero–homo binary. In making this argument de Lauretis acknowledged the importance of Eve Sedgwick and her book *The Epistemology of the Closet* (1990). In the preface to the 2008 edition of that book, Sedgwick noted that she had not used the word "queer" in the book, and raised the question of what had been so queer about her thinking. "I would say," she replied, "it's exactly this resistance to treating homo/hetero sexual categorization—still so very volatile an act—as a done deal, a transparently empirical fact about any person." To do better justice to the complexity of human sexuality, she called on progressives to challenge, rather than take for granted, "impoverished abstractions that claim to define sexuality."[25] According to Sedgwick, the period from 1880 through 1980 was the age of the "homosexual," and also (by implication) the "heterosexual." There was, to be sure, a distinction between being "gay" as an affirming, assertive, "out" identity after the 1960s, and being a "homosexual," as a diagnostic, perhaps self-loathing, identity earlier in the century. Nevertheless, in the eyes of the dominant culture this distinction was often treated as minor.

Sedgwick recognized that so long as people were being defined as "gay" or "lesbian" by the dominant culture and through self-identification, it made sense for gays and lesbians to struggle for full equal rights as citizens. But so long as the hetero–homo binary remained intact, with "hetero" defined as normal, then "homo" would be stigmatized and "othered" no matter what effort was made to reclaim and rename a homo identity with pride. In order to get beyond the limited scope of battles for civil and human rights for sexual minorities, Sedgwick concluded that the hetero–homo binary would need to be further disrupted as logically "incoherent."[26]

However, this question of the logical incoherence of the hetero–homo binary may have to be postponed, she argued, until the historical possibilities of the fight for equal rights and recognition of sexual minorities has reached exhaustion. Sedgwick at least placed the queering of the hetero–homo binary upon the horizon of possibilities, as something that is becoming "thinkable" in the postmodern age. In Butler's terms, while the "politics of identification" organized around a civil-rights agenda for LGBTQ people is progressive, equally progressive and crucial is a politics of "*dis*identification" which radically calls into question the regulatory "norms" that produce sexual identity in terms of majority–minority, hetero–homo, normal–abnormal.[27] Are we moving in the direction of a postsexual identity culture? If we are, it is clear that we are also, and at the same time, in the age of the struggle for sexual "minorities" to be recognized as "normal."

Perhaps one indication that a "queering" of sexuality is occurring in American culture is the proliferation of names that describe sexual differences. For example, in the 1970s and 1980s there were two recognized categories of sexual otherness—gay and lesbian. By the 1990s a new acronym was entering public and professional discourse: GLBT or LGBT, to include, aside from lesbians and gay men, bisexuals, and transgendered or transsexual individuals. "Transgendered" was rapidly replacing "transsexual" as the preferred term, for it located identity not in the male or female body, but rather in consciousness, and in what gender people felt "inside." Transgender, more than transsexual, also implied the possibility of a more fluid gender identity, whereas transsexual often implied a switch from one gender identity to another, thus affirming the "normal" masculine–feminine binary. The beginning of a new century brought even more sexual difference out of the epistemological closet, through naming. LGBTQ includes those who self-identify as "queer," that is, as sexually different and living, to at least some degree, outside the binary oppositions of sexual identity with a more fluid sense of desire. Most recently the term LGBTQQIA has begun to appear in sexuality education, to include (along with queer), questioning, intersexual, and asexual youth. It is hard to say when the list will stop growing, although, at a certain point an acronym loses all coherent meaning if it gets too long. When this occurs, we might also begin to question if grouping so much difference together under one acronym or mark makes sense anymore, and also whether there isn't a contradiction in the idea that clear, distinct lines can be drawn between sexualities that are, as Freud would say, so polymorphously perverse. At the same time, and inconsistent with the "queering" of sexual identity, all these various differences being named are lumped together as sexual Others, in relation to the still unquestioned heterosexual norm that does not get named.

The cultural-studies movement in the academy provided a powerful new set of lenses that links sexuality education to the study of youth culture, popular culture, and the performance of identity and difference—in ways that are either empowering and self-affirming, and that encourage a sense of agency and control, or (conversely) that keep subordinated groups "in their place" at the margins, without a sense that they can affect change. Cultural studies also suggested taking youth culture and youth voices seriously, and helping young people think about how they construct a sense of self, according to which media images, with what consequences. In a sense, cultural-studies perspectives implied a pedagogy that was about consumer protection, helping young people to become more "savvy" about the stylized images of self, the performances of self, that they consume in a highly commercialized and commodified popular culture. Among the first to recognize the central importance of popular culture and the mass media as a "hidden curriculum" that could be brought into the classroom as a text, to be critiqued to show how it represented society and various groups in society, was Henry Giroux. At Miami University of Ohio in the mid-1980s, along with Peter McLaren and Richard Quantz, Giroux began developing the components of what they called "critical pedagogy." Through a new Center for Education and Cultural Studies, they and others began to work out the basic components of a new form of curriculum and pedagogy in which the curriculum text would be popular culture and the teachers' role was to guide students in a critical reading of popular-culture texts.

The first step in any critical reading of a Hollywood movie, television show, or music video, was to locate the text within a circuit of cultural production and consumption.[28] Students needed to ask: Who produced this text? Who is its intended audience? Knowing who produces popular-culture texts is essential, of course, since that is likely to influence the message or ideology embedded in the text. So too is knowing the target audience of a popular-culture text, since popular culture is engaged with that audience in constructing the postmodern self. The media offers us images that appeal to our desires, but in ways that can be objectified and commodified, and that are not threatening to the normative culture. Aside from this effort to situate popular-culture texts within a circuit of cultural production and consumption, critical pedagogy was about engaging young people in dialogue about what they had seen or read, and helping them recognize some of the "hidden" ideological messages and "hegemonic" narratives in popular-culture texts. The decoding of texts is, of course, an interpretive process, which inevitably raises questions as to which, if any, interpretations to favor. Subjectivists favored the idea of recognizing unique interpretations of texts by individual readers, based on their own specific experiences and interests. Poststructuralists favored the idea of deconstructing the "truth games" that operated in popular-culture texts that encouraged the viewer or reader to come to certain conclusions, certain "truths" about the problem of adolescent sexuality, for example. Those more influenced by critical theory argued that popular-culture texts could be decoded as ideological texts that represented the world according to the interests and worldview of dominant groups. Giroux, who came out of this critical theory tradition, had been heavily influenced by the work of Horkheimer, Adorno, and others on the ideological critique of the "culture industry."[29] This disagreement over the interpretive process, and what it meant to interpret a popular-culture text, was one of the ongoing tensions in critical pedagogy from the start, and is perhaps irresolvable. Furthermore, all three of these approaches to getting at the "truth" about a popular-culture text have value and may be integrated.

Giroux has provided his own readings of youth culture and popular culture, and is perhaps best known for his critical books and essays on Disney culture. But throughout all his work—and this can be said for the work of most others who identify with critical pedagogy—he does not forget that the media industry is, first and foremost, an industry, engaged in appropriating, packaging, and selling objectified and commodified images of gendered, raced, classed, and sexed bodies. This becomes an increasingly important concern in an age in which the myth of childhood innocence is being replaced by the myth of the sexual child and teenager, in which the exploitation of youthful sexuality generates big profits at the expense of young people. Giroux has addressed these concerns in a number of his essays, but in one essay in particular published in 1997—"Teenage Sexuality, Body Politics, and the Pedagogy of Display"—he took them up directly, in the context of a discussion of a 1995 Calvin Klein underwear advertising campaign.[30] The Calvin Klein commercials and images featured young models, posed in such a way, Giroux observed, that they "offer both sensual pleasure and the fantasy of sexual availability." Yet, in a departure from previous advertisements that featured "buffed," middle-class adolescents and young men and women in underwear, the new campaign, according to Giroux, presented a "romanticized vision of the dangerous and seedy world of desperate kids on the make." The images were of what appeared to be poor, powerless, urban youth, fresh off the streets, and, perhaps, hustlers willing to "negotiate their sexuality as the only currency they have to exchange." Interestingly, the target audience for these advertisements is not urban, working-class youth, but rather middle-class, "preppy" youth and adults, who are buying romanticized images of urban youth as sexually desirable and exotically promiscuous. "In the slick world of advertising," Giroux wrote, "teenage bodies are sought after for the exchange value they generate in marketing an adolescent sexuality. ... This may not be pornography, but it has little to do with civic virtue or responsibility." While the Calvin Klein advertisements were viewed by some as transgressive in that they disrupted the myth of youthful innocence, Giroux concluded that the images failed to challenge conservative representations of urban, working-class youth as "sexually decadent, drug crazed, pathological, and criminal." He also suggested that such advertisements were part of a culture of pedophilia encouraged by the media industry in which children and teenagers are presented as objects of sexual desire for adults. Giroux's words were prophetic, for in 1999, when Calvin Klein launched an advertisement campaign for children's underwear, it used photographs that depicted (separately) two young boys and two young girls playing in their underwear. Although a spokesperson for Calvin Klein claimed that the advertisements were intended "to capture the same warmth and spontaneity that you find in a family snapshot," a number of critics of the advertisements noted that they featured high-definition, sexualized images of young people, and the advertisements were quickly pulled from distribution in prominent newspapers and magazines, and from the huge billboard in Manhattan's Time Square.[31]

In his critical reading of these Madison Avenue "texts," Giroux acknowledges that he does not want to fall into the company of those on the conservative, religious right who are into protecting the myth of childhood innocence and banning anything that they consider pornographic. For him, it ultimately gets down to the motives behind the sexualization of young bodies, and the effects of the sexualization of young bodies. Pornography is produced to make a profit, and it does so by selling objectified and commodified sexuality, that even turns young people into objects of adult pedophilic desire. At the same time, what is and is not pornographic is sometimes hard to tell in an age when everything is sexualized and commodified. Furthermore, pornography is, to some extent at least, in the eye of the beholder. To many people, for example, the Calvin Klein advertisements were not pornographic texts anymore than the underwear advertisements in a Sears catalogue; and, as Freud recognized, children are sexual beings even if they may express their sexuality in ways different from adults. How far do we go in seeking to protect the myth of childhood and teenage innocence? When do images of youthful playfulness and intimacy cross over the line and become pornographic? These are complicated questions for which there are no easy answers. But at least critical pedagogy has provided a new set of tools to begin addressing them.

None of this shift in the academy toward new ways of studying and teaching about sexuality made much of an impact on the field of health education, and the subfield of sex education—at least not immediately. Health was an applied field, and in an academic environment still dominated by a great wall that divides applied from liberal arts and sciences faculties, cultural studies has been a movement of the liberal arts faculty. As situated on the theory side of the theory–practice divide, cultural studies has produced a discourse that is often quite abstract and theoretical, so that it has remained largely inaccessible to practitioners. There are signs, at the same time, that the once impermeable wall that divided theoretical and practitioner faculties in the university are beginning to erode somewhat, enough at least to open a crack where cultural studies can begin to intrude and grow in applied fields—including the fields of health and sex education. The beginning of the new century marked the launch of a new journal for professional health educators, titled simply enough, *Sex Education*. It was new and different in almost every way from conventional, mainstream health-education discourse, and it marked the establishment of a beachhead of sorts within the profession for an assault on much of what the profession had come to stand for. Sex education, even among progressives, still almost always referred back to the perennial "problem of the adolescent" and his or her volatile and dangerous sexuality. Progressives and conservatives supported variations on a common solution to this problem: encourage young people to be sexually abstinent as much as possible before entering into a long-term, monogamous relationship. Meanwhile, as these two sides fought over sex-education policy and practice, sex education in any form became increasingly marginalized in a curriculum more narrowly focused on the "basic skills," with no time in the school day for such "fads and frills" as health education and physical education. And meanwhile, young people were getting most of their sex education through youth culture and the popular-culture industry, and public schools were not helping young people become critical readers of the commodified images and performances of sexuality in popular culture.

The year 2001 represents, consequently, a rather dramatic discursive shift within the field, and a move to transcend its current limits. Sex education, the new journal proclaimed, should no longer be primarily or exclusively about these perennial problems and the "facts" associated with them. Sex education was becoming something else, and that something else had to do with an understanding of sexuality as constructed within a cultural context, and thus about much more than what sex educators often mean when they use the term "sexual relations" or "sex acts." It was becoming the study of how sexuality is embodied through the way people perform identity. The body itself becomes a sexual text, coded by race, gender, class, and sexual orientation. And since these identities reflect asymmetrical power relations, the sexualized body participates in a cultural politics. It either is constructed according to dominant or hegemonic power relations, or as a challenge and resistance to these power relations—or as some of both. The socially constructed body—the real adolescent body shaped within youth culture(s), and the virtual body as it is represented and performed in popular culture and media—is the new sexuality text from this perspective. And the hope is that through a critical media literacy, young people might be able to exercise more agency in resisting commodified and objectified, and abusive and dominating images of sexuality. This is a socially reconstructive project rather than a project of adjusting the adolescent to a given adult world. It is noteworthy that this new international *Sex Education* journal was based in the UK rather than the U.S., and that most of the articles were by authors from the Anglophile world—the UK, Canada, Australia, and New Zealand. There were also articles about sex education in former British colonies in Africa, Asia, and the Near East. But a few articles by U.S. authors were included from the beginning, and the journal has—over the course of a decade—helped introduce U.S. educators to cultural-studies perspectives that have been much more widely accepted and appreciated elsewhere. In an editorial at the beginning of the first issue, Michael Reiss wrote that the journal "will aim to contribute significantly to the practice of sex education (construed broadly) and to the thinking that underpins it."[32] The key words here are "construed broadly" and "thinking that underpins it." The journal would not presume that sex education takes place only in schools or in the family. Rather, it would welcome studies that "analyse the impacts of media" on sexual behaviors and attitudes. On the other hand, it would not welcome "medical and epidemiological papers," the kind that discussed trends in the incidences of STDs, for example. The focus on STDs and reproductive biology was the old sex education; and the journal did not want to replicate the problems with that narrowing of the field of study. But why, then, pick a name for the journal—*Sex Education*—that invoked for many people the language of an earlier era? Reiss wrote that "sexuality education is preferred by many as it addresses the psychological, social and moral aspects of human sexuality." The trouble was that in some countries "sexuality education" implied a focus on sexual orientation, which the journal did not mean to imply. There was no good title, Reiss concluded, since language always came with contradictions and a history of usage that could not be ignored. Still, by naming the journal *Sex Education*, the editors hoped that term might be "reclaimed from those who would seek to position it narrowly." The purpose of the journal was to "critically examine what is meant by sex education."[33]

The first issue of the journal led with an article on the construction of heterosexual masculinity in the classroom, in which the British authors pointed to evidence that male teachers often perpetuated misogynist and homophobic beliefs and attitudes that contributed to harassment and bullying in schools. This was followed by articles from New Zealand and Russia that examined the history of battles over sex education in those countries, along with a study of sexual abuse of children in Zimbabwean secondary schools. Not all these articles were framed with the lens of cultural studies, but they did all share a concern with understanding adolescent sexuality and sex education within specific cultural contexts. Sex educators could no longer speak universalistically, that is, as if certain general principles of good sex-education programs applied to everyone, everywhere, at all times. Furthermore, all the articles politicized sex education by recognizing that it played a part in either reproducing or resisting power relations that kept some subordinated. A 2003 special issue of the journal, titled "Embodied [by] Curriculum," was more explicitly influenced by cultural-studies perspectives. That issue began with an essay that set out to "conceive sex education as encompassing education for, against and about the sexes, 'sex,' sexualities and bodies." As such, sex education aims to "deconstruct and reconstruct understandings about bodies, and how bodies are inflected by and with cultures." This was a direct challenge to the medical, health, and biological discourses of sex education that failed to appreciate how the body was not just a biological given, but rather produced along with consciousness within a culture. To treat the body as a given, and the mind as the object of education, was to "perpetuate the Cartesian dichotomy between the mind and the body."[34] In fact, the authors argued, there was a whole "hidden curriculum" of the embodied per-formance of self in schools and in other public sites, so why not acknowledge this and make it an explicit part of the curriculum? Many of the articles in the special issue were by scholars working in physical education and health education, which are generally understood to be fields in which the focus is on the body, so in some ways the issue served to reinforce the mind–body dichotomy. What emerges, however, is an argument for more holistic approaches to education to help young people become more comfortable in their bodies and to encourage them to become more self-reflective about how they perform an embodied gender self.

The reader gets some hint of what this might mean in practice in the lead article titled "Embodied [By] Dance: Adolescent De/Constructions of Body, Sex and Gender in Physical Education." The author, Libby Blume, a professor of psychology and women's studies at the University of Detroit, presents what she calls a "critical dance pedagogy" that helps young people deconstruct performances of gender and develop an "embodied knowing." As an example, she offers the following curriculum guide for a dance unit in physical-education classes in high school. Students begin by dialoging and writing about the influence of media images on their own bodies, and then dance some of these images—including parody of the images. The author references Butler's argument in *Gender Trouble* that "practices of parody" can be used to deconstruct gender categories because they call the naturalness of gender into question. "A dance that embodies 'thinness' or 'beauty' can become a starting point for girls' and boys' discussions of gendered constructions of women's bodies." To counter a homophobic construction of masculinity that says males can't touch or show "emotional relatedness," the author suggests dyadic dance activities in which students switch between same-gender and opposite-gender dyads. Dance can also be used to create improvisations related to issues in young people's lives, such as "feeling pressure to have sex before one is ready." To dance such a feeling might involve "being pushed or pulled across the room by a partner, or by moving quickly or slowly." Or students might choreograph a dance about "dating violence."[35] In dialogue after the dance, students are encouraged to "notice their own comfort with movements and how they use their body to communicate feeling strong, powerful, vulnerable, and so on.

This is followed by an article by Kristen Luschen and Lesley Bogad, feminist educators from the U.S. They begin with a discussion of dress codes in public schools as regulatory practices designed to discipline gendered sexuality rather than actually repress it or hide it. Thus, cheerleader outfits and athletic uniforms sexualize the adolescent body in a way that is considered wholesome, while "belly skirts, body piercings, brightly colored hair or gender 'inappropriate' clothing" is considered a threat to normative performances of gender and sexuality.[36] The authors then shift to a discussion of teachers, who are expected to serve as role models of gender and sexual conformity. Even when they dress in gender-conforming ways, teachers may get into trouble when their students learn that they are not "normal" in their "private" lives. If the knowledge that a teacher is gay or lesbian, for example, moves out of the "private" realm and becomes "public," that becomes a threat to the image of the teacher as a "normal" heterosexual. Similarly (and here is where the authors offer a case study), transgendered teachers face the same consequences if they are "outed." They report the case of a teacher, Dana Rivers, who was dismissed from a high school near Sacramento, California, in 1999, when her students learned that she had formerly been a man. Here the issue was not whether she performed the role of a "normal" woman teacher. It was that her public performance was inconsistent with a private reality—that she was transgendered. Once the private became public, the public image of being "normal" could no longer be maintained, and the teacher was fired for no longer serving as a good role model for students. The authors call for a reappraisal of the view of children as innocent, and "in need of protection ... from all things sexual, and in particular from those things or people that dominantly are positioned as 'marginal,' 'not normal' or even 'harmful.'"[37] The authors conclude that the public–private dichotomy helps sustain an oppressive culture of heteronormativity in schools by legitimating the dismissal of teachers whose image as role models is tarnished when their private abnormalities are revealed. This, of course, is very similar to Sedgwick's argument about the "epistemology of the closet," that it is one of the primary mechanisms for the maintenance of heteronormativity—an epistemology that also found expression in the U.S. military's "don't ask, don't tell" policy.

Increasingly, the journal of *Sex Education* has followed the general trend in cultural studies to focus more attention on the media, and to engage young people in the critical (deconstructive) reading of media images of gendered, raced, classed, and sexed bodies. A special issue of the journal in 2006, which contained papers presented at an international sex education conference held at the Institute of Education, University of London, UK, in May 2005, announced the "reframing" of sex education around the category of "culture." The key organizing principles of culture, according to Judy Hemingway, who wrote the introductory essay, is the "production, circulation, and consumption" of images that enable sense to be made of the world.[38] Movie, print, television, and web-based communication, along with the formal structures of schooling, according to Hemingway, are all engaged in shaping sexual learning. Perhaps the best example of this reframing of sex education around media studies was an article in the issue written by Sharyn Pearce from Australia, involving a critical reading of the *American Pie* teen movie series. In mapping out a critical reading of the *American Pie* movies, Pearce invoked critical pedagogy and made reference to the work of Henry Giroux in particular. "As Henry Giroux has observed," she wrote, "film is a compelling mode and form of public pedagogy … that functions as a powerful teaching machine." Film uses "spectatorial pleasure" to shape young people's sense of self in relation to others.[39] What then was *American Pie* teaching? What pleasures was it inciting in adolescent spectators in the audience? These were the questions Pearce sought to address if not answer. The first *American Pie*, released in 1999, was one of the first global box office hits, which resulted in two sequels, released at two-year intervals. In the first movie, Jim Levenstein and his high-school buddies plot to lose their virginity (without much success); in the second they host a summer party in which all kinds of sexual escapades are acted out; and in the third movie in the series (*American Pie: The Wedding*, 2003), Jim gets married with a little help from his buddies. Pearce admits that after viewing the first movie in the series, she found much to like. It may be viewed, she wrote, as a "new millennium sex manual geared for new age boys," in which gross-out comedy is used to teach adolescent males new egalitarian mores, "and, most particularly, to redefine masculinity so that desire is not dependent on oppression, nor does it resort to aggression and misogyny to maintain its sense of coherence."[40] That is, behind all the gross-out sex and adolescent humor was a sexuality curriculum of equality that signaled a new willingness among young heterosexual males to play with role reversal, to even imagine sexual desire organized around being dominated by women, or even assume the "passive" role of being made the object of a female gaze.

But after a second viewing, and after placing the first movie within the context of the overall series of three movies, Pearce revises her analysis. Although the movies are "coated with a thin sheen of permissive sex gags and gross humour," they end up promoting "traditional family values." For example, the movies endorse mono- gamy, the protagonist is a "one-girl guy," and by the third movie in the series Jim is growing up—graduating from college and getting a job—and this means "settling down" to a rather traditional marriage and future family life. Stifler is left to perform the role of a developmentally immature masculinity, who has (by mistake) sex with Jim's grandmother in a dark closet, and who upon learning the truth, comments "Hey pussy's pussy, isn't it?" But even Stifler, we are led to believe, will one day settle down, get married, and adopt family values. Pearce is left to wonder whether all the grossness and sexual humiliation in the third movie is now there to reinforce "the increasingly reactionary 'take' on married life and neoconservative values that the film seems to be espousing."[41] The *American Pie* movies are about privileged, white, male heterosexuals, who Hollywood traditionally has liked to represent as "normal" and even "typical" Americans. Homosexuals are noticeably absent, as are people of color and working-class folk in general. Ironically, Hollywood markets coming-of-age stories about privileged, white, heterosexual, American males to a global market as generalized stories of youth and growing up that everyone can relate and aspire to.

A recent sexuality-education instructional video produced by the progressive Media Education Foundation, titled *Teen Sexuality in a Culture of Confusion* (2008), offers one glimpse of what a cultural-studies sexuality education might look like for adolescents. The multicultural video begins with a comment by a white, adolescent male: "I express my sexuality even though I've never had sex." This is a telling comment, and one the entire movie will revolve around. There is "sex," which is the domain of health and biology education, and which deals with the so-called "mechanics" and "plumbing" of sex—the reproductive organs and their functions, and also sexual diseases and disorders. Then there is "sexuality," which is expressed through the body and is related to our performance of gender, along with race, class, and sexual orientation—among other things. Sexuality is culturally produced, it has emerged and evolved historically, and it is part of who we are in relation to others. In the video, Susan Douglas, a professor of media studies at the University of Michigan, comments that adolescent sexuality "expresses itself in virtually every physical way—in the way you walk, in the way you talk, in how you dress, in what you do, and how you act." The point the movie makes, by interspersing comments by cultural-studies critics with comments by young people, is that far too many adolescents consume uncritically commercialized images of adolescent sexuality in movies, television, video games, and music. The diverse group of young people interviewed in the movie speak to the power of these controlling images of sexuality and gender in their own lives, and of their attempts to take back control of their own bodies and lives. Susan Bordo, a feminist scholar remarks in the movie that, "popular culture … has a profound influence on teenagers' sexuality. That's where they get their ideas about what is attractive, what's feminine, what's masculine, what's cool, what's sexy, what's romantic." People no longer learn primarily through verbal instruction, Bordo argued, "but through pictures and images, which get directly at fantasy and desire."[42]

New cultural-studies perspectives were beginning to reframe the kinds of question academics in the U.S. raised about the "problem" of adolescent sexuality by the mid-Nineties. It was now possible to understand dominant discourses and practices of sexuality education as disciplinary, regulatory, and surveillance technologies designed to produce the "normal" adolescent, performing gendered sexuality within prescribed norms. Cultural studies also helped reveal how various marginalized Others in America have been represented according to "controlling images" of abnormality, deficiency, immorality, and sexual deviancy. The "problem" of ado-lescent sexuality was finally beginning to be a bracketed problem. That is, it was no longer an unquestioned problem, one that was simply taken for granted as a pro-blem. Rather it was understood to be a socially constructed problem that could not be separated from battles over equity, freedom, and social justice. If there was a problem, perhaps it was the socially constructed category of adolescence itself, a time when the young presumably needed special guidance and surveillance in order to ensure they successfully made it to a "normal" adulthood—usually associated with heterosexual marriage after high school or college. Foucault's work pointed toward a rethinking of a democratic sexuality ethic as an ethic of care of the self, with young people taught how to ensure their own needs are met (for example, a need for safety and protection through use of condoms), how to establish a balance in their lives in which sexuality is neither an obsession nor an absence, and how to ensure they do not enter into relationships of exploitation or domination. The cultural-studies shift thus provided a basis for a new democratic ethic that had the power to challenge the moral discourse of the religious right. Finally, cultural studies provided a new pedagogy of sexuality education organized around the idea of media literacy—learning to critically decode popular-culture texts and to critically reflect on the performance of sexuality and identity.

9

CONCLUSION

Much has changed in American attitudes toward sexuality and the sexuality of young people since 1950, yet the "problem" of adolescent sexuality hasn't been solved or resolved. As I have argued, problems such as this one are not really solvable, nor meant to be solved. Rather, they are designed first of all to define something as a problem. Throughout much of Western history since the Greeks, the problem of adolescent sexuality didn't exist because adolescents didn't exist. People in their teenage years assumed adult responsibilities and roles, including marriage and child rearing. Adolescence begins (historically) with the advent of mass secondary schooling, and perhaps the two cannot be fully separated. High schools are places designed to control, channel, discipline, and sublimate adolescent sexual desire, and to delay the onset of sexual relations until after secondary education and marriage. That hasn't changed much since 1950, even if marriage is now understood a bit more broadly in American culture—even up to the point of legitimating and valorizing same-sex marriage. The broadening of the definition of marriage is important, as is the recognition that it is no longer possible to speak of a "normal" family as health educators did in the 1950s. But it still restricts sexuality in ways that actively deny or discourage all forms of sexuality outside marriage and family life. Probably the most significant change during this study period was the emergence of alternative discourses for thinking and talking about adolescent sexuality in popular culture and, to a lesser extent, among professional educators. Even if much of the mainstream sexuality-education discourse continues its rather narrow focus on the problem of teenage pregnancy and unwed teenage mothers, the problem of STDs including HIV/AIDS, and "life adjustment" to expected gender roles, American culture today is characterized by the existence of more counterspaces and discourses than were around in the 1950s. And as mainstream sexuality education has continued to decline, these counterspaces and discourses have grown. Together, they provide new sets of conceptual lenses and new ways of "thinking" sexuality education associated with what I have called "cultural studies." At least it is possible to imagine, perched at the beginning of a new century, that the education of *eros,* as Marcuse hoped it would, might someday help build a less repressive society; and, as Foucault hoped, a less disciplinary and normalizing society. A truly democratic sexuality education would teach young people an ethic of care of the self and others, and it would engage them in a critical, deconstructive reading of sexuality and identity in popular culture.

Mainstream sexuality education continues to be most closely identified with the field of "family-life" education, a movement that emerged in the early 1960s, although one might say it was conceived out of the "life-adjustment" movement of the 1950s and carried on its themes. More than other discourses and movements in sexuality education, family-life education has stayed focused on the "normal" heterosexual family and family life as the developmentally appropriate destination of adolescence. In 1993, the two-volume *Handbook of Family Life Education* ignored homosexuality and lesbian and gay youth almost entirely, and this, no doubt, had to do with a taken-for-granted opposition between "family life" and "the gay lifestyle." Family-life educators ignored queer youth and alternatives to marriage because they presumably had little to do with family life. Coauthors of one chapter in the 1993 *Handbook of Family Life Education* argued that during adolescence "a small percentage" of young people might have "homosexual experiences," but added, reassuringly, that "most Americans marry, and of those who divorce, most remarry."[1] This legitimates a focus on the "majority" of youth who are expected to be on a "normal" path of development toward heterosexual marriage. What was new in the 1993 *Handbook of Family Life Education,* compared to an earlier time, was the inclusion of a few critical voices, particularly influenced by early feminist theories of gender. In a chapter titled "Gender Issues: A Feminist Perspective," Margaret Bubolz and Patrick McKenry find much that they like in the 1970s feminist notion of androgyny, which they argue could be liberating for young men as well as young women. Yet they critique the androgyny literature from a social-constructionist standpoint for naturalizing the categories of masculinity and femininity. The androgynous self is understood to be a mixture of masculine and feminine, yin and yang, but both are still understood as naturally given opposites, with fully functioning individuals able to integrate both masculine and feminine traits. Instead, they call for an understanding of gender that is social constructionist—although their suggested remedy seems naive. They call for a form of family-life sexuality education that "degenderizes," that is, socializes, both males and females in similar ways "so that exaggerated traditional masculine and feminine traits are no longer relevant," so that gender is removed from any preconceived "cultural correlates."[2] This, of course, is an impossible task since gender is a cultural construct, produced by culture. What is possible, however, is to shift or change the cultural correlates. Instead, the authors argue—in a way that seems to reduce gender to anatomy—that the only natural meaning gender has is "anatomical differences and reproductive organs." By treating gender as sexual organs only, supposedly young people can be led to understanding that everything else we associate with gender is arbitrary. "Sexual scripting" more than sexual biology, they argue, creates the ways people think about what it means to be a man or a woman in a cultural context. This is insightful, and consistent with performance theories of gender in some ways, although, as Butler argued in *Gender Trouble*, to treat gender as having a natural basis in reproductive organs already straps it to a set of cultural expectations that are heteronormative and family based. The transgender movement began to change all that, but transgendered bodies are not acknowledged as a possibility yet in the 1993 *Handbook of Family Life Education*. Nor is the possibility of same-sex marriages and families.

Over a decade later, in a 2007 volume on *Family Life Education: Working with Families Across the Life Span* by Lane Powell and Dawn Cassidy, little had changed—although the authors go out of their way to emphasize how much has changed in family-life sexuality education since the 1950s. Back then, the sexual climate was one of "silence, embarrassment, ignorance, and fear" and unwed teenage mothers were stigmatized as "bad girls." Now, according to the text, there is "openness about sexuality and access to good information," although this also has had the side effect of a "rise in teen pregnancies and sexually transmitted diseases."[3] If we are more open, that openness must be accompanied by a new concern that adolescents act responsibly, so that family-life sexuality education is even more important. In effect, the more progress made in fighting the early enemies of sexuality education (silence, embarrassment, ignorance, and fear) the more sexuality education is needed to fight the new enemies (promiscuity and risky behavior). The new family-life education also gets associated with providing more sexuality education for "neglected audiences and clienteles. ... Gay and lesbian couples and persons with physical disabilities are examples."[4] "Neglect" implies an inadvertent forgetting to notice or not paying sufficient attention to something, and certainly acknowledging this neglect is an important part of overcoming it. But the truth is that this neglect has been active, making invisible the sexuality of homosexuals and the disabled so as not to offend anyone, and to keep both at the margins and outside the norm. Both are constituted as abnormal groups, no longer to be neglected, but rather to receive an education targeted to their particular needs—"tailoring the message to the target audience."[5] Sex education gets represented as a product that needs to open up new niche markets if it is to succeed, in this case niche markets of abnormal Others that sex educators have traditionally neglected. As Foucault might say, no one is to be left outside the gaze of professional sex and family-life education anymore, and so this does not represent a movement beyond disciplinary and normalizing regimes in sexuality education so much as an intensification and specialization of "biopower," attaching itself to various subpopulations of sexual Others, no longer to make them "normal," but rather to manage their sexuality more effectively and efficiently as subpopulations on the margins.

Family-life education, with its emphasis on adjusting young people to their expected future roles in the "normal" family, initially seemed at odds with the scientific and fact-based perspective represented by SIECUS, which emphasized adolescents as responsible decision makers once they were given the "facts." However, as I indicated in Chapter 2, these two discourses of adolescent sexuality education began to coalesce and interweave by the late 1960s, and they have remained interwoven since. Powell and Cassidy, in their 2007 text on family-life education, argue that family-life educators share a common ground with SIECUS in advancing the idea that "[k]ids should be abstinent, but if they do have sex, they should always use condoms … [and] keep in mind that abstinence is the only means of preventing pregnancy and sexually transmitted diseases that is 100 percent effective."[6] This is the new credo of liberal and progressive sexuality and health educators, finding legislative and programmatic form in "abstinence-plus" and "comprehensive" sexuality education. While the differences between abstinence-only and abstinence-plus approaches are significant, both sides in the battle find common ground in support of abstinence as the best policy. Under President Obama and with a Democratic Congress, "comprehensive" and "abstinence-plus" approaches to sexuality education have received more policy-level support, but not at the expense of abstinence-only programs. In March, 2009, Congress passed the Responsible Education About Life (REAL) act, authorizing funds to public-school programs that provided "medically accurate, age appropriate" information about contraceptives to young people, with the stipulation that the programs had to teach that abstinence is the best and only certain way to avoid the risks of pregnancy and STDs. The acronym REAL implied that it was time to "get real" about adolescent sexuality, that it existed. And the word "responsible" implied that young people had to learn how to act responsibly, not putting themselves or others at risk, nor putting an undue burden on society for their "irresponsible" sexual behavior. These two themes—"getting real" about adolescent sexuality and promoting "responsible decision making" about sexual behavior are much better ways of framing the conversation about adolescent sexuality than beginning with "just say no." But "responsible" behavior is still defined largely in terms of delaying the onset of sexual relations and being abstinent until marriage. We need to do more than "get real" about the fact that most adolescents don't meet that standard or ideal. We need to stop holding it as a standard, stop viewing all deviations from the standard as problems. We need to begin with the assertion that adolescents have a right to a sexuality and a sex life, and this includes LGBTQ youth who get left out of the abstinence-plus discourse much as they have from the abstinence-only discourse on the basis that they are irrelevant to the primary problem at hand: teenage pregnancies.

If there is one controlling image to which the "problem" of adolescent sexuality has been attached—from the mid-20th century until today—it is that of the unwed welfare mother; and this has been a highly racialized and classed image.[7] The white middle class has rested its claims to privilege on its supposed self-discipline, on sexual responsibility rather than impulsivity. Much, consequently, has been invested in perpetuating the idea that the "problem" of unwed teenage mothers is (first of all) a problem primarily of the working class and poor—and even more particularly of urban, poor, black and Latina women, and (finally) that it is a problem of lack of self-discipline and impulsivity, of the inability to defer gratification and live by the "reality principle" instead of the "pleasure principle." In the Johnson administration, the Moynihan Report defined the problem as welfare dependency caused by a "dysfunctional" black family, and the remedy was for the black family to be rebuilt along the lines of the "normal" white, middle class, patriarchal family. In the Nixon era, the Rockefeller Commission on Population Growth reframed the problem slightly in terms of population control, in this case control of "dependent" populations to make sure their birthrates were kept in check (compared to the white middle class) and that public welfare costs to support them were kept low. In this guise, as I have argued, federal policy on sexuality education echoed the racial hygiene and eugenics movements of the early 20th century—with abortion recognized as an effective means of population control. This is certainly not the reason why women's groups fought for reproductive rights, or why the Supreme Court upheld such rights. But it does suggest that there is nothing inherently liberal or progressive about supporting abortion as a means of population control. In fact, such support can be a form of neofascism. By 1996, with the Welfare Reform Act, the problem of the unwed teenage welfare mother had not been reframed much, except that now the remedy was to be abstinence only. If we are entering an era of abstinence-plus sexuality education, the problem continues to be framed much as it has since the 1960s, and the ideology of blaming the victim continues unchecked in federal and state welfare policy. Because welfare dependency is the result of an economy that does not provide enough good jobs at livable wages, or day care for children, the problem of the welfare mother is an ongoing one in advanced capitalist societies, and it is best to understand state policy as an attempt to better manage and contain this problem than to resolve it through structural changes. To solve the problem would also require recognizing that the "normal" family is no longer the norm, and that single-parent and other nontraditional families are not inherently dysfunctional. But it has been easier and more convenient for those who control state policy to continue blaming the victim.

The case can be made that at least one "problem" of adolescent sexuality was resolved in the period since 1950—the problem of homosexuality and the homosexual. It was resolved, as I have argued, by no longer defining homosexuality as a disorder or social problem, and by reframing the problem as intolerance, narrow-mindedness, and bigotry, and, in more political terms, as homophobia and heteronormativity, the denial of full and equal rights, and social injustice and oppression. Throughout the 1950s and much of the 1960s, sex-education texts addressed homosexuality in a section on abnormal or dysfunctional sexuality, and often organized discussion around a series of questions. How can homosexuals be identified? What are the essential aspects of their disorder? Should "normal" young men and women avoid contact with known homosexuals? Does having one or more homosexual experiences make you a homosexual? These governing questions of the "problem" of the homosexual and homosexuality were endlessly debated among health and family-life educators, as I indicated in Chapter 4. All agreed, however, that homosexuality and homosexuals were a problem. If young people were exposed to known homosexuals, it could somehow influence their own sexual development in a homosexual direction. All this ended rather abruptly in the first few years of the 1970s with the declassification of homosexuality as a disorder by the American Psychological Association and American Psychiatric Association. By the late 1970s, sexuality-education discourse pretty well had made the switch to viewing homosexuality as a normal human sexual response, and homosexuals as normally happy and well-adjusted. The homosexual, the great symbol of the sexual pervert, deviant, and neurotic, became normalized in the Seventies, rerepresented as normal. Of course, this came at a price. To become normal has been to become no longer threatening to the dominant culture, to assimilate into its symbolic order. Certainly same-sex marriage may be supported not as a civil-rights issue but as the logical extension of this normalization of queerness by bringing it within the realm of the same, the realm of the intelligible.

By the late 1970s and early 1980s the road to the normalization of the homosexual and homosexuality in sexuality-education discourse was not yet complete, although some who supported the "old" interpretation of homosexuality as a disorder were still holding out. In a 1981 article in *Educational Leadership* by a sex-education teacher from New Jersey, the author writes that students may raise a number of important questions that need to be discussed openly and frankly, including: "How can you know when it [homosexual behavior] is normal and when it's an early sign of complete homosexuality?" Normal homosexuality is developmentally appropriate, "complete" homosexuality is not; and complete homosexuality is understood to be a perversion of a normal homosexuality. The failure to develop out of homosexuality is thus constituted as "abnormal," and here abnormal references "dysfunctional" more than "not the norm." This is really only a recycling of distinctions that undergirded sex education in the 1950s, that suggested the need to intervene in ways that discouraged "normal" adolescent homosexuality from becoming "complete" and thus "abnormal." In 1990, in a letter to the editor in *Educational Leadership*, a professor wrote that he was "shocked" and "dumbfounded" to read a supportive article in the journal about a resolution by the Association for Supervision and Curriculum Development (ASCD) calling for curriculum materials and programs on gays and lesbians and the equitable treatment of students who are homosexual or bisexual in all school programs. "In the schools and media," he wrote, "we actively promote the dangers of drug use. We should do no less when it comes to … tolerance for or passivity about adolescent sexual orientation or activity." To do so, the author suggested, could lead to "physical, emotional, and psychological harm—or even death."[8] This was the dying gasp of an older generation of sex and health educators who had learned the conventional wisdom of the 1950s and 1960s, and who were unable or unwilling to make the discursive shift to seeing homosexuality and homosexuals as "normal." This generation was given a space to be "shocked" and "dumbfounded"—in letters to the editors of professional journals. But very soon even such space would disappear, as the "problem" of homosexuality was reframed as the problem of homophobia.

Homophobia as a signifier shifted the problem to those who were bigoted against homosexuality and homosexuals, like the author of the letter in *Educational Leadership* in 1990. The term "homophobia" did not originate in professional discourse, but rather in the alternative media. The first print use of the word is attributed to a May 1969 issue of *Screw* magazine, where it was used to refer to the fear among "straight" men of being taken for gay.[9] By the 1970s the term was beginning to slip into professional discourse, although it was not until the 1990s that it became part of the standard professional discourse of sexuality education. There it implied a psychological disorder associated with an unnecessary and unnatural fear and aversion of homosexuality and homosexuals. Again, it is worth noting how much the tables had been turned so that the one who had the disorder was no longer the homosexual, but rather the one who had a problem with homosexuals. The term also began to enter into professional educational discourse in social studies and language arts, where it implied a cultural as well as individual psychological phenomenon, something that had to be fought by critically examining homophobia within American cultural history, showing how it has been expressed in literature and popular culture, and taken for granted in everyday life. Sexuality, through sexual orientation, began to be understood in new ways that rupture the boundaries of sexuality education in its dominant form. In a 1994 article in *Phi Delta Kappan*, John Anderson defined homophobia as a "school climate" that adversely impacts on gay and lesbian students and teachers. By shifting the discourse to focus on the "school climate," the article makes another decisive shift. It suggests by "school climate" something similar to what Pierre Bourdieu meant by *habitus*, and Jacques Lacan meant by "symbolic order." Each of these terms refers in a general sense to the taken-for-granted background of our lives, the culturally specific beliefs and knowledge and rules of interaction that are symbolically represented and ritualized in our everyday lives in various institutional sites. The family is such a *habitus*, and so too is the school, and both need to be made the subject of deliberate inquiry and reflection in order to adequately address homophobia, along with racism and sexism. At the same time, this discursive shift to define the problem as homophobia, and to recognize that it is a problem that requires addressing the school *habitus* or "climate" is not a shift that has occurred at most local schools yet, where the discourse continues to be one of tolerance for, or active silence about, homosexuality and homophobia. As Anderson concluded in 1994, "Our schools are in denial, and our administrative staff is in the deepest depths of denial," and there is little reason to challenge this conclusion today.[10] If there has been change since the Nineties, it has come because schools are being held more accountable for not allowing "bullying" to go unchecked, and for taking proactive steps to institute antibullying programs. Health professionals have, in some cases, also developed programs to help address bullying and homophobia as a developmental problem. A 1989 article on "problem sexual behavior" in school-age children and youth by Beverly Biehr lists homophobia (along with child–child sexual intercourse and child–child sexual assault) as a problem related to a failure to successfully move out of preadolescence to adolescence, from a stage of uncritically accepting parents' views on gender and sexual roles to a stage of being open to critically assessing those views and considering others. This would help those afflicted with homophobia, along with those they bully, according to Biehr, since one of the psychological costs of homophobia "is the young boys and girls who will never pursue an inner interest or talent for fear of being labeled 'tomboy' or 'sissy.'"[11] Campaigns against bullying thus provide a platform to address hegemonic masculinity that is potentially quite radical and far-reaching in its implication for reconstructing the gendered and sexed *habitus* of schooling, but even this remains an unrealized potential. So too does the promise of a queering of sexuality education that deconstructs sexual identity and gender binaries and recognizes sexuality and gender identity as more fluid and polymorphous than stable and fixed. Still, it seems likely that the future will be queer, at least in relation to the understanding of sexual identity that prevails in America today. The ever-expanding list of sexual Others in America—which by now is represented in the label LGBTQQIA (lesbian, gay male, bisexual, transgendered, queer, questioning, intersexual, and allies or asexual), seems to rupture any idea that sexual identity and difference can be neatly contained within hetero–homo, straight–gay binaries. Young people are beginning to imagine, and even demand, the right to live outside narrowly defined, oppositional categories of identity, even if we still live in an age of identity politics—whose project of rights, equity, and justice remains unfinished.

By the mid-1990s, the AIDS epidemic was still unchecked, and the only hope to stop the spread of the virus was through education. A decade of AIDS education in public schools had been organized around the assumption that young people needed factual information about the spread of the virus and how they could protect themselves so that they could make responsible choices—what we might call the SIECUS approach. As usual, there was evidence that young people did know more about how to protect themselves from HIV/AIDS after an AIDS education unit or workshop. But there was little or no evidence that this information affected their behavior. Many adolescents, especially young women, reported engaging in unsafe sexual behavior, even when they knew it was unsafe, because they lacked a sense of control over their own sexuality and bodies. The AIDS epidemic revealed the inadequacy of an information-driven, fact-based education, at least in dealing with something so complex and "irrational" as the education of *eros*. The only somewhat effective discourse and practice of AIDS education to emerge out of this period, as I indicated in Chapter 4, was community based, and developed by persons with AIDS. A 1996 text, *AIDS Education: Reaching Diverse Populations*, edited by Melinda Moore and Martin Forst, documented what had been learned from over a decade of community-based, activist-oriented movements and programs. The volume was published just before the introduction of protease inhibitors that proved effective in controlling the progression of the disease, at a time when, according to the editors, health educators were "increasingly pessimistic" about the development of either a treatment for the disease or a vaccine, and that "changing behaviors, particularly sexual behaviors that often have a deeply embedded cultural base, is a monumental task." Even the most effective community-based programs were not stopping the epidemic from "settling into spatially and socially isolated groups."[12] In the face of this catastrophe, the editors call for a redoubling of efforts at education, and "targeting" education initiatives at those "communities" most at risk (urban gay men, poor black and Latino/a communities, and intravenous drug users). The primary lesson to be learned from the most effective community-based AIDS education in changing people's behavior was that education had to take into account the "culture and social context of those at risk," and use the "cultural language" specific to that community. At the same time, AIDS educators needed to emphasize that "groups, particularly ethnic groups, should not be viewed as risk categories in and of themselves."[13] This tension between recognizing the necessary importance of identity and community in AIDS education, and at the same time recognizing that it is behaviors not group identity that puts people at risk, runs throughout the 1996 text, and is perhaps not resolvable or even in need of being resolved. It points to the need for a sexuality education that recognizes the importance of identity and community, and also troubles or unsettles the meaning of these terms as stable, unified markers of sexual behavior.

Gay Men's Health Crisis (GMHC) had, by the mid-1990s, assumed the status of an exemplary community-based program, intended to influence gay men to adopt safe-sex practices. In the first major chapter in *AIDS Education: Reaching Diverse Populations*, James Holmes and Steven Humes documented the successes of the GMHC model, and the techniques of "experiential workshops" and support groups. GMHC staff assumed (based on some solid evidence) that unsafe sexual behavior was related less to a lack of information on how to practice safe sex, than to "feelings of grief and loss, low self-esteem, societal homophobia, hopelessness about the future, survivor guilt, a tenuous connection to the gay community, and feelings of inevitability about contracting HIV."[14] Many men who came to GMHC had a negative view of themselves and their sexuality, so the first workshops in 1985 were designed to provide a space for participants to explore their feelings and attitudes in an environment where people could give and receive support for change, and where "sex-positive" attitudes could be encouraged and reinforced. Part of making the group workshops "sex positive" was the use of an erotic language of sexuality rather than a clinical, de-eroticized language—something that was called "eroticizing safer sex." The "cultural language" of sexuality of the men was used in dialogue, and dialogue centered around their own fears of sexuality, intimacy, their internalized homophobia, their anger, and their sense that AIDS could not be avoided. Slowly, within a support-group setting, "group norms could begin to be modified and mutual support for behavior change could develop."[15] Participants then began to express new needs beyond that of eroticizing safe sex, specifically the need to meet other men in nonsexual situations and learn how to "date" and even "court," and this led to workshops titled "Men Meeting Men." A third generation of workshops, beginning in 1992 and called "Keep it Up," helped participants "analyze barriers to safer sex and triggers for unsafe sex," such as alcohol and drugs, and how to negotiate sexual and intimacy needs in an open manner to protect themselves and their partners.[16] Holmes and Humes, however, do not offer up a story of success that is without qualification. They argue that the success of GMHC must be situated within the context of a second wave of HIV infection in gay communities across the nation, and thus the failure to stop the spread of HIV and AIDS. This failure was one of not examining the social construction of homosexuality, a failure to "consider the assumptions about the population for whom the program had been designed." That targeted audience consisted of "self-identified," "gay" and "bisexual" men, all of whom were supposedly characterized by a universalized gay sexuality and "cultural language." Yet GMHC emerged out of the context in order to serve a predominantly white, middle class, educated, gay community, which in reality represented only a small part of the group of self-identified gay men. It also failed to recognize the continuum of homosexual sexuality. The authors conclude that Kinsey had been right about homosexuality, that it was more polymorphous than people liked to acknowledge. Much homosexual at-risk behavior occurs among men who do not self-identify as gay, and who may even be married or in a sexual relationship with a woman. This helped explain the spread of AIDS in the black and Latino/a communities, where it was less acceptable to be "gay," and where men on the "down low" often spread the virus to their female partners. To seriously address the AIDS crisis, the fear of publicly acknowledging homosexual desires and behaviors will need to be addressed so that, as the authors say, men must develop a "willingness or ability to allow others to know about the private identity," to "come out" about homosexual desire and behavior, even if the labels "gay" or even "bisexual" may not be appealing.[17] For that to happen, of course, the immobilizing fear of homophobia must be acknowledged and overcome. The continuing spread of the HIV virus in communities of difference in the U.S. and the failure to check this spread, was, ironically, also related to the beginning of an era in which the progression toward the disease could be managed effectively by a new generation of protease inhibitors that began to dramatically reduce the death toll from AIDS in the U.S. by 1996. As public fear dissipated, the sense of crisis did as well, and with it federal monies for AIDS education—which had always been minimal.

In federal policy discourse, attention began to shift from managing AIDS within domestic subpopulations to larger concerns having to do with managing transmission of the HIV virus as a global pandemic, impacting particularly upon the developing world. This pandemic was, in a sense, symbolic of the new interconnectedness and interdependency of people in an age of global travel and border crossings of all sorts. Unless checked, the pandemic threatened to undermine development efforts in the "developing" world. Just as unchecked population growth threatened development in many areas, declining population growth because of AIDS now threatened development in other areas, particularly sub-Saharan Africa. Furthermore, the health costs of managing the disease were a tremendous drain on resources in Africa, which also stunted development. Of course, development meant economic development first and foremost, integrating the developing world into a transnational capitalist economic order, but social development—rising levels of education and women moving into the workforce—were always linked to economic development. Two organizations have played a particularly influential role in this discourse of HIV/AIDS as a global pandemic and in reframing sexuality education as a global movement: the World Bank and the Population Council. John D. Rockefeller 3rd founded the Population Council in 1952 as an international, nonprofit, nongovernmental organization headquartered in New York City, and with a focus on global "reproductive health" through contraceptives and sex education. These concerns connected the Population Council to the early 20th century eugenics or racial-hygiene movement in the U.S., and Rockefeller appointed Frederick Osborn, president of the American Eugenics Society, to lead the council. By the late 1960s, when the eugenics movement was being discredited as racist, Osborn wrote that "[e]ugenic goals are most likely to be achieved under another name than eugenics."[18] The council's journal, *Population and Development Review*, links issues of population control to social and economic development in the Third World.

It is another one of those ironies of history that an organization with links to the eugenics movement and to the interests of global capitalism in population management in the "developing world" has initiated an HIV/AIDS education initiative that most progressives in the U.S. would heartily endorse. The Population Council determined early on through research in the developing world that gender attitudes needed to change in order to effectively stop the transmission of HIV. According to a 2007 Population Council report, evidence demonstrated that women who experienced sexual coercion were less likely to use condoms, more likely to report unintended pregnancies, more likely to have multiple sexual partners, and more likely to have the HIV virus. Conversely, "young women who believe they are entitled to pleasure from their partner have greater self-efficacy such as feeling confident in knowing how to use condoms or in discussing condom use" were least likely to have the virus. The implication, according to the report, was that a paradigm shift was needed in thinking about sexuality education, toward social-studies approaches "that foster the development of critical thinking skills and emphasize learning and reflection about the ways that gender, rights, and other aspects of social context … affect sexual experience." The report called for critical reflection on how "messages about masculinity lead boys and men to 'prove' their manhood and heterosexuality, including through sexual conquest and gender-based violence," and on how young women's economic circumstances make them vulnerable to "unprotected, coerced, and/or transactional sex."[19] This comes very close to cultural-studies approaches to sexuality education that I discussed in the last chapter, with their attention to the performance of gender within power relations, and to a pedagogy of critical reflection on the messages about gender young people receive in their everyday lives. Sexuality education, in the form of this globalizing discourse of social and economic development, thus challenges many cultural traditions around the world—including those that oppress women—and this raises questions that will no doubt be the subject of much discourse in the years to come. How is it possible to construct a global democratic discourse that respects and even celebrates cultural difference and also promotes gender equity and fights homophobia and heteronormativity?

In 2009, the Population Council published a much-heralded global curriculum "for a unified approach to sexuality, gender, HIV, and human-rights education," titled, *It's All One Curriculum*. That curriculum begins with a unit on human rights, which includes reproductive rights and a right to a sexuality education. According to the text, "these human rights are universal," applying to all regardless of sex, age, marital status, sexual identity or behavior, gender identity, race, ethnicity, national or social origin, political beliefs, citizenship, religious beliefs, social or economic status, where people live, physical and mental ability, and health status.[20] The text includes activities on critically reading popular media images of what it means to be a "real" man or woman, and on "speaking truth to power," where students practice speaking up for gender equality in relationships. One activity on "feeling different" includes a homework assignment in which students are asked to think about how a minority group ("people with disabilities, people of lower social castes, ethnic or racial minorities, immigrants, sexual minorities") is treated in their community, whether their rights are sometimes violated, and whether members of that group have ever stood up to defend their rights. The follow-up activity on "feeling attracted to someone of the same sex," provides three generic, universal stories of adolescents who realize they are homosexual, none of which is situated within a cultural context, but each of which is designed to help students "empathize with them, and to correct misinformation." Teachers are advised that "if the terms used here ('gay' and 'lesbian') have negative connotations in your context, use other terms that do not carry negative connotations."[21] Of course, given that these terms do not carry positive connotations in heteronormative Western culture, it begs the question of whether the same advice might be offered to teachers in the supposedly enlightened, developed world. Still, the real phenomenon here worthy of note is that the discourse of human rights, including reproductive rights, women's rights, and gay and lesbian rights, is being carried on the back of global capitalism in the developing world. Even as global capitalism organizes the developing world as the site of the new global working class, and thus participates in oppressing and exploiting Third World peoples, it brings with it the language of universal human rights, equality of opportunity, and toleration and respect for those who are mino-rities or different from the norm. Marx understood capitalism as an oppressive and exploitive system, but also one that undermined all traditions and irrational forms of bigotry and discrimination, including gender discrimination. This in no way means that global capitalism is primarily a force for democratic progress in the developing world today, only that it does open up some space for discourses of freedom, equity, and social justice in the face of traditional bigotries and commonsense beliefs.

The long battles that defined the era of sex education, battles between social and religious conservatives on the one hand and liberals and progressives on the other, have subsided in recent years if not totally disappeared. Several factors have contributed to this decline in conflict. As federal sex-education monies became tied to abstinence-only and abstinence-in-preparation-for-marriage curricula in the 1990s, those on the religious right could declare a victory of sorts. Their sexual ideology had been enshrined in state-policy discourse and local-school practice, and at the same time sex education was being stripped from the "basic skills" curriculum—which long had been their ultimate goal. A number of states did not apply for federal monies to support sex education in protest to the abstinence-only restrictions, and family-life education programs—where sex education was often taught—were cut in many districts. Health-education certification programs are also being eliminated, so the sex-education curriculum that remains is often delivered by biology or physical-education teachers, or by members of religious groups invited into the school. Then there is the fact that the public-school curriculum has, over the past several decades, been reorganized around "basic skills," related to the needs of workers in the new global economy. Those subjects that cannot justify their existence in these economically functional terms, and in terms of raising standardized test scores in the new basic skills of math, science, and literacy, have been placed on the chopping block. In a time of shrinking budgets and a curriculum tightly coupled to standardized testing, traditional forms of sex education haven't been able to compete. Finally, reducing the size and scope of sex-education programs has been one way of managing conflict, since almost any sex-education curriculum, no matter what it teaches or leaves out, is guaranteed to spark protests from parents and community groups. The result has been that sex education as a movement in health education, with its roots in the 1950s and 1960s, has become antiquated and in need of reconceptualization and reconstruction.

As sex education as a movement was reaching its discursive limits, new movements in the academy loosely organized around cultural studies have begun to offer a counterdiscourse to reframe sexuality education and the "problem" of adolescent sexuality around a study of youth culture, popular culture, media literacy, and identity. That is the movement I sought to describe and interpret in the last two chapters. It implies reterritorializing sexuality education within social studies, literature, and history; studying the "problem" of adolescent sexuality as socially constructed and dynamic; and analyzing and reflecting on media-industry images and performances of sexuality and identity. High-school youth culture is increasingly produced by youth in relation to the culture industry, and they bring this culture industry in their backpacks, so to speak, when they come to school. School is itself a major site for the production of adolescent identity as it provides a space where youth come together to engage in their "body projects." This culture-industry "curriculum" of sexuality education, which has been reterritorialized to public schooling, is now so pervasive that it begins to make what currently passes for sexuality education largely irrelevant. If popular culture is the new text which adolescents draw upon to construct a sexual self, sexuality education must become about media literacy. That is one of the major, unavoidable conclusions of this study. It is unavoidable in that almost everyone now understands that the role of the mass-media industry in shaping, narrating, and representing adolescent sexuality is hegemonic in the strong sense of that term. That is, the media industry produces and circulates commonsense images and narratives with strong appeal to adolescents, and, because they are commonsense, they go unquestioned and are taken for granted as the way things are. It is, at the same time, impossible to unplug adolescents from the virtual world of popular culture or youth culture, as if we could somehow return to a more "innocent" age. We can at least teach adolescents to be more critical consumers of popular culture—to know what they are buying with certain images of masculinity and femininity. Then we can engage them in using the new media technologies to produce their own narratives and images of sexuality and identity that counter and parody those produced by the media industry.

Ironically, the desublimation of *eros* that Marcuse had seen as a possibility as machines took over the disciplined, repressive work of production, and individuals and groups were freer to express their desires for freedom and expressivity, has come to pass—in a somewhat different form, however, and within the logic of capitalism. As the citizen laborer has given way to the citizen consumer, capitalism has shifted toward a less repressed form, one in which appeals are made to people's long repressed desires, and this includes sexual desires. This means that capitalism in its advanced forms has opened up some space to challenge "traditional" sexual norms and mores. At the same time, it attaches people's desires to commodities and objectified images they can buy and consume as substitutes for a more authentic expression of *eros*. Once *eros* is transformed into a desire to consume images and objects, then it can be made "productive" (profitable). It can be integrated within a consumer logic of "having fun" and sexually marketing the self. The hope of many political activists in the 1960s through the mid-1970s, influenced by Marcuse, was that the youthful "sexual revolution," along with "women's liberation" and "gay liberation" movements, would challenge the established social order in such a fundamental manner that it would lead to a cultural revolution. Indeed, something of a cultural revolution did occur. But it was a revolution that was kept under control, and even capitalized on, by the culture industry. Indeed, the media industry pushed sexual revolution further, but in a direction that was less politically subversive. Young people today grow up in a culture saturated by images and performances of sexuality that leaves little (or everything) to the imagination. "Sexting" (sending sexually explicit messages or photographs, usually between mobile phones) has become a growing phenomenon among young people over the past few years (and here it can be argued that they are only following the lead of political leaders). The news media gaze now intrudes into the sexual lives of all deemed newsworthy, and has the effect of turning politics into a game of sexual "scandal" in which an enormous amount of time is devoted to reporting the minute details of sexual acts and sexual texting (as in the recent case of former New York Congressman Anthony Weiner).[22]

All this hypersaturation of the popular-culture curriculum with sexual images and narratives, all this production of sexuality as hyperreal, all this stirring of sexual desire by the media industry in order to sell people objectified and commodified virtual sex, may not have the effect those on the religious right fear, namely an increase in adolescent sexual behavior. In fact, it may be having the opposite effect, of replacing the need for embodied, intimate sexuality with virtual sexuality. According to a 2007 Center for Disease Control report, high-school students in 2007 were less likely to be sexually active compared to high-school students in 1991. For example, the 2007 groups was 12 percent less likely to have had intercourse, and the percentage who had had sexual relations with four or more partners declined by 20 percent.[23] Some of this decline in sexual behavior with others is no doubt attributable to the fact that young people today are well aware of the dangers of sexual relations, so they are more likely to abstain, and when they do have sexual relations they use a condom. Condom use among high-school students was up 33 percent since 1991. But this very real fear of sexual relations with others has played into the virtual sexuality revolution, the shift toward practicing safe sex through sexting and other forms of self-porning.

Should any of this be considered a problem? In one sense, the shift toward virtual sexuality seems to fulfill the wish of sex educators that young people abstain (as much as possible) from "having sex," and find other means (masturbation) of meeting their sexual needs. It all gets down to how we define the problem of adolescent sexuality, in what cultural and political context. The shift toward virtual, disembodied sexuality, with young people consuming images and narratives produced by a highly commercialized media industry, or at best taking back control of the new technologies to produce and distribute their own sexual images and narratives, is disturbing if the problem of adolescent sexuality is the problem of learning how to negotiate relations with unique, embodied others—what we might call mind–body subjects of desire. This desire for intimacy and embodied love is the basic bond, the glue, that builds and sustains democratic culture as a way of life and an ethic of reciprocity and caring. To have this desire blocked is also a form of alienation, a sign of a society in which more and more people are "bowling alone," and "having sex" alone.[24] In the tradition of Hegel and Marx, alienation is the production of the sensuous life-world as a world of "things," objects standing apart from the individual, to be manipulated and consumed. If the problem of adolescent sexuality is understood to be alienation, then a different set of questions and responses are called for. One set of questions and possible responses historically has been provided by a radical Freudian tradition, a psychoanalytic discourse of sexual "liberation," "freedom," and "equity" as part of a broader cultural revolution to build the expressive society out of the shell of the repressive society. For Marcuse and others, the desublimation of *eros* was to be the driving force behind the revolution that would herald a new, liberated age, when people were finally free, individually and collectively, to realize their fuller potentials as creative, sensuous subjects of their own making. This tradition, as I have said, is utopian, and we now live in a postutopian age, for both good and bad. This utopian tradition of a sexual revolution that would spark a broader cultural revolution certainly had a powerful influence in the 1960s and 1970s in the U.S. among progressives and those on the political "new left," and it profoundly changed the way people understood sexuality and sexual politics. We are still living in a post-1960s era, by which I mean we are still consolidating and extending the discursive ground, the cultural terrain, established by the end of that decade. This suggests that utopianism and idealism have important strategic and pragmatic value in advancing democratic projects. The other side of utopianism, with its thesis of sexual liberation, is that it always established the meaning of sexual liberation in a reactive manner, by negating the sexual mores and norms of advanced, patriarchal, capitalist society. In recent years, psychoanalytic critical theorists such as Gilles Deleuze have argued that "reactive" politics is the politics of the "slave" who imagines and longs for a day when the master's disciplinary power and authority is cast off.[25] Such a politics, from this perspective, remains stuck in the need to define itself in reaction to its Other; and to this extent it can never achieve a final victory since it needs its Other to know itself. The alternative to disciplinary power, as Foucault would say, is not the lack of discipline, but a different kind of discipline of the self. A more radical democratic politics would need to get beyond the binary logic of sexual repression versus sexual liberation, to construct an active sexuality that is not merely reactive. This was Foucault's project as well in his history of sexuality, and he saw in the ancient Greek construction of sexual desire as *eros* the possibility of moving beyond merely reactive thinking and acting, to recognize desire as neither good nor bad, healthy nor unhealthy—a force that could heal and also potentially kill. *Eros* was a life force, a will to power, and thus the active force that drew people together in love and intimacy, and community. The Greeks also understood *eros* as a force that could lead people to nihilistic excess, obsessive desire, and a lust for power. *Eros* represented a desire that if unchecked, could even lead whole communities into a form of collective insanity, as in the *eros* that gripped the Greeks when they decided to go to war against a much larger and powerful Troy because of a collective obsession for Helen. *Eros* could also take the form of a lust for political power or wealth.[26] Consequently, it was never for the Greeks a question of liberating or freeing *eros*. As Foucault indicated, *eros* was not to be freed so much as educated in an ethic and a discipline of "care of the self," aimed at maintaining physical and psychic health and healthy relations with others. This might be considered an individual project, but it is also, in its most democratic forms, a collective public project of education as upbringing—or *paideia*—in which the young are "produced" as subjects of particular forms of democratic sexuality and desire, which also means as active subjects of their own desires.

NOTES

Introduction

1 For a history of early discourses in sexuality education, see Dennis Carlson, "Conflict and Change in the Discourse on Sexuality Education," *Educational Theory*, 41 (no. 4, 1991), 343–59.

2 Michel Foucault, *The History of Sexuality: An Introduction*, Vol. 1 (London: Penguin, 1998), 137–40.

3 See Dennis Carlson, "Gay, Queer, Cyborg: The Performance of Identity in a Transglobal Age," *Discourse: Studies in the Cultural Politics of Education*, 22 (no. 3, 2001), 297–309.

4 W.E.B. Dubois, *The Souls of Black Folk* (New York: Simon & Schuster, [1903], 2005). For a discussion of the social construction of adolescence and the adolescent as a "problem," see Bernadette Baker, *In Perpetual Motion* (New York: Peter Lang, 2001).

Chapter 1

1 Alfred Kinsey, *Sexual Behavior in the Human Male* (Philadelphia, PA: W.W. Saunders, 1948); and *Sexual Behavior in the Human Female* (Philadelphia, PA: W.W. Saunders, 1953).

2 Sigmund Freud, *Beyond the Pleasure Principle* (New York: W.W. Norton, 1961), first published in 1920; and *Civilization and Its Discontents* (New York: W.W. Norton, 1961), first published in 1930.

3 Freud, *Civilization and Its Discontents*, 124.

4 Freud, *Beyond the Pleasure Principle*, 4.

5 Freud, *Civilization and Its Discontents*, 36–37.

6 This is an idea more specifically developed by Anna Freud. See Elisabeth Young-Bruehl, *Anna Freud: A Biography, Second Edition* (New Haven, CT: Yale University Press, 2008).

7 Freud, *Civilization and Its Discontents*, 81.

8 Herbert Marcuse, *Eros and Civilization: A Philosophical Inquiry into Freud* (Boston, MA: Beacon Press, 1955), 5.

9 Marcuse, *Eros and Civilization*, 201.

10 Marcuse, *Eros and Civilization*, 208.

11 Kinsey, *Sexual Behavior in the Human Female*, 476.

12 Kinsey, *Sexual Behavior in the Human Female*, 511.

13 Kinsey, *Sexual Behavior in the Human Female*, 132.

14 Kinsey, *Sexual Behavior in the Human Female*, 167.

15 Kinsey, *Sexual Behavior in the Human Male*, 325.

16 Kinsey, *Sexual Behavior in the Human Male*, 651.

17 Ibid.

18 Clyde Kluckhohn, "The Complex Kinsey Study and What It Attempts to Do," *New York Times Book Review* (September 13, 1953), Book Review, 3ff.

19 Kluckhohn, "The Complex Kinsey Study and What It Attempts to Do," Book Review, 38.

20 William Cochran, Frederick Mosteller, & John Tukey. *Statistical Problems of the Kinsey Report on Sexual Behavior in the Human Male* (Washington, DC: American Statistical Association, 1954), 22.

21 See Miriam Reumann, *American Sexual Character: Sex, Gender, and National Identity in the Kinsey Reports* (Berkeley, CA: University of California Press, 2005); and Vern Bullough's review of Reumann's book in *Journal of Sex Research*, 44 (no. 2, 2007), 213–14.

22 "Postal Ban Urged on Kinsey's Book," *New York Times* (August 30, 1953), 78.

23 Erich Fromm, "Sex and Character: The Kinsey Report Viewed from the Standpoint of Psychoanalysis," in Jerome Himelhoch & Sylvia Fava (ed.), *Sexual Behavior in American Society* (New York: W.W. Norton, 1955), 301.

24 Fromm, "Sex and Character: The Kinsey Report Viewed from the Standpoint of Psychoanalysis," 305.

25 James Maddock, "Sexuality Education: A History Lesson," *Journal of Psychology and Human Sexuality*, 9 (no. 3/4, 1997), 1–22.

26 Quoted in Herbert Kliebard, *The Struggle for the American Curriculum, 1893–1958* (New York: RoutledgeFalmer, 2004).

27 Lester Kirkendall, "Sex Education," *NEA Journal* (December, 1951).

28 Child Study Association of America, *What to Tell Your Children About Sex*, (New York: Duell, Sloan & Pearce, 1954), v.

29 Child Study Association of America, *What to Tell Your Children About Sex*, x.

30 Child Study Association of America, *What to Tell Your Children About Sex*, 4.

31 Child Study Association of America, *What to Tell Your Children About Sex*, 81.

32 Child Study Association of America, *What to Tell Your Children About Sex*, 99.

33 Child Study Association of America, *What to Tell Your Children About Sex*, 95.

34 Child Study Association of America, *What to Tell Your Children About Sex*, 96–97.

35 Dorothy Baruch, *New Ways in Sex Education: A Guide for Parents and Teachers* (New York: McGraw-Hill, 1959), 24.

36 Baruch, *New Ways in Sex Education*, 219.

37 Edward Olsen, "A Curriculum Not for Celibates, *Phi Delta Kappan*, 34 (no. 6, 1953), 246–47.

38 Herbert Spencer, "What Knowledge Is of Most Worth?", *Westminster Review*, 72 (July, 1859); quoted in Olsen, 246.

39 Helen Manley, *A Curriculum Guide in Sex Education* (St Louis, MO: State Publishing Co., 1964), 7.

40 Manley, *A Curriculum Guide in Sex Education*, 41.

41 Manley, *A Curriculum Guide in Sex Education*, 61.

Chapter 2

1 Mary Calderone, "Sexual Behavior: Whose Responsibility," *Phi Delta Kappan*, 46 (no. 2, 1964), 71.

2 Calderone, "Sexual Behavior," 69. Quotes from Arnold Toynbee's *New York Times* essay are cited as they were quoted in Calderone.

3 Calderone, "Sexual Behavior," 71.
4 See Mary Breasted, *Oh! Sex Education!* (New York: Praeger, 1970), 233–34.
5 Ira Reiss, "Sex Education in the Public Schools: Problem or Solution?", *Phi Delta Kappan*, 50 (no. 1, 1968), 52.
6 Reiss, "Sex Education in the Public Schools: Problem or Solution?"
7 John Gagnon, "Content: Stereotypes Style: Castrated Freud," *Phi Delta Kappan*, 49 (no. 9, 1968), 542.
8 Lester Kirkendall, "Changing Sex Mores and Moral Instruction," *Phi Delta Kappan*, 46 (no. 2, 1964), 68.
9 Quoted in Breasted, *Oh! Sex Education!*, 112.
10 Breasted, *Oh! Sex Education!*, 34.
11 Breasted, *Oh! Sex Education!*, 110–11.
12 See Jeffrey Moran, *Teaching Sex: The Shaping of Adolescence in the 20th Century* (Cambridge, MA: Harvard University Press, 2000), 176.
13 Quoted in Breasted, *Oh! Sex Education!*, 33.
14 Quoted in Breasted, *Oh! Sex Education!*, 34.
15 This address before the 1969 Convention of the American School Health Association was published. See Gere Fulton, "Sex Education: Some Issues and Answers," *Journal of School Health*, (May, 1970), 263–68.
16 Fulton, "Sex Education: Some Issues and Answers," 263.
17 Birgitta Linner, *Sex and Society in Sweden* (New York: Pantheon, 1967).
18 Fulton, "Sex Education: Some Issues and Answers," 264.
19 Fulton, "Sex Education: Some Issues and Answers," 265.
20 Fulton, "Sex Education: Some Issues and Answers," 266.

Chapter 3

1 The Moynihan Report was republished in its entirety in Lee Rainwater & William Yancey, *The Moynihan Report and the Politics of Controversy* (Cambridge, MA: MIT Press, 1967), 39–124. Quotations cited from the report are from this source. Rainwater & Yancey also include a number of other documents that I cite, including: President Johnson's Howard University address, reactions to the report by civil-rights leaders, and reactions by scholars such as William Ryan & Charles Silberman.
2 *The Moynihan Report*, 51.
3 *The Moynihan Report*, 54–58.
4 William Ryan, *Blaming the Victim* (New York: Pantheon, 1971).
5 *The Moynihan Report*, 248.
6 *The Moynihan Report*, 252.
7 "An Address by Dr. Martin Luther King, Jr.," in Lee Rainwater & William Yancey, *The Moynihan Report and the Politics of Controversy*, 402–9.
8 James Farmer, "The Controversial Moynihan Report," is two articles that appeared in Farmer's column "The Core of It" on December 18 and 25, 1965. Farmer's articles are reprinted in Rainwater & Yancey, *The Moynihan Report and the Politics of Controversy*, 409–13.
9 Richard Nixon, "Special Message to the Congress on Problems of Population Growth," (July 18, 1969), The Nixon Foundation Library. Retrieved April 2, 2009. http://www.presidency.ucsb.edu/ws/index.php?pid=2132#axzz1Zr72s9iJ
10 Quoted in Constance Nathanson, *Dangerous Passage: The Social Control of Sexuality in Women's Adolescence* (Philadelphia, PA: Temple University Press, 1991), 23. See also *New York Times* (May 6, 1972, 1–5).
11 Susan Gustavus, "Commission Report: Implications for Women," *Social Science Quarterly*, 53 (no. 3, 1972), 473.

12 Gustavus, "Commission Report: Implications for Women," 470–71.

13 Gustavus, "Commission Report: Implications for Women," 473.

14 Ozzie Edwards, "The Commission Recommendations from the Standpoint of Minorities," *Social Science Quarterly*, 53 (no. 3, 1972), 465.

15 See Dennis Carlson, "Tales of Future Past: The Living Legacy of Eugenics in American Education," *Journal of the American Association for the Advancement of Curriculum Studies*, 5 (February, 2009), 1–10.

16 Edwards, "The Commission Recommendations from the Standpoint of Minorities," 467–68.

17 Arthur Dyck, "Ethical Assumptions and Implications of the Population Commission's Report," *Social Science Quarterly*, 53 (no. 3, 1972), 459–64.

18 Foucault developed the idea of "biopower" in a number of places in his later work. See Michel Foucault, *Security, Territory, Population: Lectures at the College de France 1977–1978* (New York: Palgrave Macmillan, 2009). For a discussion of biopower in the health field, see Robin Bunton & Alan Petersen (ed.), *Foucault, Health and Medicine* (New York: Routledge, 1997).

19 Martha Ward, "The Politics of Adolescent Pregnancy: Turf and Teens in Louisiana," in W. Penn Handwerker (ed.), *Births and Power: Social Change and the Politics of Reproduction* (San Francisco, CA: Boulder Press, 1989), 151.

20 Christopher Lasch, *The Culture of Narcissism: American Life in an Age of Diminishing Expectations* (New York: W.W. Norton, 1979).

21 Willard Richan, *Beyond Altruism: Social Welfare Policy in American Society* (New York: Haworth Press, 1988), 160.

22 Cited in Richan, *Beyond Altruism: Social Welfare Policy in American Society*, 161.

23 Richan, *Beyond Altruism: Social Welfare Policy in American Society*, 167–69.

24 See Linda Hendrixson, "Pregnant Children: A Socio-Educational Challenge," *Phi Delta Kappan* (May, 1979), 64.

25 Constance Nathanson, *Dangerous Passage: The Social Control of Sexuality in Women's Adolescence* (Philadelphia, PA: Temple University Press, 1991), 224.

26 Melvin Zelnick, John Kantner, & Kathleen Ford. *Sex and Pregnancy in Adolescence* (Beverly Hills, CA: Sage, 1981).

27 See Nadine Brozan, "More Teen-Agers Are Pregnant Despite Rise in Contraception," *New York Times* (March 12, 1981). Retrieved May 26, 2010. http://www.nytimes.com/1981/03/12/garden/more-teen-agers-are-pregnant-despite-rise-in-contraception.html?scp=1&sq=&st=nyt

28 John Burt & Linda Brower, *Education for Sexuality: Concepts and Programs for Teaching* (Philadelphia, PA: W.B. Saunders, 1970), 345.

29 Clint Bruess & Jerrold Greenberg, *Sex Education: Theory and Practice* (Belmont, CA: Wadsworth, 1981), 102.

30 Douglas Kirby & Judith Alter, "The Experts Rate Important Features and Outcomes of Sex Education Programs," *Journal of School Health* (November, 1980), 497.

Chapter 4

1 *New York Times*, "Word for Word: 'Deviates' and 'Inverts'," (April 12, 2009), WK3.

2 See David Brown (ed.), *The Hippies: By the Correspondents of Time* (New York: Time Incorporated, 1967), 4.

3 Frederick Kilander, *Sex Education in the Schools: A Study of Objectives, Content, Methods, Materials, and Evaluation* (Toronto: Macmillan, 1970), 4–5.

4 Kilander, *Sex Education in the Schools: A Study of Objectives, Content, Methods, Materials, and Evaluation*, 307–9.

5 John Burt & Linda Brower, *Education for Sexuality: Concepts and Programs for Teaching* (Philadelphia, PA: W.B. Saunders, 1970), 360.

6 Burt & Brower, *Education for Sexuality: Concepts and Programs for Teaching*, 361.

7 Burt & Brower, *Education for Sexuality: Concepts and Programs for Teaching*, 360.

8 Quoted in Gregory Kimble & Michael Wertheimer (ed.), *Portraits of Pioneers in Psychology*, Vol. 4 (New York: American Psychological Association, 2000), 263.

9 "Gay Is Okay with APA: Medical News & Perspectives—August 12, 1998 Forum Honors Landmark 1973 Events." Retrieved May 7, 2010. http://www.soulforce.org/article/642. This is a primary source for my discussion of the change in the American Psychiatric Association in the early 1970s, including quotes from Melvin Sabshin.

10 For an analysis of Bieber's role in opposition to the APA resolution to declassify homosexuality as a disorder, see "The A.P.A. Normalization of Homosexuality and the Research Study of Irving Bieber," National Association for Research and Therapy on Homosexuality. Retrieved May 7, 2010. http://www.narth.com/docs/normalization.html

11 Lloyd Campbell, "Sex Education: Let's Get On With It," *Phi Delta Kappan*, (December, 1973), 245.

12 Jack Megenity, Jean Megenity, & Barbara Barnum, "A Workshop in Human Sexuality for Parents," *Educational Leadership* (October, 1973), 26–29.

13 Clint Bruess & Jerrold Greenberg, *Sex Education: Theory and Practice* (Belmont, CA: Wadsworth, 1981), 172–73.

14 Bruess & Greenberg, *Sex Education: Theory and Practice*, 172.

15 Bruess & Greenberg, *Sex Education: Theory and Practice*, 8–9.

16 Thomas Szasz, *Sex By Prescription* (Garden City, NY: Anchor Press, 1980), 22.

17 Quote is from William Masters & Virginia Johnson, *Homosexuality in Perspective* (Boston, MA: Little Brown, 1979), 227. Quoted in Szasz, *Sex By Prescription*, 39.

18 Szasz, *Sex By Prescription*, 39.

19 Szasz, *Sex By Prescription*, 45.

20 Willard Waller, *The Sociology of Teaching* (New York: Wiley, 1965), 147–48.

21 Craig Rimmerman, *From Identity to Politics: The Lesbian and Gay Movements in the United States* (Philadelphia, PA: Temple University Press, 2001), 129–31.

22 "A Homosexual Teacher's Argument and Plea," *Phi Delta Kappan* (October, 1977), 93–94.

Chapter 5

1 Carol Reeves, *The Language of Science* (New York: Routledge, 2005), 16. See also Michael Scarce, *Medical Bias in the Health Care of Gay Men* (New York: Routledge, 1999).

2 William Bennett & Gary Bauer, *What You Need to Know About AIDS* (Ann Arbor, MI: Servant Books, 1989), x.

3 Bennett & Bauer, *What You Need to Know About AIDS*, 137.

4 William Bennett, "AIDS: Education and Public Policy," *International Review of Natural Family Planning*, Vol. 11 (New York: St John's University, 1987), 94.

5 Quoted in Douglas Feldman, *Global AIDS Policy* (New York: Bergin & Garvey, 1994), 164.

6 From the Surgeon General's report, published in Inge Corless & Mary Pittman-Lindeman, *AIDS: Principles, Practices, and Politics* (New York: Taylor & Francis, 1989), 94–97.

7 Quoted in Anne C. Lewis, "A Dangerous Silence," *Phi Delta Kappan* (January, 1987), 348.

8 For a review of the controversy surrounding Koop's report, see "AIDS", *Mother Jones*, 12 (no. 8, 1987), 33ff.

9 Lewis, "A Dangerous Silence," 348.

10 Craig Rimmerman, *From Identity to Politics: The Lesbian and Gay Movements in the United States* (Philadelphia, PA: Temple University Press, 2001), 87.

11 Randy Shilts, *And the Band Played On: People, Politics, and the AIDS Epidemic* (New York: St Martin's Press, 1987).

12 Rimmerman, *From Identity to Politics: The Lesbian and Gay Movements in the United States*, 94–95.

13 "AIDS Victim Kept from School in Indiana," *New York Times* (August 1, 1985), A15.
14 "Boy With AIDS to Get Schooling by Telephone," *New York Times* (August 25, 1985), 22.
15 "AIDS Victim Starts School over Telephone," *New York Times* (August 27, 1985), 19.
16 See Dudley Clendinen, "Schools in New York Will Admit an AIDS Pupil but not 3 Others," *New York Times* (September 8, 1985), 1.
17 "The Law on the Side of Young AIDS Victims," *New York Times* (September 23, 1985), A18.
18 James Barron, "AIDS Sufferer's Return to Classes Is Cut Short," *New York Times* (February 22, 1986), 6.
19 "Parents Drop Effort to Bar AIDS Student," *New York Times* (July 19, 1986), 8.
20 "14-Year-Old Boy With AIDS Attends School After 2 Years," *New York Times* (August 26, 1986), B3.
21 "Schools Bolster AIDS Curriculums," *New York Times* (September 10, 1987), B11.
22 John O'Connor, "Review/Television: AIDS and Hemophilia," *New York Times*, (January 16, 1989), C16.
23 Dirk Johnson, "Ryan White Dies of AIDS at 18; His Struggle Helped Pierce Myths," *New York Times* (April 9, 1990), D10.
24 Albert Camus, *The Plague* (New York: The Modern Library, 1948), 228–29.
25 These are the words of Philip Kayal, *Bearing Witness: Gay Men's Health Crisis and the Politics of AIDS* (Boulder, CO: Westview, 1993), 181.
26 Kayal, *Bearing Witness: Gay Men's Health Crisis and the Politics of AIDS*, xviii–xix.
27 Paulo Freire, *Pedagogy of the Oppressed, 30th Anniversary Edition* (New York: Continuum, 2000).
28 Jacques Derrida, *The Eyes of the University* (Stanford, CA: Stanford University Press, 2004), 83.
29 See the introductions in Dennis Carlson & C.P. Gause (ed.). *Keeping the Promise: Essays on Leadership, Democracy, and Education* (New York: Peter Lang, 2007); and Greg Dimitriadis & Dennis Carlson (ed.). *Promises to Keep: Cultural Studies, Democratic Education, and Public Life* (New York: RoutledgeFalmer, 2003).
30 Sally Munt, *Queer Attachments: The Cultural Politics of Shame* (Burlington, VA: Ashgate, 2007), 66.
31 Lauren Berlant & Elizabeth Freeman, "Queer Nationality," in Michael Warner (ed.), *Fear of a Queer Planet: Queer Politics and Social Theory* (Minneapolis, MN: University of Minnesota Press, 1993), 201.
32 Warren Johansson & William Percy, *Outing: Shattering the Conspiracy of Silence* (Binghamton, NY: The Haworth Press, 1994), 263.
33 Augusto Boal, *Theatre of the Oppressed* (London: Pluto Press, 2000).
34 Frederick Corey, "Gay Life/Queer Art," in A. & M. Kroker (ed.), *The Last Sex: Feminism and Outlaw Bodies* (New York: St Martin's Press, 1992), 121. For a further discussion of Corey's essay and ACT UP, see Dennis Carlson, "Gay, Queer, and Cyborg: The Performance of Identity in a Transnational Age," *Discourse: Studies in the Cultural Politics of Education*, 22 (no. 3, 2001), 297–310.
35 Corey, "Gay Life/Queer Art," 122.
36 Corey, "Gay Life/Queer Art," 126–27.
37 Patricia Lather & Chris Smithies, *Troubling the Angels: Women Living with HIV/AIDS* (Boulder, CO: Westview, 1997), 194–96.
38 Quoted in Lather & Smithies, *Troubling the Angels: Women Living with HIV/AIDS*, 198.
39 See Ivory Toldson, Aba Essuon, & Kamilah Woodson, "HIV/AIDS in the Black Community," in Ronald Braithwaite (ed.), *Heath Issues in the Black Community* (New York: Jossey-Bass, 2009), 363.
40 Toldson, Essuon, & Woodson, "HIV/AIDS in the Black Community," 367.
41 Toldson, Essuon, & Woodson, "HIV/AIDS in the Black Community," 363–64.
42 Toldson, Essuon, & Woodson, "HIV/AIDS in the Black Community," 371.

43 Inge Corless & Mary Pittman-Lindeman, *AIDS: Principles, Practices & Politics* (New York: Taylor & Francis, 1989), 519.

44 "Black Causus Leads Drive to Declare AIDS Crisis Among Blacks a Public Health Emergency," *Jet*, 94 (no. 12, 1998), 37–38.

45 Beverly Wright & Randall Yates, "AIDS and Homophobia: A Perspective for AIDS Educators," *Feminist Teacher*, 4 (no. 2/3, 1989), 10.

46 Wright & Yates, "AIDS and Homophobia: A Perspective for AIDS Educators," 11–12.

47 Phyllis Gorman, "Educating Students About HIV/AIDS," *Feminist Teacher*, 4 (no. 2/3, 1989), 13.

48 Christina Frazier, "AIDS and AIDS Phobia Prevention Education in a Midwestern Conservative, Low Incidence Area," *Feminist Teacher*, 4 (no. 2/3, 1989), 16.

49 See Jessica Fields. *Risk Lessons: Sex Education and Social Inequality* (New Brunswick, NJ: Rutgers University Press, 2008).

50 See J. L. Carroll, "An Exploration of AIDS Education and Teaching Methods," *AIDS Care*, 3 (no. 1, 1991), 101–4.

51 This perspective on AIDS education is represented in the World Bank report, *Education and HIV/AIDS: A Window of Hope* (Washington, DC: The World Bank, 2002), 30.

Chapter 6

1 Janice Irvine, *Talk About Sex: The Battle Over Sex Education in the United States* (Berkeley, CA: University of California Press, 2004).

2 Karen O'Connor, *No Neutral Ground? Abortion Politics in an Age of Absolutes* (Boulder, CO: Westview, 1996), 90.

3 Roger Levesque, *Sexuality Education: What Adolescents' Rights Require* (New York: Nova Science Publishers, 2003), 67.

4 Quoted in Joseph Piccione & Robert Scholle, *Combating Illegitimacy and Counseling Teen Abstinence: A Key Component of Welfare Reform*. A Backgrounder Report on Sex Education and Abstinence, Backgrounder no. 1051, 21pp. (Washington, DC: The Heritage Foundation, August, 1995).

5 See Wanda Pillow, *Unfit Subjects: Educational Policy and the Teen Mother* (New York: RoutledgeFalmer, 2004), 178–79.

6 Robert Rector, *Combatting Family Disintegration, Crime, and Dependence: Welfare Reform and Beyond* (Washington, DC: Heritage Foundation, 1995), 1.

7 Charles Murray, "The Coming White Underclass," *The Wall Street Journal*, October 29, 1993.

8 Charles Murray & Richard J. Herrnstein, *The Bell Curve: Intelligence and Class Structure in American Life* (New York: Free Press, 1994).

9 Rector, *Combatting Family Disintegration*, 28–29.

10 Rector, *Combatting Family Disintegration*, 16.

11 Naomi Farmer, "Illegitimacy," *Sex and Society*, 2, (2009), 399–401.

12 Advocates for Youth, "The History of Federal Abstinence-Only Funding," (Washington, DC: Advocates for Youth, July, 2007). Retrieved May 7, 2011. http://www.advocates foryouth.org

13 See Robert Thomas, *Sex and the American Teenager: Seeing Through the Myths and Confronting the Issues* (New York: Rowman & Littlefield, 2009), 204.

14 See Josh McDowell. *Why True Love Waits: The Definitive Book on How to Help Your Kids Resist Sexual Pressure* (Carol Stream, IL: Tyndale House, 2002), xviii–xix.

15 Quoted in Dagmar Herzog, *Sex in Crisis: The New Sexual Revolution and the Future of American Politics* (New York: Basic Books, 2008), 117–18.

16 "Why self control, not birth control." Retrieved September 24, 2010. http://www.sexrespect.com/Contraception.html

17 McDowell, *Why True Love Waits: The Definitive Book on How to Help Your Kids Resist Sexual Pressure*, xix–xx.

18 Phyllida Burlingame, *Sex, Lies, and Politics: Abstinence-Only Curricula in California Public Schools* (Oakland, CA: The Applied Research Center, 1997). For a discussion of *Sex, Lies, and Politics*, see Priscilla Pardini, "A Look at the Sex Respect Curriculum," *Rethinking Schools: Online.* Retrieved September 28, 2010. http://www.rethinkingschools. org/restrict.asp?path=archive/12_04/sexrespe.shtml

19 See *Sex and Society*, Vol. I: *Abstinence-Gender Identity* (New York: Marshall Cavendish Reference, 2010), 115.

20 McDowell, *Why True Love Waits: The Definitive Book on How to Help Your Kids Resist Sexual Pressure*, 36–38.

21 McDowell, *Why True Love Waits: The Definitive Book on How to Help Your Kids Resist Sexual Pressure*, 39–40.

22 Nancy Gibbs, "The Pursuit of Teen Purity," *Time* (October 20, 2009).

23 Felicia Mebane, Eileen Yam, & Barbara Rimer, "Sex Education and the News: Lessons From How Journalists Framed Virginity Pledges," *Journal of Health Communication*, 11 (2006), 583–606.

24 Mebane, Yam, & Rimer, "Sex Education and the News: Lessons From How Journalists Framed Virginity Pledges," 595.

25 Mebane, Yam, & Rimer, "Sex Education and the News: Lessons From How Journalists Framed Virginity Pledges," 596.

26 Hannah Bruckner & Peter Bearman, "After the Promise: The STD Consequences of Adolescent Virginity Pledges," *Journal of Adolescent Health*, 36 (April, 2005), 271–78.

27 Bruckner & Bearman, "After the Promise," 277.

28 Bruckner & Bearman, "After the Promise," 277.

29 Sexual Information and Education Council of the United States, "Virginity Pledgers More Likely to Engage in Risky Sexual Behavior Including Oral and Anal Sex." Press Release, March 18 (2005).

30 Matt Apuzzo, "Study: Many Who Pledge Abstinence Substitute Risky Behavior," Associated Press wire service, March 18 (2005).

31 *San Francisco Chronicle*, "Key to Sex Education: Discipline or Knowledge," May 22 (2005).

32 The Heritage Foundation, "Adolescent Virginity Pledges, Condom Use, and Sexually Transmitted Diseases among Young Adults." Presented at the National Welfare and Evaluation conference, June 14 (2005).

33 The Heritage Foundation, "Adolescent Virginity Pledges, Condom Use, and Sexually Transmitted Diseases among Young Adults," 6.

34 Cited in Bruckner & Bearman, "After the Promise," 271.

35 Janice Irvine, *Talk About Sex: The Battle Over Sex Education in the United States*, 187–88.

36 See Jen Gilbert "Can Sex be Educated and Can Education be Sexed?". Curriculum in Motion: A Moment of Celebration, Critique and Contemplation, 30th Conference on Curriculum Theory and Classroom Practice, October 15–17, 2009.

37 Irvine, *Talk About Sex*, 189.

38 Linda Berne & Barbara Huberman, "Sexuality Education," *Phi Delta Kappan*, 77 (no. 3, 1995), 2.

39 Lois Weis (with Doris Carbonell-Medina), "Learning to Speak Out in an Abstinence Based Sex Education Group: Gender and Race Work in an Urban Magnet School," *Teachers College Record*, 102 (no. 3, 2000), 646.

40 Weis (with Carbonell-Medina), "Learning to Speak Out in an Abstinence Based Sex Education Group: Gender and Race Work in an Urban Magnet School," 623.

41 Ibid.

42 All quotes are from H.R. 1551, Responsible Education About Life Act, as passed by the U.S. House of Representatives, March 17, 2009.

Chapter 7

1 Foucault, *The History of Sexuality: An Introduction*, Vol. 1, 7.
2 Foucault, *The History of Sexuality: An Introduction*, Vol. 1, 25–26.
3 Foucault, *The History of Sexuality: An Introduction*, Vol. 1, 26.
4 Foucault, *The History of Sexuality: An Introduction*, Vol. 1, 54.
5 See Dennis Carlson, "Tales of Future Past: The Living Legacy of Eugenics in American Education," *Journal of the American Association for the Advancement of Curriculum Studies*, 5 (February 2009), 1–10.
6 Foucault, *The History of Sexuality: An Introduction*, Vol. 1, 28–29.
7 Foucault, *The History of Sexuality: An Introduction*, Vol. 1, 19.
8 Foucault, *The History of Sexuality: An Introduction*, Vol. 1, 67.
9 Foucault, *The History of Sexuality: An Introduction*, Vol. 1, 121–22.
10 Foucault, *The History of Sexuality: An Introduction*, Vol. 1, 57.
11 Michel Foucault, *The Use of Pleasure, The History of Sexuality*, Vol.2, translated by Robert Hurley (New York: Random House, 1985), 4.
12 Foucault, *The Use of Pleasure*, 6.
13 Foucault, *The Use of Pleasure*, 36.
14 Foucault, *The Use of Pleasure*, 23.
15 Foucault, *The Use of Pleasure*, 192.
16 Foucault, *The Use of Pleasure*, 19–20.
17 Quoted in Foucault, *The Use of Pleasure*, 120.
18 Foucault, *The Use of Pleasure*, 20.
19 Michel Foucault, *Care of the Self, The History of Sexuality*, Vol. 3, translated by Robert Hurley (New York: Random House, 1986), 51.
20 Foucault does not use the term *vita activa* although the notion of "care of the self" is clearly linked to the idea of an active, vigorous, productive life in both one's role in the family and the state. For a discussion of the meaning of this term in Roman culture, see Hannah Arendt, *The Human Condition* (Chicago, IL: University of Chicago Press, 1958).
21 Foucault, *Care of the Self*, 135.
22 Foucault, *The Use of Pleasure*, 57.
23 James Sears (ed.), *Sexuality and the Curriculum: The Politics and Practices of Sexuality Education* (New York: Teachers College Press, 1992).
24 Debra Haffner, "Forward," in Sears (ed.), *Sexuality and the Curriculum*, viii.
25 Peter McLaren, "Forward: Border Anxiety and Sexuality Politics," in Sears (ed.), *Sexuality and the Curriculum*, xi. Quotation from Terry Eagleton, *The Ideology of the Aesthetic* (London: Basil Blackwell, 1990), 13.
26 James Sears, "Dilemmas and Possibilities of Sexuality Education: Reproducing the Body Politic," in Sears (ed.), *Sexuality and the Curriculum*, 17.
27 Michelle Fine, "Sexuality, Schooling, and Adolescent Females: The Missing Discourse of Desire," *Harvard Educational Review*, 58 (no. 1, 1988), 32.
28 Lynn Phillips & Michelle Fine, "What's 'Left' in Sexuality Education?" in Sears (ed.), *Sexuality and the Curriculum*, 243–44.

Chapter 8

1 Judith Butler, *Gender Trouble* (New York: Routledge, 1990), xxvii.
2 Butler, *Gender Trouble*, xxvii–xxix.
3 Butler, *Gender Trouble*, 25.
4 Sara Salih, "On Judith Butler and Performativity," in Karen Lovass & Mercilee Jenkins (ed.). *Sexualities and Communication in Everyday Life: A Reader* (New York: Sage, 2006), 55–68.
5 Karen Martin, *Puberty, Sexuality, and the Self: Boys and Girls at Adolescence* (New York: Routledge, 1996), 9.

6 Martin, *Puberty, Sexuality, and the Self*, 121.
7 Martin, *Puberty, Sexuality, and the Self*, 126.
8 See Chris Shilling, *The Body and Social Theory* (London: Sage Publications, 1993); and Joan Brumberg, *The Body Project: An Intimate History of American Girls* (New York: Random House, 1997).
9 Brumberg, *The Body Project*, xxv.
10 Patricia Hill Collins, *Black Feminist Thought: Knowledge, Consciousness, and the Politics of Empowerment* (New York: Routledge, 2000), 52.
11 Foucault uses the term "history of the present" in *Discipline and Punish:* The Birth of the Prison (New York: Vintage, 1995).
12 Collins, *Black Feminist Thought*, 284.
13 Patricia Hill Collins, "Reply to Commentaries: Black Sexual Politics Revisited," *Studies in Gender and Sexuality*, 9 (2008), 79.
14 bell hooks, "Misogyny, Sexism, & Gangsta Rap—Who Takes the Rap?," *Z Magazine*, 7 (March 4, 1994).
15 Oliva Espin, *Latina Realities: Essays on Healing, Migration, and Sexuality* (Boulder, CO: Westview, 1997), 89.
16 See Gloria Anzaldua, *Borderlands/La Frontera: The New Mestiza* (San Francisco, CA: Aunt Lute Books, 1987). See also, Gabrieta Arredondo (ed.), *Chicana Feminisms: A Critical Reader* (Durham, NC: Duke University Press, 2003).
17 R.W. Connell, "Hegemonic Masculinity," *Gender & Society*, 19 (no. 6, 2005), 829–59.
18 R.W. Connell, *The Men and the Boys* (Oxford, UK: Polity Press, 2000), 46. See also Tony Coles, "Negotiating the Field of Masculinity: The Production and Reproduction of Multiple Dominant Masculinities," *Men and Masculinities*, 12 (no. 1, 2009), 30–44.
19 Coles, "Negotiating the Field of Masculinity," 38.
20 William Pinar, *The Gender of Racial Politics and Violence in America: Lynching, Prison Rape, and the Crisis of Masculinity* (New York: Peter Lang, 2001).
21 Pinar, *The Gender of Racial Politics and Violence in America*, 29.
22 Pinar, *The Gender of Racial Politics and Violence in America*, 921.
23 Pinar, *The Gender of Racial Politics and Violence in America*, 1152.
24 De Lauretis, "Queer Theory, Lesbian and Gay Sexualities," *Differences*, 3 (2), iii–xviii.
25 Eve Sedgwick, *The Epistemology of the Closet* (Berkeley, CA: University of California Press, 1990, 2008), xvi.
26 Sedgwick, *The Epistemology of the Closet*, 85. See also Judith Butler, "Capacity," in Stephen Barber & David Clark (ed.), *Regarding Sedgwick: Essays on Queer Culture and Critical Theory* (New York: Routledge, 2002), 109–20.
27 Judith Butler, *Bodies that Matter: On the Discursive Limits of "Sex"* (New York: Routledge, 1993).
28 See Richard Peterson (ed.), *The Production of Culture* (London: Sage, 1976).
29 Theodor Adorno, *The Culture Industry: Selected Essays on Mass Culture* (New York: Routledge, 2001).
30 Henry Giroux, "Teenage Sexuality, Body Politics, and the Pedagogy of Display," *Education/Pedagogy/Cultural Studies*, 18, (no. 3, 1997), 307–31.
31 See "Calvin Klein: A Case Study," Media Awareness Network, http://www.media-awareness.ca/english/resources/educational/handouts/ethics/calvin_klein_case_study.cfm (March 8, 2010).
32 Michael Reiss, "Editorial," *Sex Education*, 1 (no. 1, 2001), 6.
33 Michael Reiss, "Editorial," 7.
34 Will Letts & Connie Nobles, "Introduction—Embodied [By] Curriculum," *Sex Education*, 3 (no. 2, 2003), 91.
35 Libby Blume, "Embodied [By] Dance: Adolescent De/Constructions of Body, Sex and Gender in Physical Education," *Sex Education*, 3 (no. 2, 2003), 99.

36 Kristen Luschen & Lesley Bogad, "Bodies that Matter: Transgenderism, Innocence and the Politics of 'Unprofessional' Pedagogy," *Sex Education*, 3 (no. 2, 2003), 146.

37 Luschen & Bogad, "Bodies that Matter," 149.

38 Judy Hemingway, "Reframing Sex Education," *Sex Education*, 6 (no. 4, 2006), 314.

39 Sharyn Pearce, "Sex and the Cinema: What *American Pie* Teaches the Young," *Sex Education*, 6 (no. 4, 2006), 370. Pearce cites Henry Giroux, *Breaking Into the Movies: Film and the Culture of Politics* (Maldon, UK: Blackwell, 2002).

40 Pearce, "Sex and the Cinema: What *American Pie* Teaches the Young," 368.

41 Pearce, "Sex and the Cinema: What *American Pie* Teaches the Young," 371.

42 Transcripts for Teen Sexuality in a Culture of Confusion. Media Education Foundation (Northampton, MA: 2008). Retrieved July 2, 2010. http://www.mediaed.org/assets/products/220-P-V/transcript_220-P-V.pdf.

Chapter 9

1 John Engel, Marie Saracino, & M. Betsy Bergen, "Sexuality Education," in Margaret Arcus, Jay Schvaneveldt, & J. Joel Moss (ed.), *Handbook of Family Life Education: The Practice of Family Life Education*, Vol. 2 (London: Sage, 1993), 63–64.

2 Margaret Arcus, Jay Schvaneveldt, & J. Joel Moss (ed.), *Handbook of Family Life Education: Foundations of Family Life Education*, Vol. 1 (London: Sage, 1993), 140–41.

3 Lane Powell & Dawn Cassidy, *Family Life Education: Working With Families Across the Life Span* (Long Grove, IL: Waveland, 2007), 155.

4 Powell & Cassidy, *Family Life Education*, 165.

5 Powell & Cassidy, *Family Life Education*, 167.

6 Powell & Cassidy, *Family Life Education*, 166.

7 See Stephanie Troutman, "The Cautionary Whale, Viking, Vessel, Planet or Saint? Adolescent and Maternal Configuration in *Juno* and Beyond," in Dennis Carlson & Donyell Roseboro (ed.), *The Sexuality Curriculum and Youth Culture* (New York: Peter Lang, 2011), 246–60. Troutman provides a critical reading of the 2007 movie *Juno* and the trope of the "monstrous" pregnant teenage body, and resistance and subversion of that trope in popular culture.

8 Letters to the editor "Resolution Conflict," *Educational Leadership*, September, (1990), 93.

9 See Gregory Herek, "Beyond Homophobia: Thinking About Sexual Prejudice and Stigma in the Twenty-First Century," *Sexuality Research & Social Policy*, 1 (no. 2, 2004), 6–24.

10 John Anderson, "School Climate for Gay and Lesbian Students and Staff Members," *Phi Delta Kappan*, 76 (no. 2, 1994), 151–55.

11 Beverly Biehr, "Problem Sexual Behavior in School-Aged Children and Youth," *Theory into Practice*, 28, (no. 3, 1989), 224.

12 Melinda Moore & Martin Forst, "Introduction," in Moore & Martin (ed.) *AIDS Education: Reaching Diverse Populations*, (Westport, CT: Praeger, 1996), 3–4.

13 Moore & Forst, "Introduction," 5.

14 James Holmes & Steven Humes, "Successes and Failures in the Gay Community: HIV Prevention Workshops at Gay Men's Health Crisis," in Moore & Forst, "Introduction" 14.

15 Holmes & Humes, "Successes and Failures in the Gay Community," 15.

16 Holmes & Humes, "Successes and Failures in the Gay Community," 17–18.

17 Holmes & Humes, "Successes and Failures in the Gay Community," 19.

18 Quoted in Betsy Hartmann, "Everyday Eugenics," *Znet*. Posted September 22, 2006. Retrieved November 27, 2006. http://www.zcommunications.org/everyday-eugenics-by-betsy-hartmann

19 Nicole Haberland & Deborah Rogow, "Sexuality and HIV Education: Time for a Paradigm Shift." Promoting Healthy, Safe, and Productive Transitions to Adulthood. Population Council, Brief no. 22, August 2007.

20 *It's All One Curriculum: Guidelines and Activities for a Unified Approach to Sexuality, Gender, HIV, and Human Rights Education* (Population Council, New York, 2009).

21 *It's All One Curriculum,* 62–63.

22 For a complex analysis of "sexting" that draws upon Foucault's notion of "care of the self," see Joshua Garrison, "The Self-Porning of American Youth," in Carlson and Roseboro, *The Sexuality Curriculum and Youth Culture,* 348–62.

23 Reported in the *New York Times,* "Teenagers Changing Sexual Behavior," August 26, 2008, D7.

24 This is a metaphor popularized in cultural studies by Robert Putnam, *Bowling Alone: The Collapse and Revival of American Community* (New York: Simon & Schuster, 2000).

25 See Gilles Deleuze, *Neitzsche and Philosophy* (New York: Columbia University Press, 1983). In philosophy, Nietzsche is most associated with this effort to move beyond, or at least around, a narrow reactive politics of negation.

26 Bruce Thornton, *Eros: The Myth of Ancient Greek Sexuality* (Boulder, CO: Westview Press, 1997), 14.

INDEX